RUSSIAN CITIZENSHIP

Russian Citizenship

FROM EMPIRE TO SOVIET UNION

Eric Lohr

HARVARD UNIVERSITY PRESS

Cambridge, Massachusetts, and London, England

2012

Library of Congress Cataloging-in-Publication Data

Lohr, Eric.
    Russian citizenship : from empire to Soviet Union / Eric Lohr.
        pages ; cm
    Includes bibliographical references and index.
    ISBN 978-0-674-06634-2 (hardcover : alkaline paper)
    1. Citizenship—Russia—History.   2. Citizenship—Soviet Union—History.
3. Naturalization—Russia—History.   4. Naturalization—Soviet Union—History.
5. Russia—Emigration and immigration—History.   6. Soviet Union—Emigration and
immigration—History.   7. Minorities—Legal status, laws, etc.—Russia—History.
8. Minorities—Legal status, laws, etc.—Soviet Union—History.   I. Title.

    JN6583.L64 2012
    323.60947—dc23

                                                            2012008910

To Anya

Contents

RUSSIAN CITIZENSHIP

Introduction

This book is the first to tell the history of the interface between Russian citizens and foreigners, focusing on the era from the 1860s great reforms to Stalin's sealing the country off from the world in the early 1930s. It is grounded in case studies of group and individual immigration, emigration, naturalization, and denaturalization—including the stories of Jews, Muslims, Germans, Armenians, and other minority groups.

Two types of boundaries are central to the narrative. We normally think of physical boundaries around a country as the delimiters of sovereignty, but sovereignty also extends to embrace all of a country's citizens regardless of their place of residence. States can regulate entry into and exit from their citizenries in much the same way that border guards regulate entry and exit from the country. In short, one can imagine a "citizenship boundary" as the interface between citizenries and the reach of their countries' claims of sovereignty. This book focuses on this citizenship boundary, seeking its origins and asking how it was conceived, crossed, documented, controlled, and evaded.

The physical border around the country is an important part of the story as well. Borders certainly affected the flows of people—especially by the twentieth century. But in the Russian case, the site of actual control was less along its thousands of kilometers of external border than in the form of documents issued in bureaucratic offices, and inducements, sanctions, and other measures that gave certain groups incentives to migrate or change their citizenship status. Thus, while border guards and checkpoints are important, more time will be spent with police officials in charge of settlement policies, conducting campaigns to improve passport and registration systems, deciding which ethnic and religious groups should be allowed into the country, and which should be allowed, encouraged, or compelled to leave.

Although citizenship has been a hotly contested issue throughout the post-Soviet space since 1991, the history of citizenship in the region has received very little attention.[1] However, there has been an explosion of interest in citizenship in various national contexts over the past two decades since the collapse of the Soviet Union created dozens of new states and the European Union added a new transnational citizenship on top of the old national citizenships of the continent.[2] One of the goals of this book is to add the Russian case to this rapidly growing literature.

To this end, I try to identify broad trends and patterns in Russian law and practice through a fairly broad swath of its history, attempting to establish the key elements of what we might call the "Russian citizenship tradition." The citizenship history of any country, more than most topics, is full of contradictions and exceptions. In fact, the researcher constantly faces the problem that normative laws often provide only indirect evidence about actual practices (think about the scale of undocumented immigration even in modern states with their advanced technologies of enforcement). Moreover, individual and group cases that create archival records almost by definition are exceptions to the normal practice. Finding the norm in a sea of exceptions is one of the more challenging tasks of writing citizenship history. I have tried to do this by working extensively in the records of the Department of Police, attempting to discern how officials sought to control the border, register immigrants, and deal with the other aspects of citizenship in practice. The book strives to find general enduring features of citizenship practice in order to build up an ideal-type model of the Russian case to facilitate comparison to other countries. It also includes several excursions into detailed case studies and examples to illustrate the complexities of actual citizenship practices and to emphasize that there were almost always exceptions to the general rules.

This methodological issue itself changes as one moves through history. One of the themes of this book is that a key aspect of old regime subjecthood was its embrace of exceptions, of what I call "separate deals" with different immigrant groups, social orders, and national and religious minorities. These separate deals gave very different combinations of rights and obligations before the law. The ideal of modern citizenship as equal rights and obligations for all citizens fundamentally challenged the idea of exceptions and the separate deals paradigm.

In order to see how the Russian citizenship tradition compares to others, the book makes occasional reference to citizenship histories elsewhere in the world. There are many interesting and surprising specific points of comparison and contrast. On the whole, the book argues that Russia's citizenship history up to 1914 is more comparable to other countries' than scholars have thought—until the drive toward autarky from 1914 to the 1930s set it completely apart.

This book defines the term "citizenship" as many others do, in a narrow sense, as a status denoting membership in a country, usually documented with a passport or comparable document. "Subjecthood" is used in the same way, to refer simply to the membership status of the subjects of the tsar. The focus throughout is on the "citizenship boundary," the line between members and nonmembers, on the rules and practices that define the boundary, and on the various ways citizenship status was acquired, lost, ascribed, or removed.

There are of course other ways to define "citizenship." Much writing and thinking about the concept has focused on the rights that accrue to citizens. In fact, according to a common ideal-type definition, citizenship is "a personal status consisting of a body of universal rights (i.e., legal claims on the state) and duties held equally by all legal members of a nation-state."[3] This sets a high bar. No country has ever had full citizenship according to this definition, because no country has ever established perfectly equal rights and obligations for all its members. But Russia was further from the ideal than most countries. It was not a nation-state with a unified citizenship, but rather a sprawling multiethnic empire where people were relatively rightless subjects of an autocratic tsar or Soviet leader. This simple fact may account for what I have found to be a remarkably widespread instinctual reaction to my topic that "Russian citizenship" is an oxymoron. Add to this the idea that nationality is defined in the formal terms of state membership in the West, but increasingly in terms of ethnicity and culture as one moves east, and there is a powerfully engrained sense that Russian citizenship is not a viable concept.[4]

The history of the concept in Russia actually deepens the problem. For most of the late imperial period, the term citizenship (*grazhdanstvo*) was used almost exclusively by liberal and radical opponents of the regime, and it carried a polemical edge, as an idea, program, and reminder of the rightlessness inherent to contemporary subjecthood (*poddanstvo*). In striking contrast to most other countries and even empires like Britain and Austria-Hungary, the very term for citizenship became an abstract concept that its leading legal philosopher, Vladimir Gessen (also a leader of the liberal Constitutional Democratic Party), grounded in principles of natural law rather than in practical juridical and constitutional law categories.[5] Gessen deepened this unworldly meaning of *grazhdanstvo* by grounding his juridical philosophy of citizenship in a neo-Kantian revival of natural law. The rights of the citizen (*grazhdanin*), he argued, derived not from inherited legal precedents and traditions but from universal *a priori* natural rights. So while there is a large gulf in all countries between the idealized vision of citizenship as the perfect equation of the rights and obligations of all individuals before the law on the one hand, and extant citizenship or subjecthood on the other, this gulf was both conceptually and practically wider in imperial Russia than in most other cases. Ironically, perhaps in part because the term *grazhdanstvo* remained unsullied by the compromises and realities of legal interpretation and practice, its meaning actually remained closer to the ideal-type definition cited above than it did in other countries.[6]

This said, taking a rights-based approach to citizenship, one could frame an analysis of Russian citizenship as a study of the transition from an old regime subjecthood based on a society of social orders toward a new regime of citizenship based on the principle of equal rights and obligations for all individuals in the country. This story is so complex and overwhelmingly important that a study of citizenship could easily become a social and legal domestic history of peasants, nobles, and merchants during the transition to a new era. The social and legal history of this transition has been told often and well.[7]

But the field of citizenship studies more often than not defines "citizenship" in a very different way, as the institution delineating membership in a state. Using this definition, this study can focus on the standard questions of citizenship studies—naturalization, denaturalization, immigration, emigration, and border policies—topics that have received very little attention from scholars of Russian history.

The February 1917 revolution brought the liberals to power. One of their first acts was to declare equal rights for all citizens, thus definitively marking the terminological switch from subjecthood to citizenship. I follow this terminological history in my use of the two words, but by doing so emphatically do not mean to imply a sudden conceptual shift in 1917. In many ways, Russian subjects in 1906 were closer to Gessen's notion of citizenship (*grazhdanstvo*) as an ideal type of equalized rights and obligations for all state members than Soviet citizens were in 1926.

All this is not to say that rights and obligations will be excluded from this study. Rather, the book treats the citizenship boundary as the dependent variable, the central analytical focus. Rights and obligations of various groups are often important independent variables in the analysis, crucial to explaining the twists and turns of policies along the citizenship boundary.

CITIZENSHIP AND DOMESTIC RUSSIAN HISTORY

The book begins with the origins and evolution of Russian subjecthood policy and practices up to the mid-nineteenth century. Russia was not defined by xenophobia, isolation, and relatively closed subjecthood boundaries in the centuries prior to the twentieth century. To be sure, nativist pressures from society and parts of the administration were episodically very strong, and the book looks closely at these phenomena. However, more often than not, the state overruled these forces in the name of modernization. Early in its history, it developed what I call an "attract and hold" approach to subjecthood policy. There was a persistent shortage of people and a sense that immigration and naturalization helped expand the economic power of the empire, while emigration and denaturalization were to be avoided for the same reason. This changed in the nineteenth century as rural overpopulation became a problem, but the approach had remarkable staying power. I argue that "attract and hold" remained a defining feature of Russian citizenship policy right up to 1914.

The detailed analysis begins with Tsar Alexander II's great reforms in the 1860s that ended serfdom and set Russia on the path to modernization and industrialization. One of the first acts of the great reform era was a reform of citizenship laws, making it easier for foreigners to immigrate and conduct business in Russia. The link between modernization and intensified interaction with the outside world was established and became the key to most aspects of Russian citizenship policy for the next half century. In retrospect, this period can be seen as Russia's first era of globalization. In just a couple decades, border crossings changed from rare, group events to normal, daily, individual occurrences on a mass scale. If in the 1850s there were roughly 40,000 total registered border crossings by foreigners and Russian subjects combined, by the mid-1860s, there were closer to 100,000; by 1900 four million, and more than ten million in 1909 (see Tables 1 and 3–7 at the end of the book). This study of the interface between citizens and foreigners also yields new insights into four interrelated problems of Russian history: the role of nationality, population policy, the nature and relative strength of the state, and strategies of economic modernization.

The problematic relationship between citizenship and nationality is a central theme of the book. At least since the French Revolution—long considered one of the key founding events for modern citizenship—there has been a close relationship between citizenship and nationality. Naturalization became essentially an oath of political allegiance to the revolution. In theory, those who refused to naturalize in the 1790s were forced to leave France.[8] Thenceforth, the boundary between citizens and foreigners grew in conceptual and practical significance, and the principle that only citizens were members of the nation became firmly established. According to Rogers Brubaker's classic typology, citizenship and nationality were linked in a very different way in Germany, where birth and bloodline became the operative principles in naturalization policy. This policy made it easy for Germans living abroad for generations to retain, renew, or reacquire citizenship, while making naturalization very difficult for non-Germans even if they were born on German soil. But the important point is that both in Germany and France, the state strove to fuse its concepts of citizenship and nationality. In fact, as a matter of principle and definition, all "nation-states" to one degree or another try to fuse citizenship and nationality.

Conversely, one would expect that "empire-states" would try to avoid linking their principles of citizenship/subjecthood with nationality. This was indeed largely true for the Russian Empire through most of its history. It was not a nation-state and did not want to become one. However, I will argue that throughout the period under consideration, national goals crept into imperial immigration, naturalization, and emigration policies. In part, this was a function of the international, interrelational aspect of citizenship. Because Russia shaped its citizenship boundary through interaction with other nation-states (especially along its crucial border with Germany), the national principles embodied in citizenship practices abroad influenced Russian subjecthood practices. This is just one example of the many ways in which Russian citizenship policy was entangled with that of other countries.[9] But it was also a product of insecurities about ruling borderlands with large and growing non-Russian populations. This was most powerfully on display in the Far East, where the fears of Asian demographic dominance led officials to push hard to limit immigration and naturalization, but it was a factor in the Caucasus and on the western borders as well.

There is a long-standing presumption in nationality studies—traceable perhaps to Hans Kohn—that in the West, nationality was a legal institution based on the individual–state relationship and was essentially a contractual membership issue; while in the East, nationality was defined by culture, ethnicity, and blood. In citizenship studies, Brubaker entrenched the related distinction between the ideal types of assimilationist France in the West, where the *jus soli* principle of ascribing citizenship to all foreigners born on French soil prevailed versus the ethnic exclusivity of Germany in the East, where the *jus sanguinis* principle allowed only the descendants of citizens to automatically acquire citizenship, excluding the sons and daughters of foreigners born on German soil.[10]

Andreas Fahrmeir, Patrick Weil, and others have already begun to break down this ideal-type distinction between the French and German cases.[11] My book will further challenge this geographical dichotomy by presenting the case of a surprisingly strong assimilationist *jus soli* tradition in the East. In this and other ways, it will argue that the two halves of the continent were less different, more comparable, and more a part of a single citizenship history than was previously thought.

Imperial subjecthood and migration policies toward Jews are often the great exception to general policies, and they receive much attention in the book. Jews made up over 40% of all emigrants from the empire from 1860 to 1920, and nearly every law on naturalization, denaturalization, immigration, or emigration under the old regime included a general clause written in universalistic terms, but followed by "commentary" *(primechanie)* that laid out very different rules for Jews. For example, Catherine the Great's famous 1762 manifesto declared that Russia welcomed all European immigrants "except Jews" *(krome zhidov)* to come settle in Russia. Foreign Jews were banned from naturalizing and sharp restrictions were imposed on their immigration or travel to the empire. Likewise, while Russia's general policy was to prevent emigration, in 1892 the regime began to allow and even encourage Jewish emigration. While the regime found many ways to write separate laws and rules for Jews, in many ways, general citizenship and migration policies were inextricably tied up with imperial restrictions on the Jews until the 1917 revolutions cut through the Gordian knot of interrelated regulations.

Sociologists have used several metaphors to describe what states try to do through their citizenship policies—the best known of which are penetration or embrace.[12] In a previous book, I argued that during World War I, the state strove to nationalize economy and society. In this book, I use the related metaphor of the filtering state. I argue that the regime used citizenship policy as a filter, blocking unwanted nationalities, religions, and character types from entering while setting the outgoing filter to hold in the nationalities it wanted, allowing others to slip out. Then in the Soviet era, the filtering process changed to class criteria. Workers of the world were in principle (much less in practice) invited to immigrate and naturalize while bourgeois, noble, clerical, and other citizens could be deprived of the rights of citizenship. A mass denaturalization in 1921 turned millions of refugees into stateless exiles. The citizenship boundary served as a locus for state attempts to filter and channel population movements that were largely driven by economic and other forces outside the state's control. While much of this movement occurred despite rather than because of state policy, one can easily underestimate the significance of the filtering function. In several of the case studies that follow, we will see that different policies could easily have changed the international migrations of hundreds of thousands of individuals.

THE STATE

One of the big questions of Russian history deals with the capacity of the state. Was it strong or weak? Could it exert full sovereignty and control over the boundary between its citizens and foreigners, or were its often relatively extensive *claims* of control actually a sign of its relative weakness? Were its borders rigid or porous? These are important questions that bedevil discussions of borders and citizenship in all countries. The answers are complex, and they emerge through close analysis of both stated policy goals and actual practices (to the extent that such are accessible to the historian). As a preliminary generalization, I can say that citizenship and border controls meant more and were more effective than most scholars have thought. But, while the recent fashion for stressing the inexorable expansion of the state as it strove to incorporate individuals ever more firmly in its nets of knowledge and control describes the *intentions* of officials well, it can miss the great chasm between intentions and results.[13]

The broad variety of sources consulted for this study helps to bridge this chasm—but it remains a daunting challenge. The archival records of the ministries of internal affairs and foreign affairs, and those of the military allow this study to go beyond the analysis of laws and statutes to see the often quite different realities on the ground. Colorful stories of bribery, fake passports, emigrant smuggling rings, and internal reports such as one estimating that 80 percent of all emigration was undocumented and illegal emphasize that one cannot understand a citizenship history by looking at laws alone. They also suggest that state control of the citizenship boundary was very far from absolute. On the other hand, the impact of laws is easily underestimated because so often it is measured in counterfactuals—of the millions of people who might have crossed the border, naturalized, or taken a second citizenship had the rules been different. There is no way to measure these migrations and immigrations that did not happen, but they had a huge impact on the shape of the citizenry.

The imperial regime backed away from the "attract and hold" and *jus soli* principles at the core of the prewar Russian citizenship tradition in its response to the pressures of World War I. The government banned naturalization, interned foreign citizens from enemy states, nationalized their properties, and stressed ethnic criteria to an unprecedented degree in citizenship policy. The February 1917 revolution declared a sweeping transformation of Russian citizenship, abolishing all the differentiations in rights and obligations on the basis of ethnicity, religion, and social status. However, in large part because the war was still under way, its impact on the citizenship boundary was not as complete as it seemed. When the Bolsheviks seized control, they quickly reintroduced differentiation in rights and obligations, this time based on class. At first, they opened the country to easy immigration and naturalization for workers from abroad. But, during the civil war, control over immigration, emigration, denaturalization, and naturalization was gradually centralized and became extremely tight. After a brief relative relaxation of these controls in the mid-1920s as part of an attempt to promote foreign participation in the Soviet economic recovery, the country launched a full-scale, unprecedented attempt to industrialize based on domestic resources. In the context of a war scare, autarkic industrial mobilization, and an intensive campaign against the flight of hard currency and people, Stalin closed down the citizenship border, making it extraordinarily difficult to immigrate, emigrate, or denaturalize.

*　　*　　*

All countries define their own citizenship traditions through a long progression of choices made through their history. In most cases, there is a legible record of these choices in the form of a continuous juridical chain of precedents, court rulings, and interpretations. Thus, detailed analysis of seventeenth-century British court cases on naturalization is self-evidently part of the story of American citizenship, as are the provisions of the Napoleonic Code in the French. Countries with a continuous legal history thus have a traceable path along which certain principles emerged, evolved, and influenced the contemporary legislation and statutes on citizenship.

In this sense, Russia poses a problem. The 1917 revolutions declared the entire pre-revolutionary legal apparatus null and void, and started from an entirely different set of principles and operating procedures. Of course there were occasional holdovers (like Sergei Kishkin and Vsevolod N. Durdenevskii) from the old juridical establishment who brought and applied juridical knowledge across the 1917 divide. But, the striking fact is discontinuity—not only in the underlying principles—but more significantly, in practices.

This is especially apparent in the unprecedented swing toward autarky in the late 1920s. This book argues that this was not a return to pre-1860s or medieval Russian isolation, but rather a distinctly Soviet decision that amounted to a dramatic break from Russian traditions. Taking a long view, the Soviet era from Stalin to Gorbachev thus appears to be in many ways a half-century detour. From the late 1980s through to the present day, new problems and dilemmas have emerged. They are not easily seen in historical context because they are so different from the issues of the Soviet era. But sometimes, the strongest continuities and parallels are not found in the most recent decades. If we think about the pre-Stalin history of Russian citizenship as creating not a set of legal precedents, but rather, in a more anthropological sense, a national "citizenship tradition," we will be better prepared to see the commonalities in the problems and dilemmas Russia faces in its contemporary approach to citizenship. So as we enter the seemingly very different world of Russian subjecthood in centuries past, we may well see a bit of the present.

ONE

Boundaries and Migration before 1860

For most of Russian history, religion, social order, guild, and other member-ships were far more important than the difference in legal status between subjects and foreigners for determining rights and obligations. However, the subjecthood boundary was more significant than scholars have assumed, and remains largely unstudied. The institution of subjecthood emerged as a meaningful delineator of status and means of controlling movement in the centuries prior to the great reforms of the 1860s.

From the beginning of recorded history in the lands of Rus', long-distance international trade has been the key to political and economic success in the lands that later comprised the Russian Empire. It is something of a myth that Russia was an autarky cut off from the world by the Mongol con-quest of 1241. Trade and interaction with foreigners flourished, especially through the southern steppe to Central Asia, Persia, the Black Sea, and on to the Mediterranean in the first century or so after the conquest, under what some historians have called the "Pax Mongolica."[1] The Hanseatic League maintained a vibrant trade in the north. Russia was not an autarky from its very origins. In fact, a leading expert on foreigners in Muscovy ar-gues that there were no effective limits on the entry of foreigners—regardless of nationality or religion—during the Kievan and appanage periods.[2]

However, the new principality of Muscovy did not participate in the great era of empire building and internationalization during the sixteenth through seventeenth centuries that completely transformed the nature of international exchange and interaction in the Atlantic world. In fact, while populations were increasingly crossing borders, trading, and moving about in Europe, Russia was solidifying and intensifying the controls of serfdom, tying people ever more tightly to their localities and to their landlords.[3] The entire social and legal order came to be centered upon the goal of bonding serfs to their masters and to their villages. Movement outside of the immediate vicinity of the village became ever more tightly regulated, requiring an internal passport and permission of the landlord and local authorities.[4] The increasingly tight controls the regime placed on the population and its ability to move included sharp constraints on foreign travel and elaborate measures to prevent emigration. Yet, from the seventeenth century on, Muscovite policy quite consistently strove to encourage immigration for service to the tsar.[5] Together, these policies formed a consistent population policy that can be described simply as a policy of "attract and hold" for peoples of nearly all types. This is the most enduring and deeply rooted population policy in Russian history and it is much closer to the early modern policies that prevailed in Europe than to the autarchies of fifteenth–nineteenth-century China and Japan, or twentieth-century Stalinism.

KEEPING RUSSIAN SUBJECTS IN

The subjecthood boundary had little practical or theoretical relevance to the policy of "attract and hold." The state banned emigration and did not recognize loss of Russian subjecthood through naturalization abroad. So in principle, a runaway serf, if caught or turned over to Russia by a foreign power, would be returned to his master. Likewise, nobles and civil servants in the elite who left without permission could be subjected to penalties upon their return or capture. However, it was not along the subjecthood boundary that these issues were usually decided. The external boundary was extremely porous, and controls over peasant emigration—or any movement within the country—had far more to do with the commune and the principle of collective responsibility. All obligations of tax, labor, and share of harvest were owed by the commune as a whole to the landlord or the state. Departure of anyone—particularly of the young, able-bodied males who comprise the bulk of all emigrants from all countries in all times—would severely hurt the ability of the commune to meet its overall obligations.

The state encouraged the strengthening of the commune as a means of control over movement. Peter the Great introduced the first Russian "passport" *(pasport)* not as a document to define who was a subject and who was not, but rather as a document that limited a peasant's movement to a defined radius around his place of residence.[6] It was not a national identity document or a means to travel abroad but rather a tool for the police to assist in enforcing the bondage of peasants to their villages. The passport system was reformed but this key function was not eliminated.[7]

The Russian tsars developed elaborate and fairly effective means to hold their elites in service to the tsar and prevent their defection to neighboring states. For example, they enforced a law that properties belonging to any Russian-subject landlord abroad continuously for more than five years (or three years for members of any other social order) could be confiscated and transferred to state institutions without compensation.[8]

From the fifteenth through the seventeenth centuries, there was a fairly intense competition between the Polish-Lithuanian Commonwealth, Muscovy, and to a lesser degree the Ottoman Empire, for servitors.[9] The Muscovite system of serfdom itself emerged in part out of tsars' attempts to entice servitors to stay by giving them unlimited control over the populations on their estates and the incomes they were able to squeeze out of these populations.[10] This enticement was mixed with extremely sharp restrictions on noble foreign travel. Noble clans were held collectively responsible for anyone who left Muscovite service and the country without permission.[11] Even foreign subjects in Muscovite service were often denied requests to travel abroad, and had to put up family members as a pledge that they would return.[12]

Peter the Great opened the door to the first substantial travel abroad by nobles and merchants for education and trade as part of his strategy of economic modernization. While such travel grew rapidly and became a staple of eighteenth-century noble education, the number of Russians traveling abroad remained relatively small compared to the great expansion in foreign travel and international migration that was under way in Europe. The system of control over emigration was fairly effective considering its extremely rudimentary nature. It relied almost entirely on social, political, and administrative controls rather than guarded borders around the state.

FOREIGNERS IN MUSCOVY

The predominant image of Muscovy prior to Peter the Great is one of a religious, inward-looking society cut off from outside influences, suspicious of and impenetrable to foreigners. Certainly there is a degree of truth to this generalization. Foreigners were only allowed into the empire to trade with the express permission and actual stamp of approval of the tsar. Those who entered the country (primarily for trade and service to the military) wore distinguishing clothes and lived in separate "foreign" settlements under fairly strict oversight and control. In 1526, in the wake of a major struggle against purported heresy, Muscovy banned Jews from entering the kingdom, a ban that remained on the books until the late eighteenth century. Likewise, one of the most consistently repeated regulations in the full collection of Russian laws was a categorical ban on the entry of Jesuits into the empire.[13]

However, historians have been revising the image of an autarkic Muscovy suddenly opened up to foreign influence and interaction in the eighteenth century, beginning with Peter the Great. S. P. Orlenko argues that the restrictions of separate settlements, clothes, and the like did not reflect deep Muscovite traditions, but rather were reactions to the rapidly growing interaction of Muscovy with the West in the seventeenth century. These restrictions, A. S. Muliukin contends, ran contrary to the traditions of the previous centuries, in which foreigners were actually given many privileges to draw their skills and trade to Muscovy.[14] Moreover, Orlenko finds so many individual exceptions that he concludes: "the limitations on the rights of immigrants from West Europe [in the seventeenth century] were strict only on paper."[15]

Foreigners were in fact a key factor in Muscovite modernization from the sixteenth century onward. The role of resident foreign mercenary officers and soldiers was particularly significant in the introduction of the gunpowder revolution and the "new-formation" regiments. From 1640–70, the number of foreign officers in Russia ranged from 4,000 to 7,000.[16] Foreign trade accounted for a large part of seventeenth-century tax receipts and was largely run through resident foreigners.[17] Moreover, foreigners played very prominent roles in building Russian factories, developing mines, iron works, armament factories, and other industries.[18]

Despite the centrality of foreigners to military and economic modernization, Muscovy kept them at arm's length. Orlenko argues that the church hierarchy was by far the most important institutional source pushing for restrictions of foreigners in order to preserve the Orthodox faith against heresies and foreign competition. Non-Orthodox foreigners could not enter a church, could not marry an Orthodox Russian, and had no access to the formal elite institutions of the country.[19]

Russian merchants often mobilized against foreign-merchant competition and their agitation was one of the reasons for a growing welter of restrictions faced by foreigners, including limits on the types of goods that could be sold, a ban on owning serfs or slaves, limits on the ability to trade with other foreigners, sharp restrictions on areas to live and trade, a ban on retail trade (foreigners could only buy or sell wholesale), and above all, much higher taxes. The tax differential grew sharply in the latter half of the eighteenth century.[20] However, Russian merchant opposition to foreigners was by no means universal or constant. While competition with foreigners bred opposition, many Russian merchants developed close trade and commercial relations which gradually expanded into cultural, political, and personal spheres. Thus, Russian merchants could be a force for both restriction and openness.[21]

The tsar exercised great arbitrary personal powers over foreigners and their activities. His permission was required for each individual case of a foreigner entering service, opening an enterprise, or entering or leaving the kingdom. By the second half of the seventeenth century, the tsar far more often used these powers to protect and promote the role of foreigners in Muscovy than he did to restrict them.[22]

Foreigners were often required to live in special foreign settlements outside the city and to wear distinguishing clothes. They went to their own churches, and lived by a set of rights and obligations different from those of Russian urban populations. Formal subjecthood status was only one of a list of social, religious, cultural, linguistic, and other factors dividing foreigners from Russians; naturalization did not automatically overcome these divisions.

In contrast, the process of conversion to Orthodoxy was much more practically and symbolically linked to gaining membership in the state and society. Upon conversion, the foreigner as a general rule left the foreign settlement, switched to Russian clothes, and gained most of the rights and obligations of a native Russian of his station. For example, the regime put significant pressure on prisoners of war to convert, at times requiring conversion as a prerequisite for release from captivity—but then using the newly baptized individual's Orthodox status as a justification for holding him in service to the tsar. This was the cause of many seventeenth-century diplomatic disputes.[23] Muscovites of all ranks considered Orthodoxy to be a far more significant indicator of membership than the formality of taking an oath to the tsar.[24] Dmitrii Tsvetaev, one of the leading experts on the history of Russian naturalization, goes so far as to claim that "naturalization was completely unknown to the law of the Muscovite era. As once was the case in Byzantium, in Moscow, conversion to Orthodoxy was a means to enter Russian subjecthood. Membership in the Russian Church was identified *(otozhdestvliaetsia)* with membership in the Russian state."[25] Muscovy encouraged conversion by offering promotion in rank for military servitors, and pay increases and other privileges for foreigners in other types of state service.[26] In principle, land and serf labor were only granted to foreigners who converted, though the need for foreigners and lack of money to pay them apparently led to many exceptions to this general rule.[27]

Despite all the attention the regime placed on conversion, only a small proportion of foreign servitors converted.[28] The small conversion rates can be attributed to three factors. First, the Russian Church refused to recognize the validity of Protestant and Catholic baptism; in Muscovy, conversion from these Christian faiths required not only chrismation, but also a full baptism. Second, conversion did not bring full membership. Converts were generally treated as "newly converted" *(novokreshchennye)*—a sort of halfway stage to full membership in the Orthodox core community. In popular lexicon, not only the newly baptized foreigners, but also their children and descendants were often referred to by the somewhat pejorative Russian term *nemchiny*. Third, conversion could become a serious barrier to leaving the empire. New converts required special permission from the tsar to do so.[29] In short, conversion to Orthodoxy did not bring full membership, but rather an intermediary denizen status.

Despite all these limitations on the rights and ability of foreigners to become full Orthodox subjects, Muscovy generally enthusiastically encouraged conversion and naturalization, even offering substantial monetary rewards and explicit political protection to newly converted and naturalized individuals.[30] Conversion to Orthodoxy undoubtedly was in many ways the most significant means to membership, but Tsvetaev goes too far in claiming that "naturalization was completely unknown to the law of the Muscovite era."[31] In fact, subjecthood distinctions were more significant than most scholars have thought. Margarete Woltner claims that already in the seventeenth century consistent semantic distinctions were made between the largely Russian-subject "Muscovite Germans" *(Moskovskie nemtsy)* and "foreigners of the old immigration" *(inozemtsy starogo vyezda)* on the one hand and more recently arrived foreign subjects on the other.[32]

The differences between the legal position of foreigners and subjects were particularly substantial for merchants in Muscovy. For much of the Muscovite era, the great majority of foreign-subject merchants were restricted to settling in border cities—primarily Arkhangelsk, Astrakhan, Novgorod, and a few others.[33] They could not travel outside their prescribed town or abroad without official documents giving approval. Likewise, other merchants were given permission to trade throughout the empire only if bilateral treaties with other powers guaranteed such a right, or if they were granted this privilege (along with others) in a special individual charter (*gramota*) signed by the tsar.[34] The charter could be granted to an individual or to a firm and it was legally revocable at the tsar's will. Thus all foreign merchants in the interior of Muscovy operated with few legal protections, under privileges granted as exceptions to the general ban on foreign involvement. In times of internal and international strife, when tensions with the outside world ran high (like the late 1640s and 1650s), the regime could conduct quite drastic revocations of foreign merchant privileges without breaking any legal principles. However, while consciousness of subjecthood status was strong in Muscovy, Muliukin strongly argues that in practice foreigners generally had more freedom of movement and other privileges in Muscovy than foreigners enjoyed in most other European states.[35]

Woltner makes a strong case for the gradual emergence of principles of *jus soli*—often referred to as "automatic" naturalization of the children of foreigners solely due to the fact of their birth on Muscovite territory—regardless of whether they had converted to Orthodoxy. She argues that this principle emerged through a series of seventeenth-century decisions to deny permission to the sons of foreigners to travel, treating them as Russian subjects without the right to leave, culminating in Peter's 1722 decree that sons of foreigners in service were automatically considered to be subjects of the tsar.[36]

France created the paradigm of a sharp conceptual and practical distinction between secular citizenship and religious subjecthood from the late eighteenth century through the revolution. Woltner and others have perhaps read a similar transition into Russian old regime reforms from Peter I onward. One of the reasons for the wide range of opinions on the relative significance of conversion versus naturalization is that the form and function of the two procedures were similar, unclearly defined, and often overlapping. In Russia, the oath of subjecthood borrowed freely from the Orthodox liturgical creed and was far from a secular alternative to conversion. Conversion and naturalization coexisted in Muscovy and imperial Russia, with the balance tipping toward naturalization only toward the end of the nineteenth century.

The most powerful policy tool used by Muscovy to draw foreigners was the grant of privileges. Again, there is a misperception that foreigners were a beleaguered, relatively repressed minority in Muscovy until the enlightened absolutist tsars of the eighteenth century reversed the old policies and extended an open invitation to foreigners. The 1649 Law Code explicitly guaranteed equal treatment to Russian subjects under the law and guaranteed access to markets and trade.[37] Those in civil or military service to the tsar also were able to demand monetary and physical punishments from anyone who legally dishonored them.[38] While foreigners could not own Russian Orthodox serfs,[39] the land estates granted to them in escheat (upon condition of loyal service) were given legal protections that were nearly as extensive as those granted to Russian subjects.

As was true of the *pomestie* service holdings of Russian subjects, these lands were held only conditionally upon loyal service, and in principle they reverted to the crown for redistribution upon the death of the servitor. No one—foreigner or Russian subject—held a *pomestie* estate in absolute ownership with unlimited power to determine its new owner after the death of the servitor. But land belonging to foreigners was protected collectively by the stricture against granting foreigners' service holdings to Russian subjects. The following clause in the Law Code says a lot about the Muscovite approach to foreigners: "Grant foreigners' [service landholdings] to foreigners with small or no service landholdings. Do not grant foreigners' service landholdings to anyone besides foreigners. Do not grant Russians' service landholdings to foreigners."[40] Their position was generally protected and at least equal to that of Russian subjects of comparable estate and service rank.

Foreigners were often granted reduced customs duties and sometimes allowed to produce alcoholic beverages and to possess and consume tobacco (not a minor privilege, as penalties for tobacco use could include cutting off the nose of the offender). They generally received higher salaries in the army or in other work.[41] Indicative of the general policy was the clause of the 1649 Law Code that prescribed that foreigners were to receive payment before Russian subjects from debtors who owed money to both.[42] This was part of a consistent policy of supporting the establishment and development of foreign trade in Russia.[43]

There was opposition to the privileges and prominence of foreigners, particularly from Patriarch Joachim, who left a "testament" on his 1690 death bitterly denouncing the policy of hiring foreigners and tolerating non-Orthodox faiths that has been portrayed as "the 'last gasp' of Old Russia."[44] Likewise, Muscovite merchants periodically petitioned the tsar to eliminate the privileges their foreign competitors received. These petitions suggest that foreigners were adept at gaining preferences well beyond the ones they officially enjoyed by bribing officials, avoiding customs duties, and manipulating the market.[45] The merchant and church opposition to the privileges of foreigners were largely ignored by the government, but in times of domestic strife and foreign wars, tsars sometimes temporarily gave way. Foreigners faced substantial popular hostility and sanctions during the Time of Troubles, and especially during the popular Moscow uprising of 1648. In that year, the merchants demanded the expulsion of foreigners from Moscow, and gained the tsar's partial acquiescence when he expelled the English merchants in the city to Archangelsk after the execution of King Charles I in 1649.[46] Agitation against the privileged position of foreigners continued until the tsar finally responded in 1652 by forcing all foreigners in Moscow to sell their homes in the city and move to the new special foreigner suburb. But, Samuel Baron has shown that this was a much less drastic measure than previously thought, and that it was as much a function of a major set of domestic reforms of the time as it was a response to popular agitation. These reforms related to the tsar's attempt to raise revenue by declaring the transfer of 1,400 urban boyar and merchant lands to the tsar, and the imposition of taxes on formerly exempt individuals. But foreigners were allowed to keep their households and tax exemptions, adding fuel to already burning resentments. The tsar's response itself—sending foreigners to a special suburb—was an act that fit well with the general pattern of Moscow's social geography. It was consistent with the tendency of the 1649 Law Code to classify people and settle them into occupationally and socially homogenous suburbs. In short, while antiforeign sentiments ran high during the urban and religious unrest of 1648 and the 1650s, even the dramatic expulsion of foreigners to the new foreign suburb hardly changed the fact that foreigners remained a privileged group within Muscovy. The tsar retained his reliance on foreign troops—they proved to be much more reliable than the native musketeers (*streltsy*) and nobles (*dvoriane*)—and continued to encourage foreign merchants to come to Muscovy to trade and invest.[47]

THE APOGEE OF THE ATTRACT AND HOLD POLICY

A widely cited April 16, 1702, decree of Peter the Great declared an open invitation to foreigners to come to the empire to trade, promising them a generous mix of privileges and rights.[48] While this decree, and Peter's reign as a whole did not mark so radical a break with the past as scholars have often claimed, Peter's reign did bring several important changes. Prior to Peter, only merchants or individuals entering Muscovite military or civilian service were allowed to immigrate and, once they did, they served the tsar with very few legal protections or rights, including even a lack of the right to leave service and the country without the tsar's written permission (and such permission was not always granted).[49] His manifesto of 1702 inviting merchants, artisans, and military servitors built upon and more aggressively pursued the common seventeenth-century strategy of granting concessions and exemptions from taxes to foreigners in order to induce them to immigrate.[50] Immigration policy was pragmatic and targeted specific modernization goals. For example, while the standard inducement to foreigners to settle in Russia was a ten-year exemption from taxes and other obligations to the state, foreign merchants and entrepreneurs received special thirty-year exemptions for settling in certain targeted areas.[51] The two biggest changes for all foreigners were the explicit new guarantees of the freedom to practice their religion, and to exit the country.[52] Foreign entrepreneurs acquired an unprecedented level of codified protection under the Manufacturing Statute of 1723.[53]

While the 1702 decree and subsequent Petrine government practices moved toward heightening the importance of the citizenship boundary, they at the same time codified and regularized the "separate deals" approach to defining the status, rights, and duties of categories and nationalities of foreigners. This paradigm has been developed and discussed by Andreas Kappeler and others as a way to understand the processes of conquest and expansion of the empire through the flexible means of imperial co-optation of local elites. It can also be applied fruitfully to a conceptualization of immigration. Nearly every group entering the empire negotiated a "separate deal" with the tsar that created a mix of rights and obligations before the law and the Russian state that was distinct and different from the laws and rights pertaining to the tsar's other subjects of similar social standing. In other words, there was no universal citizenship; only separate citizenship deals that applied to separate groups.

Why? The answer is fairly straightforward. First, the entire Russian legal system was based on the concept of legally separate groups. The estate (*soslovie*) system was structured on both the broad legal distinctions between nobles, peasants, merchants, and clergy—and upon an intricate list of legal distinctions between various gradations and subgroups within and outside these four major social estates. Even Petr Guliaev, one of the first to use the modern concept of "the citizen"—saw no contradiction between defining citizenship as "general rights and obligations common to all," while still dividing the book into four parts, each describing the unique rights and obligations of a separate *soslovie* group.[54]

Both laws and naturalization records show that the most important moment for the foreigner entering the empire was not taking the oath of subjecthood, but rather his or her ascription to an estate institution. All foreigners wishing to naturalize were required to "choose their way of life" (*izbrat' svoi rod zhizni*) and acquire permission to pursue it and be registered in it. For nobles, the key moment was gaining permission to enter a local noble corporation. For merchants, the key was gaining entry into a guild or merchant association. Foreign peasants and farmers rarely if ever entered Russian peasant institutions. Instead, they came in groups after negotiating their own separate legal deal and were usually placed in the omnibus *soslovie* category of "colonist" (*kolonist*). In all cases, it was unclear if it was necessary to take an oath to the tsar, and naturalization itself seems to have been only of secondary importance; far more important was entry into a social order.[55]

Just as Peter the Great's domestic subjecthood policy operated within the separate deals paradigm, so too the paradigm applied to foreigners according to their separate countries. The key to categorical national differences often came from bilateral trade agreements with foreign powers. Most-favored-nation principles were not well established prior to the 1860s, and thus there was substantial variation in legal status according to country of origin. Moreover, while pragmatic motives of developing commerce and economy were usually at the forefront, great power politics could also be a significant factor. For example, through much of the eighteenth century, Russia granted Armenians particularly favorable deals in order to stimulate the development of trade through Astrakhan and other southern trade centers, while at the same time expanding Russian influence. In Astrakhan, Armenian naturalization was encouraged by granting a denizen status to new subjects that allowed them to continue to enjoy the full benefits and exemptions that foreigners enjoyed after taking the oath of subjecthood, thus avoiding the main barrier to naturalization in imperial Russia—the fact that the foreigners often lost more privileges and rights than they gained when they became subjects. By gaining the sworn loyalty of the Armenian commercial diaspora, the thought was that Russia would be able to extend its influence into both Persia and the Ottoman Empire. Russian officials tried to keep their immigration inducements and naturalizations secret in pursuit of these strategic goals.[56]

Peter I also introduced important conceptual changes in naturalization policy and practice. First, he increased the ceremonial and practical significance of acceptance of Russian subjecthood. In 1700, he tried to clarify the relationship between naturalization and conversion to Orthodoxy by making the former a legal consequence of the latter.[57] He likewise tried to make naturalization a requirement of service at a high level (anyone in the colleges). This was particularly important for foreign military personnel. In 1710, there were more than twice as many foreign infantry and cavalry generals as native-born Russians in the army, and means were needed to assure their loyalty.[58] Neither attempt succeeded immediately, but both pointed toward future changes. The most important opposition to Peter's 1719 attempt to make naturalization a requirement for high-rank civil service came from the recently annexed Baltic German elites. They feared that it would lead to a loss of the privileges they had retained after annexation and led a successful effort to block the initiative. In the end, Margarete Woltner estimates that only a tenth of foreigners took the oath of subjecthood, while the vast majority remained foreign subjects who only took "oaths of service" *(prisiagi na vernost' sluzhby)*.[59] Foreigners retaining full foreigner legal status took only an oath of "temporary" service.[60] Those who took an oath of "eternal" service became what citizenship literatures refer to as "denizens"—people in an intermediary status between foreigners and full subjects. While they were technically still foreigners, in practice the regime often treated them like Russian subjects. For example, the regime denied those in eternal service the right to freely leave the country that foreigners on a temporary oath continued to exercise.[61]

The 1830 case of a foreign soldier in a military settlement in Elizavetgrad illustrates the significance and ambiguities of this system. A subject of Saxony, Second Lieutenant Frantsil entered Russian service in 1810, taking only the temporary oath of loyal service. In 1830, he declared to his commander his desire to "permanently remain in Russia as a loyal subject of the emperor."[62] He took an oath that must have been composed on the spot, for it did not correspond to either the official oath of subjecthood or the oath of eternal service. But interestingly, although the ceremony was registered as a naturalization, the text was much closer to the oath of eternal service. It does not seem that the officials involved saw much of a difference between the two types of oath.[63] The other interesting aspect of this case is that after twenty years in Russia, Frantsil suddenly decided that it was important to formally undergo a new naturalization procedure. Why? Though the answer does not appear in the records, it is likely that it was related to the outbreak of revolution in the Kingdom of Poland. Throughout the nineteenth century, war was the occasion for major increases in naturalization activity—perhaps to prove one's loyalties, perhaps due to pressure from Russian officials. Regardless, it is clear that there is a correlation, and that naturalization was more than a simple cost-benefit decision—it also had much to do with proving loyalties in extraordinary times.

CREATING THE PHYSICAL BORDER AROUND THE EMPIRE

An important part of the citizenship boundary is the physical boundary around the country and its institutions to prevent (or enable) movement of foreigners in and movement of Russian subjects out. In the twentieth century, the physical border became the most important site of control over movement and the primary place where citizenship laws were enforced. Russia's modern hard border institutions have a history going back to the early eighteenth century, but it is easy to exaggerate their significance in the early modern period. Peter Sahlins has shown how even the presumably most stable, modern, and firm border in Europe—in the Pyrenees between Spain and France—was actually only defined and hardened much later than most scholars had assumed.[64] This point holds even more for the vastly longer borders of the Russian Empire, which was largely without natural barriers like the Pyrenees, and which had only a relatively sparse government and population to enforce border rules.

The most basic border institutions only began to appear in the eighteenth century, primarily in order to fight against contraband and customs evasion on imports and exports. In 1724, in order to protect and stimulate the growth of domestic industry, Peter the Great raised import duties sharply. Previously, neither import nor export duties were high enough to give rise to a significant illegal trade to evade them, but the 1724 tariff changed the situation. Peter took measures to stop it, cutting down forest along the border with Poland, and posting units of four to eight soldiers in small border posts along the border. He gave them the task not only of controlling and taxing imports and exports, but also of catching runaways from the increasing burdens of serfdom.[65] Peter's successors reduced tariffs, and thus border enforcement declined in significance until tariffs were sharply increased again in the reign of Elizabeth. In 1754, she took the important step of abolishing all internal tariffs within the empire, conceptually and practically shifting the focus on import duties to the external boundary of the empire. But it took a long time before serious efforts were undertaken to actually control the border. In 1782, the first statute for the border guard allotted only one patrol for every five kilometers, and relied heavily on local resident volunteers and settlements of Cossacks that the regime strove to establish at regular intervals along the border.[66] The military did what it could to help police the borders, both to secure and protect the border regions and to help enforce its constant struggle against flight from conscription. Most sources suggest that despite all these measures, the border remained far from effectively guarded.[67]

Until well into the nineteenth century, the customs border guard was the primary institution responsible for controlling exit from the borders of the country by Russian subjects and for ensuring that all individuals leaving the empire had a *zagranichnyi pasport,* which literally translates as "foreign passport." For much of Russian history, the *zagranichnyi pasport* was usually only valid for a single trip out of the country, and it was usually retained by border guards upon return to the Russian Empire. Its function was closer to an "exit visa" than a modern passport. However, it was not attached to a domestic passport and it fulfilled the function of a passport for the traveler or emigrant, so it was always something more than an exit visa. In the early twentieth century, far-reaching proposals envisioned transforming the document by unifying its function with that of the domestic passport, and by switching the purpose of the document from permission to leave to a form of individual identification and a means for the regime to register the location and identities of its citizens. Since neither "foreign passport" nor "exit visa" is a fully accurate translation, I leave the Russian term untranslated in the text [for economy, I use the colloquial short form *zagranpasport* (plural: *zagranpasporta*)].

Attempts to enforce the border increased exponentially in times of war. One of the first major attempts to police the borders came during the era of the Napoleonic Wars. In 1809, the government became concerned about reports of large numbers of Polish peasants and impoverished Russian-subject Polish nobles (*szlachta*) fleeing to find refuge in the relatively free Grand Duchy of Warsaw, where they could enter military or civilian service. In order to counter this perceived military threat, the regime created an armed border guard with full authority to shoot Poles trying to slip across the border. The primary concern here was military—that these Poles would join a potential enemy army and simultaneously deprive the tsar of recruits. Men of service age captured while trying to cross the border were sent directly into the ranks of the Russian army.[68] For all the significance of this new border guard, it probably did little more than add a bit of uncertainty for those planning to emigrate. Only two battalions were deployed over a border stretching hundreds of kilometers.

But after the wars ended, the military continued to play a significant and growing role in border control. By 1827, the border guard troop strength reached 3,200, a number which grew steadily throughout the century, reaching 12,100 by 1898.[69] The state's capacity to guard its external borders and check the flows of goods and people expanded as a result. The border guards increasingly got involved in efforts to check the documents of Russian subjects leaving the country, and in intercepting attempts to cross the border illegally, without proper documents. Likewise, they were responsible for checking the documents of individuals trying to enter the empire, taking particular care to deny entry to vagrants.

Though attention to the enforcement of borders increased rapidly, Russia's external borders remained relatively porous. Underground contrabandists created major smuggling operations, bribing border guards and local officials, and operating brazenly throughout the nineteenth century. In the 1830s, there were even skirmishes and a few full-scale battles between smugglers and border troops.

One of the primary aims of the rudimentary institutions of border enforcement prior to the 1860s was holding serfs in the country. However, in practice the external border was far less important to this end than local controls on movement. In fact, in Russia the passport—that institution that documents the possession of citizenship status in modern states and declares to the world the state's support of the bearer's right to travel—was introduced in Russia in 1719 as a means to limit movement to a defined distance from an individual's place of residence and thereby to stop deserters from the army or serfs running from their landlords.[70] In that sense, the Russian domestic "passport" served the opposite function from the *zagranpasport,* holding people to their locales, not giving them permission to pass through international borders.

But what about nobles and other elites? Here, there was an uneasy balance in official policy between two contending impulses. Peter the Great famously broke with Muscovite traditional hostility toward elite travel abroad by encouraging Russian nobles and merchants to travel to Europe for education and training as part of his comprehensive program of modernization.[71] But the regime remained highly suspicious and was careful to try to prevent its subjects from becoming politically and morally corrupted by such travel. The yearly reports of both the Ministry of Foreign Affairs and of the Third Section of the Imperial Chancellery included special sections that often remarked on the "moral climate" in various countries of Europe. During the French Revolution, Tsars Catherine and Paul so sharply limited foreign travel of elite Russians that it was nearly cut off entirely. Wars also led to the sharp curtailment of foreign travel. Even in peacetime, the regime was leery of countries like France, and often denied the applications of Russian students for foreign passports to travel for study because "the moral climate there would not be healthy for our youth."[72]

Another major bias toward restricting travel came from the perceived threat to the regime posed by the Polish revolutionary national movement. In the wake of the 1830–31 Polish rebellion, the Ministry of Internal Affairs required special background checks on all applications for foreign passports for travelers from the western borderlands. The intent was to prevent contact between Russian-subject Poles and Polish revolutionaries abroad, though in practice it was also used to limit travel of Jews across the international border. Fighting revolution and preventing cross-border contact of national groups divided among empires were constant concerns of the Department of Police and the military.[73]

While the physical border grew steadily in significance, and the number of guards and troops assigned to policing the border grew rapidly through the eighteenth and nineteenth centuries, it must be remembered that this was a tremendously long border, and any determined emigrant or immigrant could easily evade border guards with just a bit of extra risk and cost. The physical boundaries around the empire were not central to the subjecthood boundary or to policies on immigration or emigration until state capacity increased markedly in the twentieth century. This distinguishes Russia from countries like Australia, Britain, Japan, and the United States, where water boundaries facilitated a close association between the physical and citizenship boundaries. Access to U.S. citizenship was controlled more by Ellis Island gatekeepers than by naturalization laws and regulations. With its long land borders and incapacity to control them, the Russian Empire depended more heavily on its policies.

TWO

Annexation and Naturalization

The Russian Empire added far more subjects to its ranks through annexation and ascribed subjecthood than through voluntary immigration and naturalization by choice. How did these people become Russian subjects?

We might start by venturing a few generalizations about the pre-1860 practices of naturalizing annexed populations. First, there was a deeply established principle of the immediate application of *automatic* naturalization, that is, at the date of annexation all individuals present on the territory were declared to be Russian.[1] This fits well with the enduring "attract and hold" theme of Russian population policy. Second, naturalization policies tended to follow a general pattern corresponding to other occupation policies. Initially, in most cases, Russia pursued an approach that was relatively tolerant of local particularities. Local elites were allowed to keep their social orders and many of their powers as the regime strove to co-opt them into the imperial system. As the empire expanded, each new population—or more accurately—each *soslovie* (social estate) in each newly acquired territory received its own particular "separate deal." In other words, "naturalization" of an annexed population rarely meant the full grant of the same mix of rights and obligations that applied to subjects in other parts of the Russian Empire. That said, it is important to reiterate that this was not so much a sign of different subjecthoods for each imperial acquisition as it was the general nature of "subjecthood" throughout the empire. "Subjecthood" in the core of the empire also was marked by separate deals for different social, religious, and immigrant groups. However, in the decades following each annexation pressures to eliminate separate deals and move toward a more universal set of rights and obligations (i.e., toward a more unified concept of subjecthood) tended to increase. Pressures to eliminate separate deals increased substantially when the 1860s great reforms introduced the modern ideological and legal concepts of citizenship (with its stress on equal rights and obligations for all) into the practices of subjecthood.

According to leading late imperial juridical scholars, the annexation of Ukraine in 1654 established the imperial paradigm for naturalization during the process of annexation.[2] After a series of Cossack rebellions against the Polish-Lithuanian Commonwealth, the Hetman of the Ukrainian Cossacks, Bohdan Khmelnytskii, signed a formal agreement with the Ottoman Porte accepting vassal status and protection within the Ottoman Empire. The agreement quickly foundered and in January 1654 Khmelnytskii called an assembly of the Cossack elite and declared an alliance with the Muscovite tsar. However, problems arose at the oath-taking ceremony. According to the report of the tsar's emissary, Vasilii Buturlin, Khmelnytskii asked him to take an oath on behalf of the tsar swearing to uphold rights, privileges, property ownership, noble and burgher charters.[3] "But Buturlin refused to swear in the name of his monarch, arguing that the tsar, unlike the Polish king, was an absolute ruler and that it was below his dignity to take an oath to his subjects."[4] Khmelnytskii ultimately gave way and took the oath to the tsar without a reciprocal oath. Shortly afterwards, Muscovite officials went to 117 Ukrainian towns, and administered the oath to 127,000 people.[5] The meaning of this agreement and these oaths has been the subject of intense dispute among historians ever since. Ukrainian historians have argued that Khmelnytskii saw this as a typical short-term oath of revocable contractual alliance between the Hetman and a neighboring sovereign against common enemies. The tsar saw it as a binding eternal act of naturalization of the Hetman and all his people.[6] The Cossack leaders of Ukraine drew on two sources for their interpretation. First, there was a long tradition of Cossack leaders negotiating temporary or long-term alliances with the Polish-Lithuanian kings, Crimean khans, the Muscovite tsars, or the Ottoman sultan. These agreements were in constant flux and alliances often shifted. The Muscovite approach in 1654 was thus completely out of touch with long-established patterns of diplomatic practice. Second, the Ukrainian Hetmanate was strongly influenced by the political ideals of the Polish-Lithuanian Commonwealth—a powerful military, political, and cultural force at the time. The notion of allegiance in the commonwealth was much more rooted in feudal concepts of a legal contract that bound both the subject and the sovereign. As George Vernadsky has argued, the treaty was likely appealing to the Cossacks precisely because it offered more privileges than anything the Polish commonwealth was offering at the time.[7] According to the commonwealth tradition, the tsar was as bound by the agreement as the Ukrainian subjects were to him.

For a century after the 1654 agreement, each time a new Hetman was appointed, Moscow was quick to confirm the "fundamental law" of Ukraine and the privileges and autonomies that it defined.[8] The treaty explicitly recognized the right of the Cossack army to elect its Hetman and protected local control over many governmental and social affairs. Moreover, article 3 of the 1667 Truce of Andrussovo granted the Zaporozhian Sich free lands a status as subject both to Muscovy and Poland, in which the Cossacks there owed common service against Turkish and Tatar attacks.[9] Even the border between Muscovy and Ukraine was maintained by a boundary and customs office that was not abolished until 1754.[10]

However, both Buturlin's refusal to formalize limits on the tsar's authority in Ukraine and the language of the 1654 documents themselves suggest that Muscovy saw the agreement as a full and permanent naturalization and incorporation of the population into the Russian Empire right from the start. The 1654 oaths referred to "eternal subjecthood" *(vechnoe poddanstvo)* to the tsar, not to anything contractual, limited, or conditional.[11] The extensive autonomies Ukraine continued to practice after 1654 were gradually whittled away by the tsars until they were finally fully abandoned and the Hetmanate was abolished and absorbed into the Russian Empire in 1764.[12]

Although Ukrainian autonomy only lasted a century, Boris E. Nolde argues that the experience created a new paradigm that was applied elsewhere, that a "system of Russian regional autonomies . . . functioned for the first time in Ukraine."[13] The duration of tolerance of autonomies varied from one annexed area to the next. For example, Kurland and the lands of Belarus were acquired in the seventeenth century; in both cases all people resident on the territory at the time of annexation were simply ascribed to Russian subjecthood status.[14] But they retained a very different mix of privileges and rights compared to other subjects of the empire. In Kurland, these privileges were remarkably extensive, including the retention of Magdeburg law in the cities and most of the powers of the local nobles and burghers, as well as the granting of a lucrative monopoly on foreign trade and shipbuilding. The autonomies granted to this region lasted quite a bit longer than in Ukraine.

Finland's autonomy was even more impressive. Annexed in 1809, the Grand Duchy of Finland retained its own citizenship underneath the scepter of the tsar. Through the nineteenth-century Finland expanded the role of its parliament and the rule of law, including expansions of the equality and quantity of rights for each Finnish citizen. This created an unusual situation where a more free and rights-based Finnish citizenship existed within Russian subjecthood. These rights adhered not to all residents of Finland on a *jus soli* basis, but rather, to all Finns, including many natives of Finland who had taken up residence within the empire outside Finnish territory.

Core Russian subjects who moved to Finnish territory without Finnish citizenship faced a very extensive list of limitations on their ability to manage businesses, work in state institutions, or teach in schools; they could not participate in elections to the Finnish parliament, could not serve in the Finnish civil service, and faced other serious restrictions. Because of these limitations, and importantly, because the Finnish welfare system was much more extensive than anything in the rest of the empire, the stakes of granting Finnish citizenship status were high. In practice, it was very difficult to acquire. Russian subjects had to maintain six years of continuous residence, and workers and merchants had to pay a huge 1,000 ruble contribution to a workers' welfare fund as part of the naturalization process.[15] Oleg E. Kutafin claims that it was generally much more difficult for Russian subjects to acquire Finnish citizenship than it was for foreigners from Western Europe.[16] It was certainly harder for Russian subjects to acquire Finnish citizenship than American, French, or Austrian citizenship.

This set of special privileges and exemptions from the obligations of Russian subjecthood came under increasing pressure from both conservative nationalists and liberal proponents of the ideals of universal citizenship in the late nineteenth century. Conservative and liberal critics alike pointed out that Finnish residents enjoyed all the privileges of "core" Russian subjects (such as the right to purchase estates in the Polish provinces), yet were also exempt from many of the obligations, enjoyed more rights, and did not have to undergo any kind of naturalization or registration to exercise the privileges of Russian subjecthood.

Committees in the government and the elected Russian State Duma both proposed to eliminate the separate status of Finnish citizenship, in various ways proposing that Finnish citizens and Russian subjects be made equal under civil law. But, for all the noisy debates such proposals stimulated, the autonomies and separate deals remained largely intact until the end of the empire.[17]

No other territory had its own subjecthood or as extensive and long-lasting separate deals as Finland. But some regions retained exemption from central obligations of subjecthood. For example, Finland, Bessarabia, and many of the residents of Siberia, Central Asia, and the Caucasus retained exemptions from conscription and other basic obligations of citizenship through the end of the nineteenth century.[18]

The Ukrainian pattern of eventual repeal of autonomies, exemptions, and separate deals was more common. For example, the Baltic provinces annexed in 1710 lost their exemption from the poll tax in 1783, and from conscription in 1796. The provinces of Bessarabia (present-day Moldova), acquired in 1812, provide another example. They received exceptional legally defined autonomy in an 1818 charter, including retention of nearly complete local control over tax and legal systems, and very broad powers to a council of boiars. Although this charter was repealed in the 1820s, serfdom was never introduced into the region, and the social structure remained very distinct from the rest of the empire. Facing severe shortages of labor, local officials even allowed the region to become a haven for runaway Russian and Ukrainian serfs in the decades prior to emancipation.[19] However, the experiment in local autonomy did not last long. The administration in Bessarabia quickly asserted the autocratic paradigm, erasing many of the autonomies of the 1818 charter in a new 1829 charter. Even during the decade of autonomy, the central government controlled immigration and emigration policy, overruling boiar resistance to pursue an aggressive and successful policy of attracting Bulgarian, Czech, German, and other foreign settlers to the region with large land grants, exemptions from taxes and military service, and other exemptions from the general obligations of subjecthood.[20]

One curious case that illustrates how distinct policies of naturalizing annexed territories could be from general naturalization policies was that of the Central Asian Jews, acquired in a series of conquests from the 1850s to the 1880s. The parts of Central Asia that were annexed and fully incorporated directly into the empire were ascribed subjecthood on a full *jus soli* basis. Thus, in remarkably sharp contrast to the general ban on the naturalization of foreign-subject Jews and strict prohibitions on conversion to Judaism in the empire as a whole, Jews resident in this territory of the Turkestan general governorship at the time of annexation "received Russian citizenship and [those who had converted to Islam] were able to return to Judaism."[21] This is a remarkable contrast to the general ban on the naturalization of foreign-subject Jews and strict prohibitions on conversion to Judaism in the empire as a whole.

In a unique arrangement, the emirates of Bukhara and Khiva (formally acquired by Russia and given protectorate status in 1867 and 1873 respectively) retained their own subjecthoods and their subjects were treated as foreigners in nearly all respects when they crossed the border between the emirates and the empire proper.[22]

Another important exception to the general story of annexation and naturalization is the politics of negotiating naturalization with prominent clan and local leaders along the frontiers of Russian expansion into Central Asia and the Caucasus. From the late eighteenth century through the mid-nineteenth century, viceroys, generals, and local governors-general often negotiated deals that led to the naturalization of important leaders with the implied or explicit assumption that their people were naturalized along with them. This sometimes was an explicit policy of the tsar to facilitate expansion. An April 1884 incident during the Russian expansion into Central Asia shows how local groups and Russian officials could seize the initiative from central authorities on such naturalization decisions. In this case, the Russian general Aleksandr M. Dondukov-Korsakov conducted negotiations and administered the oath of Russian subjecthood to a group of Turkmen of the Saryk tribe living outside the borders of the empire. The central government, especially the Ministry of Foreign Affairs, was upset, and wrote to Dondukov-Korsakov that his acceptance of Saryks into Russian subjecthood "was considered undesirable." But in the end, reluctant central authorities accepted his preemptive naturalization of the Saryks. The act caused serious diplomatic complications with Britain, and the Ministry of Foreign Affairs argued strenuously that Dondukov-Korsakov should refrain from accepting any more Turkmen tribes into Russian subjecthood.[23] This case shows that naturalization was not always simply a matter of policy composed in the Kremlin and imposed on annexed territories, but was sometimes a negotiated policy in which local authorities could shape policy in response to their interpretations of local conditions.

ANNEXATION AND NATURALIZATION AFTER 1860

This brief overview has revealed a great diversity of annexation and naturalization practices prior to the great reforms of the 1860s. But there are two general recurrent elements that defined the Russian tradition of naturalization after annexation: (1) ascription of subjecthood to the entire population at the moment of occupation and (2) the "separate deal" model of granting permanent or temporary privileges and exemptions from the obligations of all-imperial subjecthood. The great reforms challenged the second element with the notion that all subjects should share an equal set of rights and obligations before the law. Important challenges also came from international developments in the laws and customs of warfare during the nineteenth century. According to Gerhard Von Glahn, "common practice prior to the drafting of the modern rules governing belligerent occupation entitled an occupant to force the inhabitants of an enemy territory under his control to swear an oath of allegiance to the sovereign of the occupying forces." International law moved away from this practice, posing a challenge to blanket ascription of citizenship to the entire population after annexation.[24]

The concept of a legal distinction between occupation and annexation grew in nineteenth-century legal thought. While many theorists and more practitioners continued to believe that ascribed subjecthood at the date of annexation was fully legitimate, arguments that individuals should be granted the option of choosing their subjecthood gained increasingly broad acceptance, along with the related notion of the plebiscite as a means of drawing boundaries. Both worked their way into practice. After extensive use by the French in the revolutionary era, the plebiscite fell out of use in Europe, revived for the first time in the 1860s annexation of Savoy and Nice to France and in the unification of Italy.[25] The expectation that populations would be granted a choice of subjecthood and/or a vote to determine the fate of their region became more broadly accepted, as evidenced by the outcry over the lack of a plebiscite in Alsace and Lorraine after German annexation in 1870.[26] Finally, the Hague Regulations of 1899 declared unequivocally in article 45 that "it is forbidden to force the population of an occupied territory to swear allegiance to the hostile power."[27]

These international changes combined with the domestic Russian shifts in the concepts and practices of citizenship and naturalization to create a new environment for the treatment of annexed populations. Two very different cases show how the process worked in detail.

CHINESE IN RUSSIA AFTER THE 1858 TREATY OF AIGUN

At the same time that Russia launched the great reforms of subjecthood, it also annexed a vast expanse of territory from the Chinese Empire along the Amur River to the Pacific (223,018 square miles by the 1858 Treaty of Aigun and 124,179 by the 1860 Treaty of Peking).[28] Although Russian fur traders and military governors had encroached upon this territory from the seventeenth century through the nineteenth, the regime was not eager to upset relations with China, which saw the Far East as its sphere. Moreover, in the conservative era of Nicholas I, the influential Russian Minister of Foreign Affairs Count Karl Nesselrode, "argued that Siberia should remain a 'deep net' into which troublemakers could be securely consigned." Acquiring the Amur, he warned, would untie the net and allow dangerous people out and subversive ideas in.[29] However, the combination of Chinese civil war, the threat of British and other great-power expansion in China, and the aggressive foreign policy entrepreneurship of Russian military men on the ground (who had the good excuse for overstepping their mandates that they could not wait three months for correspondence from Petersburg)—all proved to be too tempting to resist.

Although the map shows this border to be a contiguous segment of the Russian Empire's border, it was quite literally on the other side of the world, with a completely different set of issues and dynamics from the other borders of the empire. Until the completion of the Trans-Siberian railway in the early twentieth century, it took months of arduous travel to get to the region from European Russia, and many preferred to take the quicker and easier route by ship around India (and until the completion of the Suez Canal, around the Horn of Africa). One Russian administrator in the 1870s even preferred to get to Vladivostok by ship, train, and ship via New York and San Francisco. In short, the Far East border was in practice no more contiguous to Russia than Australia was to Great Britain.

The annexation of this vast territory brought with it only an extremely small Chinese-subject population, estimated at just over 6,000 settled and two or three thousand itinerant Chinese (including Manchu, Han, and Daurians) in the entire vast region in 1858.[30] But this small population was next to a troubled, but still powerful nation. Russian authority was tenuous, its administrative structure rudimentary, and its levers of control few. This is the key reason why China was able to extract a set of limits on the Russian annexation that were unprecedented and without parallel in the history of

Russian annexation. Basically, the Treaty of Aigun recognized Russian annexation of the territory but left the Chinese population in Chinese subjecthood. Most authors estimate that the Russian population in the Amur region was two or three times greater than the Chinese population on the eve of annexation.[31] Article 1 of the treaty guaranteed that the Chinese in the region would retain their Chinese subjecthood indefinitely and that they would be under the authority of Chinese officials, owing all their taxes and state obligations solely to the Chinese government: "Manchurian residents on the left bank of the Amur from the Zeia river to the village Khormoldzin are to be left forever in their former places of residence, under the rule of the Manchurian government, without insult or repression from the Russians."[32] The supplementary treaty of Peking (November 2, 1860) more broadly guaranteed the right of all Chinese residents of territories ceded to Russia to continue their way of life without hindrance or subjection to Russian taxes or other obligations.[33] Moreover, the property of all Chinese subjects in Russia was protected by the 1858 Treaty of Tian'-tszin.[34] In the decades following the treaty, the Chinese government closely guarded these privileges, extracted huge payments of taxes in the form of foodstuffs and raw materials, and even required these Chinese subjects to report for labor duties like road construction on the Chinese side of the border.[35] The grant of such an extraterritorial status to the Chinese in the Zeia River region was a peculiar arrangement without analog in the history of Russian annexations. According to S. C. M. Paine and T. N. Sorokina, China insisted upon this provision because China saw the treaty as a temporary expedient to be reversed later, and thought of its continuance of tributary relations with the Chinese population as a means to maintain old-style relationships until the region was reconquered.[36]

Whatever the motive, the provision had significant theoretical and practical implications. While other Russian annexations brought automatic naturalization of the entire population of the territory on a *jus soli* principle, the Treaty of Aigun guaranteed the exclusion of all residents from Russian subjecthood not just in the present, but on a *jus sanguinis* principle covering future generations. Naturalization of these Chinese as Russian subjects was neither explicitly banned by Russian law, nor was it banned by the Treaty of Aigun, but it does not seem to have happened except in extremely rare and extraordinary cases.[37] One of the few explicit statements of policy on Chinese naturalization came in an 1886 conference of governors of the Far East, which issued an impossibly stringent set of preconditions. The conference resolved to consider applications only if Chinese subjects 1) lived in the region not less than five years, 2) converted to Christianity, 3) married a Russian woman, *and* 4) cut their traditional Chinese braided hair.[38]

In theory, the Treaty of Aigun set up a permanent foreign population with extraterritorial rights and immunities from Russian rule. In practice, this meant that Chinese subjects continued to pay taxes and other obligations to the governors of Chinese border provinces, and were extradited to China for nearly all criminal matters. Russian administrators chafed at these limits on their authority. Already in 1883, they succeeded in reversing the extradition requirement of the treaty, bringing the Aigun Chinese under the jurisdiction of Russian courts for most crimes.[39] In the 1890s, Russian officials continued to whittle away the extraterritorial status of the Aigun Chinese.[40]

When Governor-General Dukhovskoi finally conducted the census in 1893, he found that of 20,273 Chinese permanent residents, 16,102 were 'trans-Zeia Manchurians' under the authority of the Chinese officials. He concluded that these figures proved that new immigrants were falsely claiming to have been in Russia since 1858 or to be the descendents of such individuals. He proceeded to simply ignore their special status and used administrative means to treat them all like other foreigners. This caused many—often successful—diplomatic protests from China. The situation remained tense and in limbo until the extraordinary events of the Boxer Rebellion.[41]

In June 1900, Chinese began to attack Russian guards and personnel along the Far Eastern Railway in Manchuria. In the same month, the governor of Aigun called Chinese men aged eighteen to forty living in the Russian Empire to military duty. Many left suddenly, with their families and possessions. The crisis peaked first in the small city of Blagoveshchensk, which was located far to the west of Aigun, but had a large population of Chinese merchants and laborers, and served as the base for many Chinese gold prospectors. For several weeks, rebel forces in China gathered along the Amur at and around the city. Nervous Russian officials reported the spread of propaganda among the Chinese populations on the Russian side of the border and despite public declarations that the government would protect the rights of foreign-subject Chinese, secretly began to consider internment, expulsion, or other measures. As tensions mounted, some Chinese began to spontaneously depart the region for China. On July 1, 1900, the Chinese rebels shelled Blagoveshchensk sporadically, and two days later the military governor of the Amur region, Konstantin Nikolaevich Gribskii, ordered the mass deportation of the entire Chinese population. More than three thousand Chinese from the region were quickly rounded up by military and police forces, driven to an abandoned town, and between July 4 and July 8 were forced into the Amur River. Reports indicate that only a few hundred made it across the river alive.[42]

In the midst of these events, from July 5–10, 1900, nearly the entire population of the trans-Zeia Chinese left the Russian Empire. A special commission that investigated the areas of former Chinese settlement in September 1900 concluded that seventy-six settlements were burned to the ground, and only ten were not destroyed, leaving 114,500 desiatin (124,800 hectares) deserted. The land was quickly transferred to Cossacks and the treasury for redistribution. It was a remarkably swift and decisive conclusion to the experiment in Chinese extraterritoriality in the Russian Far East.[43]

The 1858–60 annexation of Chinese territory in the distant and sparsely populated Far East was exceptional. It was the only major annexation not to ascribe Russian subjecthood to the entire annexed population at a set date, instead setting up an unprecedented experiment in extraterritoriality. The experiment failed spectacularly. Russian administrators could not accept Chinese claims to the taxes, services, and loyalties of the annexed Chinese populations. When crisis hit four decades after annexation, the administration drove the population out of the country. This decision was taken in the context of a broader administrative and public campaign to restrict Asian immigration to the Far East (described in Chapter 3). In the end, this case proved to be an exception that proved the rule for Russian annexation and ascribed naturalization.

THE PROVINCES OF KARS, BATUM, AND ARDAHAN

The second case involves the 1878 annexation of three provinces (Kars, Batum, and Ardahan) at the end of a war with the Ottoman Empire. It also broke with the Russian tradition of ascribed subjecthood after annexation, but in a very different way, by introducing a formal procedure allowing individuals in the annexed population to opt for the subjecthood of their choice. The populations of these three regions were diverse, but there were two major groups. First, the predominantly Muslim Adzhars and Laz—both linguistically related to the main Georgian linguistic groups—lived in all three provinces, but were most concentrated in the Batum province. Second, Armenians were most concentrated in the Kars and Ardahan regions, with a substantial population in urban areas throughout the region.[44]

There is general agreement that the war and its aftermath saw an influx of Armenians into the Caucasus from the Ottoman side of the border, and the movement of several thousand Muslim Kurds from the Russian side to Anatolia along with the retreating troops. But, there are sharply conflicting reports of the movements of Laz and Adzhars. Standard Georgian and Adzhar accounts stress the hostility of the population toward Ottoman rule, citing an Adzhar uprising in 1875 against an Ottoman attempt to order Adzhars to serve in the army in the Balkans. Merab Vachnadze and Aslan Kh. Abashidze both claim that the retreating Ottoman army expelled rural Adzhars to the Ottoman Empire, while several scholars point out the warm attitude of the Georgian intelligentsia toward bringing Adzhars into Georgia and the Russian Empire.[45] Conversely, Justin McCarthy and others claim that Russian repression drove thousands of Adzhars and Laz to follow within three years. British diplomats reported intense dissatisfaction with Russian rule among the Laz and Adzhars, not least because of widespread rumors that the Russians would forcibly convert the Muslims to Christianity, and because of the deportation of the chief mullah of Adzharia to Siberia.[46] The truth is probably somewhere between portrayals of a happy reunion of Georgians under the Romanov scepter on the one hand and the picture of a bitterly resisted conquest of Muslim Laz and Adzhars leading to a voluntary mass emigration of both on the other.

In any event, the question of the subjecthood of the annexed populations in the three provinces remained to be determined. Reports suggest that when the Russian army and administrators came to the newly conquered regions in August 1878, General Sviatopolk-Mirsky gathered the beks and elders of the former Laz Sandjak at Churuk-Su and simply declared that "their country had come under Russian authority, they were no longer subjects of the Sultan, and should be true only to their new fatherland; that for all their needs they should turn to the Russian authorities." He concluded by advising them to "return home and immediately start their peaceful pursuits."[47] However, in contrast to the typical annexation pattern, no oaths of subjecthood were administered. Article 7 of the 1879 Treaty of Constantinople finally clarified the situation. It set a period of six months, during which residents of the annexed territories were free to pick the country and subjecthood of their choice, but were required to sell their properties, renounce their Russian subjecthood, and leave the empire if they chose to become Ottoman subjects. Anyone residing in the annexed provinces on the day the six-month period expired was automatically considered naturalized as a Russian subject (whether an oath was administered or not).[48]

Why was this unique clause included in the treaty? While the clause undoubtedly facilitated Muslim departures from the region, its motives were not necessarily directed at encouraging the separation of Muslims and Christians. Rather, there is a curious connection to abstract theoretical debates among Russian international law experts that had been bubbling through the 1860s. According to Vladimir Grabar, an influential group of scholars were arguing that "population is not a mere appurtenance of territory, a thing without rights. Theoretically, it is desirable that they express their will, their consent or non-consent, to a change of state power by means of a vote of the whole people or plebiscite."[49] Such changes in thinking were apparent throughout Europe, where the "influence of the growing belief in self-determination and the principle of plebiscites as a condition of transfer of territory" proved significant in an 1860s dispute between Prussia and Austria over control of Schleswig and Holstein provinces.[50] Likewise, the practice of granting residents of annexed territories the option to retain their prior citizenship and leave the region by a set deadline was granted to the residents of Alsace-Lorraine in article 2 of the 1871 Treaty of Frankfurt, and was becoming a normal clause in treaties governing annexations.[51] In short, the nature of sovereignty was changing in international law and practice by the time of the annexation of Kars, Batum, and Ardahan.

Article 7 was path-breaking in the history of Russian practices in the sense that it created a real legal mechanism for an unprecedented exercise of individual will and choice in defining the subjecthood of the annexed populations—and it offered the same choice to Muslims and Christians, Adzhars and Kurds. Likewise, in 1878 the Russian Ministry of Internal Affairs extended an open offer of naturalization to Ottoman prisoners of war regardless of whether they were Muslim or Christian.[52]

Another important consideration for the regime was avoiding dual subjecthood. Article 7 itself led to a long series of diplomatic exchanges with the Ottoman Empire over precisely this issue. In the decades that followed, it became clear that many Armenian and Greek Ottoman subjects had briefly traveled to the annexed provinces toward the end of the six-month period before the deadline to choose their subjecthood, received documentation of their status as Russian subjects during the blanket naturalization, and then returned to Anatolia as foreigners.[53] In the decades that followed, they used and abused extraterritorial rights granted to Russian subjects under the capitulatory regime and frequently turned to Russian consulates for diplomatic protection. Russia consistently provided such diplomatic support but, interestingly, the objections of liberal Russian international lawyers to this breach of the basic principles of international citizenship law had some impact, leading to investigations and some denaturalizations of these individuals.

The greatest test of the naturalizations of the three provinces came thirty-six years after the annexation, with the Ottoman declaration of war on Russia in October 1914. For a few weeks at the end of that year, Ottoman troops occupied parts of the three provinces, losing the region to Russia again in January 1915.[54]

In the aftermath of the brief Ottoman occupation, the local Christian population and the press accused Muslims of disloyalty. Viceroy Illarion Ivanovich Vorontsov-Dashkov responded by deporting about 6,000 Russian-subject Muslims to the uninhabited Nargen Island in the Caspian near Baku in January 1915, under the accusation of aiding Turkish troops during the occupation.[55] In the same month, Vorontsov-Dashkov's assistant for civilian affairs Pederson sent a proposal to the Council of Ministers to deport the entire Muslim population of Kars and Batum provinces to the Russian interior and to permanently remove their Russian citizenship, with the goal of permanent expulsion from the territory of the empire at the end of the war if it did not prove possible to do so beforehand.[56] The proposal received strong support in the Council of Ministers, but it ultimately failed. Georgian deputies in the Russian State Duma quickly mobilized in opposition. They protested that many of the Muslims already deported and the vast majority of those targeted by the proposal were not Turks or Kurds, but rather Adzhars, and as such were "Georgian despite their Muslim religion, and therefore loyal Russians."[57] As a result of their protests, Grand Duke Georgii Mikhailovich presided over an investigation which concluded that there was "absolutely no hostile relationship to the troops or administration on the part of the Adzhars."[58] The minister of foreign affairs and the minister of justice also argued that international law did not allow for either such a mass unilateral denaturalization or for the deportation from a country of its own citizens. This was both a matter of firmly established international law and a practical concern, since such an action could spur the Ottoman Empire to retaliate with mass expulsions of Armenians and others at the end of the war.[59]

Curiously, then, this case in the Caucasus ended much better than the Far East example. In the Caucasus, the optation procedure sifted out populations effectively. The naturalization of 1879 was recognized in both Russian and international law. This contrasts sharply with the case in the Far East. In both these cases, formal citizenship status mattered a great deal. Ottoman subjects in the three provinces were all arrested and interned, while most naturalized Russian-subject Muslims in the area were left alone. It is not difficult to speculate that if universal naturalization had not been part of the resolution, a mass internment or violent mass expulsion could have resulted.

The examples in this chapter show the power of the "attract and hold" and "separate deals" principles in the formulation of naturalization policy in annexed territories. From seventeenth-century Ukraine to eighteenth-century annexations in the Baltic region, to the nineteenth-century acquisitions in Central Asia and Finland, the regime generally applied automatic and universal naturalization to everyone present or residing on the territory at the time of annexation. This inclusive practice fits well with the "attract and hold" principle of maximizing the number of subjects of the tsar. In order to facilitate this approach, the regime proved willing to apply a variant of the separate deals paradigm, allowing newly naturalized subjects to retain old privileges, exempt them from key obligations of general Russian subjecthood like military service and taxes, and even in some cases, to retain their own subjecthood. The package of privileges and obligations that came with subjecthood was nearly as varied as the territories acquired. Each region and each social and religious group within each region had its own separate deal defining these privileges and obligations. This was a defining feature of old-regime subjecthood, and one of the most successful tools of Russian empire builders.

But the separate deal paradigm eventually came under pressure in every case from an opposite drive toward administrative uniformity throughout the empire. The autonomy of the Ukrainian Hetmanate was eroded step by step until it was abolished entirely a century after annexation. The pattern repeated itself to a greater or lesser degree in other annexed lands as well. The anomalous, exceptional case of the annexed trans-Zeia Chinese in the

Far East did not prove tenable in the long run. In all these cases, it is important to stress that the motive was not just administrative uniformity, but also the introduction of the principles of modern citizenship. The great reforms were grounded in the idea of moving toward equal rights and obligations for all citizens. This idea added liberal and moderate support in the administration and the broader Russian public for action to eliminate the old separate deals in annexed lands. Likewise, as the 1878 example showed, in its last significant annexation, the regime paid unprecedented attention to the choices of individuals. Citizenship, it seems, had become too significant to simply ascribe it to an entire population.

THREE

Immigration and Naturalization

In contrast to much of Europe, population, not land, was the most-valued resource through most of Russian history. Long after Western Europe moved away from serfdom, Russia introduced and strengthened it in the fifteenth–eighteenth centuries, largely in order to keep its peasants in place so that their surplus could be directed toward the building of armies and the few other things the early modern Russian state did.[1] If anything, the rapid expansion of the empire to the south and east during this period to incorporate the vast Eurasian steppe with its rich soils added to the overwhelming official desire to attract and hold its people in the country. For centuries, population drained from the poor grey forest soils to the rich black earth of the steppe, and, starting in the eighteenth century, the government launched an aggressive program of attracting farmers from Europe to settle the steppe as well. For Catherine the Great and the economic thinkers of her era, population was the source of wealth, and any person— even if Muslim, Protestant, Mennonite, or Jewish—was worth keeping in order to expand the prosperity of the empire. Bodies were good too for security reasons. In the eighteenth century, the empire was desperate to populate and till the vast, largely uninhabited southern steppe in order to claim it for good from the Ottoman Empire and the nomadic societies that conducted pastoral migrations, long-distance trade, and the occasional raid or war against farming communities and their Russian sponsors. Russia's rulers also believed that the steppe had to be won in order to hold its core population in place. Large and growing Cossack communities on the steppe not only preyed on Russian trade and settled communities, but also provided a home for runaway serfs. Later, in the nineteenth century, concerns about the strength of the Russian hold over the Far East prompted a persistent drive to settle more people there.[2]

The most dramatic example of this population policy involved the renowned December 4, 1762, manifesto of Catherine the Great, which invited foreigners to come to Russia and settle untilled lands, offering generous inducements and permanent exemptions from core obligations like military service.

> Upon Our ascension to the All-Russian Imperial Throne, the main rule we put forth was our Motherly concern and labor for the tranquility and well-being of the entire expanse of the Empire entrusted to Us by God, and for the increase of its inhabitants. As many foreigners petition for Us to allow them to settle in Our Empire, so We most graciously declare that foreigners of various nations, except Yids [*krome zhidov*], looked upon with our usual Imperial grace, are accepted for settlement in Russia, and most solemnly confirm that that all who come to Russia will be given Our Monarchic kindness and goodwill, in the hope that they, having received Our Motherly munificence, will take care, having settled in Russia, to live in peace and prosperity, for the good of all of society.[3]

Foreigners could purchase unpopulated lands, and in fact the regime went to great lengths to draw foreigners to Russia to purchase and settle empty lands on its vast steppe from the middle of the eighteenth century to the early nineteenth century.[4]

While the demand for people was powerful and persistent in the *longue durée* of Russian history, there were many important limits to the *type* of people considered to be desirable or acceptable. For example, foreign clergy were always a serious concern for the regime. All immigration laws, going back at least to the 1649 Law Code banned the entry of any member of the Jesuit order into the empire.[5] Likewise, particularly in the wake of the 1830 and 1863 Polish rebellions, tight controls were imposed over the entry of any Catholic clergy. Foreign dervishes were not so strictly banned from entry, but they were not allowed to naturalize.[6] Even the entry of foreign Orthodox monks and priests from the Ottoman Empire, Bessarabia, and elsewhere was tightly regulated.[7] Various laws and administrative regulations banned the issuance of visas to foreign gypsies. Local officials were granted authority to deport them from the country or to the interior as vagrants.[8]

The most important restrictions of all in terms of their severity and number of individuals affected applied to Jews. But they were not as ancient or automatically applied as popular and scholarly writings often imply. For example, during the first few decades after the 1772–95 annexations of the Polish-Lithuanian Commonwealth—the region where most of Russia's Jews lived—there were no explicit special limitations on the immigration of foreign Jews. An 1804 statute even explicitly guaranteed that foreign-subject Jews settling in Russia or visiting for commercial reasons came under the same laws applying to other Russian subjects.[9] However, things changed in the 1820s. In 1824, the Committee of Ministers banned all foreign Jews from permanent settlement in the empire. In 1828, the prohibition was extended to Russian-subject Jews from the Russian kingdom of Poland.[10] These restrictions evolved along with the growth of an entire complex of restrictions on residence that confined most Russian-subject Jews to the shtetls, cities, and towns of the western borderlands of the Russian Empire (a region defined roughly by the western border of the empire prior to the first partition of the Polish-Lithuanian Commonwealth in 1772, and widely known as the Jewish Pale of Settlement). In order to prevent foreign Jews from getting around these regulations, an 1833 decree required all immigrants to present documented proof that they and their families were really Christians.[11]

Despite much international pressure, the regime introduced more restrictions in the late nineteenth century. Foreign Jews were only allowed to settle in Russia in exceptional cases requiring the approval of the Ministry of Internal Affairs and only if they fell into one of the following categories:[12] (1) rabbis considered necessary by the government, (2) medics for the army and navy, (3) those with intentions to found factories (except breweries) and bringing a minimum of 15,000 rubles to invest (if they built the factory within three years, they could apply for naturalization, if they did not they were to be expelled from the country), or (4) craftsmen and masters.[13]

Naturalization was extremely difficult for immigrant Jews. By an 1896 decision the only categories of foreign Jews who could become Russian subjects were those building factories, craftsmen and masters, and Central Asian Jews wishing to enter guilds in Orenburg province.[14] The Department of Police files contain many cases of the discovery and deportation of individuals who had acquired visas on their passports without notation that they were Jewish, or came to Russia with passports falsely using Christian names. When the police discovered such individuals, they deported them from the country by administrative order.[15]

Another concern of the regime was to prevent any foreign atheists from entering the country. In practical terms, every foreigner had to indicate his religion both when applying for a visa in a Russian consulate abroad, and upon registration with local officials upon arrival in Russia—and the religion was written upon the individual's visa. Several individual cases established the policy that atheism or even agnosticism (declaring "no faith") was not allowed.[16]

These examples illustrate some serious limits on the general policy of "attract and hold." The regime went to great lengths to draw the immigrants it wanted but at the same time insisted on filtering out those it did not. Numerically, from the 1750s to the 1850s the large majority of all immigrants were farmers attracted by free land, and exemption from taxes and military service. Toward the middle of the nineteenth century, as untilled arable land disappeared, the regime's priorities switched from attracting farmers to attracting people who could contribute to industrialization.

The state had attempted to attract merchants, entrepreneurs, skilled laborers, professionals, etc., to Russia's cities for centuries. But in contrast to the fairly large-scale immigrations to open lands in the Russian steppe, the scale and scope of immigration to Russia's cities and industrial areas was limited by several important factors. First and most obvious was simply the small scale of Russian industrialization and urban growth. Second, the old regime imposed many serious limitations on the rights of foreigners for political reasons. One of the central themes of the reign of Nicholas I was the struggle to save Russia from the threat of liberal revolutionary ideas from abroad, and his police took many measures to control, oversee, and limit travel abroad and the activities of foreigners within Russia—especially in urban areas. The systems of control came to be widely seen as part of the reason for Russia's relative economic backwardness by the end of his reign. Third, precisely the type of immigrant who would be most useful—the commercial diaspora Jews, Armenians, or religious minorities—were most suspect in the eyes of the police.

THE FORGOTTEN GREAT REFORMS

All this changed after the humiliating defeat in the Crimean War. Tsar Alexander II launched a series of reforms that culminated in the law of February 10, 1864, which "opened up a new era in the history of Russian laws on subjecthood [*poddanstvo*]."[17] These laws—truly among the most overlooked of the great reforms—had important theoretical and practical ramifications. The initiators of the reform clearly planned for a radical break with the past, as a means to open up the country to foreigners who would help in the drive to industrialize and modernize the country. To a certain degree, it was a new variant of the eighteenth-century population policy of attracting foreigners. While the eighteenth-century policy aimed to draw farmers to populate and till the steppe, the 1860s reforms of subjecthood and naturalization aimed primarily at drawing investors, engineers, merchants, and skilled workers.

The reform began with a series of decisions in the late 1850s to roll back the draconian politically oriented restrictions on the entry of foreigners into the country that had been imposed in response to the 1831 Polish rebellion, the 1848 revolutions, and the general suspicion of the "ill intentions" of foreigners that prevailed in the administration of Nicholas I.[18] The government declared its complete break with the approach of the previous tsar shortly after Alexander II's accession, declaring that "restrictions on the commercial rights of foreigners living here permanently or temporarily in order to protect Russian merchants [only] harm Russian exports and competitiveness abroad."[19] In 1857, spurred to action by a French request, the government abolished the double tax on French citizens in urban estates, and lifted a number of other restrictions as well.[20] Other countries appealed for the same relief for their citizens in Russia on the most-favored-nation principle. Step by step, the Russian Ministry of Foreign Affairs played a very active role, initiating and negotiating a set of new trade treaties with individual states that led to a broad expansion of the rights of most foreigners in Russia. Each was concluded on the principle of reciprocity, bringing improvement of the legal position of Russian subjects abroad as well.[21] Each time, the most-cited reason for the government's support for the agreements was that it could facilitate international trade and economic development.[22] While the domestic context of a new reformist tsar explains why these important reforms occurred when they did, the broader global context should also be kept in mind. France led the way by abolishing legal restrictions upon foreigners from the 1760s through revolutionary era (concluding with the abolition of the special "foreigner tax" known as the *droit d'aubaine* in 1819). Austria had equated the civil rights of foreigners with natives in the 1790s, and the general trend throughout Europe in the following decades was toward greater equality of rights between subjects and foreigners.[23] Then, according to John Torpey, the 1860s saw the emergence of broad European consensus "that economic liberalism was the surest recipe for prosperity."[24] In Eric Hobsbawm's words, "the remaining institutional barriers to the free movement of the factors of production, to free enterprise and to anything which could conceivably hamper its profitable operation, fell before a world-wide onslaught."[25]

Another law in 1857 created greater legal security for foreign-owned capital investments by easing the rules on inheritance and the burdensome taxes that foreigners had to pay to liquidate property in Russia and depart the country.[26] These taxes ranged from 10–20 percent depending upon the length of time of residence in the country. As with the double tax on foreigners, a series of bilateral agreements quickly eliminated these inheritance and expatriation taxes. A decree of May 16, 1866, simply recognized the results of a wave of bilateral agreements by officially abolishing all these taxes for all foreigners.[27]

The Ministry of Internal Affairs argued that easing documentary and police requirements on foreigners on a permanent basis had to wait for the new statute on passports and other legislation closely tied to the reforms required by the emancipation of the serfs. However, Alexander II did not want to wait that long. He pushed the agenda forward by issuing an important law of June 7, 1860, which substantially relaxed passport requirements and police oversight and granted a series of new rights to foreigners, especially foreign merchants, in Russia.[28] This law explicitly repealed the restrictive January 1, 1807, decree that had established a set of restrictions on the entry of foreigners and new requirements to register and maintain police oversight over foreign residents.[29] The 1860 law declared the principle that "all foreigners coming to Russia for trade, agriculture and industry were granted the same rights [in civil law] enjoyed by Russian subjects."[30] One of the most important principles the decree established was the ability of foreigners to acquire landed property.[31] The language of the June 7, 1860, decree itself speaks clearly to the underlying motives for these reforms:

> The Manifesto of January 1, 1807 (No 22418) established a few limits on the commercial rights of foreigners living permanently or temporarily in Russia. Now, with the constant improvement of the means of communication and under the rapid growth of international trade relations, such restrictions no longer correspond to the demands of the times. On the other hand, in the

main European capitals our subjects are being allowed, along with all foreigners in general, to engage in commercial affairs with equal rights to native residents. Taking into account the useful influence that easier access to foreign capital may have on all branches of the national economy, and wishing to give a new signal of our desire to increase trade, agriculture, and industry in the Empire, and also to demonstrate our fairness in relations with foreign powers, we grant foreigners in Russia the same rights that our subjects already have acquired in the main European states.[32]

The new attitude toward immigration quickly infused all branches of the government. Even the 1861 annual report of the agency responsible for border control and oversight of foreigners broke with its traditionally negative attitude toward immigration. Based on the year's experience with a new influx of foreigners, it claimed that "there was no sign among foreigners living in Russia of ill-will toward their chosen second fatherland. On the contrary, most were fully satisfied with the privileges and improvements in their position granted by the government."[33] The main concern was that Poles and liberals were coming into the country; but the report claimed most of these were individuals without a defined occupation, and thus were not difficult to distinguish from the useful majority.[34]

A series of other measures facilitated easier travel and trade in the empire by foreigners. For example, in 1861 new rules allowed merchant ships to enter the ports of Arkhangelsk and Onega, allowing free entry without the previous requirement that passports be checked. The 1860 temporary rules on foreign passports allowed foreigners to enter the empire twice with a visa issued by Russian consuls abroad (in effect turning all Russian visas into double-entry visas). An 1861 decree of the tsar not only eliminated old bans on foreigners entering the empire through the Far East, but also created duty-free trade cities for foreigners in the Pacific coastal region.[35]

But old attitudes in the bureaucracy toward foreigners did not change overnight, as a special circular of the Department of Police in 1861 "on the unacceptability of slowness in the affairs of foreigners" made clear. The circular noted that foreigners' inheritance appeals and other matters had often "languished for several years due to the inertia of lower level officials," and that such languor would no longer be accepted in light of the new policies directed toward attracting foreigners to participate in the Russian economy.[36]

Local peasants and officials by no means greeted the immigrants with enthusiasm—sometimes expressing open hostility. For example, residents of Voronezh blamed a rash of fires on the recent arrival in the province of 160 foreign wage laborers in agriculture, most of whom had not settled into full-time jobs. The Ministry of Internal Affairs agreed to deport these foreigners from the country in response to local opposition—but only if such deportations did not violate international rules and agreements with countries to which they were to be deported.[37] In the end, most of the deportation orders seem to have been overturned. In the early stages, the new openness was a policy imposed from above.

The emancipation of the serfs also had a direct impact on the position of foreigners. Prior to 1861, one of the key restrictions on the rights and economic activities of foreigners had been a ban on their ownership, leasing, or hire of agrarian, household, or possessional serfs. After 1861, foreign nobles and merchants were free to hire Russian-subject laborers, and thus the competitive position of foreigners in Russia suddenly improved relative to Russian-subject merchants, factory owners, and nobles. Moreover, a decree issued the same day as the February 19, 1861, emancipation decree opened up the possibility for landlords to lease land to foreigners for up to thirty-six years. This was an important stimulus for immigration in the following decades.[38] These policies both encouraged immigration and created openings for unnaturalized foreigners to thrive in the economic elite.

The new law also created favorable conditions for a major new phenomenon in the history of Russian immigration: an influx of agricultural workers from abroad. According to the Third Section of the Imperial Chancellery annual report for 1862, many landlords quickly took advantage of the new laws, "bringing in foreign workers from abroad, both to increase the area under tillage and to create a positive impression on our peasants, presenting a good example of labor, morals, and improving the land through sound agricultural methods."[39] In the era of serfdom, agrarian immigrants were given or sold land and enrolled in the "colonist" estate. After emancipation, some landlords felt that there was not sufficient low-wage labor to work the lands they received in the emancipation settlement and turned to foreign workers. To facilitate an influx of foreign labor, the 1864 law allowed foreign workers to apply for Russian subjecthood immediately upon arrival in Russia by expedited procedure that bypassed the legal requirement of five years' residence in the country.[40]

For most other foreigners, the 1864 law kept in place a two-year exemption from taxes *(podat)*. In practice, because the requirement of joining a tax-paying social body *(podatnoe obshchestvo)* was relaxed in this period, foreigners were often *de facto* able to continue past the two-year deadline and avoid paying taxes indefinitely.[41]

An important 1865 bilateral agreement with Belgium extended the granting of equal rights in civil law for individuals to joint-stock companies, trade and industrial partnerships, and financial institutions. It declared that such entities founded in Belgium "may enjoy in Russia all the rights, including the right of court defense, outlined in Russian law [for Russian firms], on the condition that such companies and partnerships legally founded in the Russian Empire enjoy the same rights in Belgium."[42] At the same time, the tsar empowered (and encouraged) the Ministry of Foreign Affairs to conclude similar agreements with other states in cooperation with the Ministry of Finance—which it quickly did.

One of the central aims of these reforms was to facilitate an immigration of merchants, entrepreneurs, technicians, and managers from abroad. From an analysis of the details of important new commercial laws of January 1, 1863, and February 9, 1865, I. V. Potkina concludes that there was an important conceptual shift in the legal position of foreigners in the Russian Empire from conditional, individually negotiated "separate deals" to normative principles that opened institutions to foreigners and put them on an equal footing compared to Russian subjects. Prior to these laws, foreigners had either to naturalize and acquire permission to enter a Russian merchant estate or be ascribed to the "foreign guest" *(inostrannye gosti)* social category. For the latter, conditions of economic activity were based on detailed individual contracts signed by the tsar in every single case. Akin to the Muscovite era principle of conditional ownership embodied in the *pomestie* estate, "rights" of ownership and economic activity were not legal rights if one assumes that laws must have a universal normative content. Instead, they were more akin to individual, revocable, separate deals of the tsar with select foreigners. Moreover, all foreigners in the "foreign guest" category faced a large number of restrictions that tipped the competitive field to the favor of Russian subjects.[43] Likewise, in the nineteenth century prominent foreign investors, businessmen, scholars, and artists could be granted the title of "honorary citizen," which brought rights nearly equal to that of a subject, with the important exception that it did not give rights to will property to descendants on the same basis as subjects. Foreigners who did not naturalize or acquire one of these special statuses were allowed to invest in factories and enterprises in Russia for ten years, at the end of which they had to either naturalize or sell their properties.[44]

The new laws allowed foreigners to enter Russian merchant guilds (*tsekhy*) directly, without naturalizing, as a means to attract foreign investment and to bring foreigners out of their isolated legal and social status in the urban economy.[45] Foreigners were no longer to be granted denizen status through special privileged titles granted on a case-by-case basis, but rather were to be granted broad, legally defined rights shared by all foreigners. The reform proved quickly to be very successful toward that end—much to the chagrin of increasingly vocal Russian opponents.

REFORMS OF NATURALIZATION

Prior to 1860, there were distinct and important differences in the legal status, rights, and obligations of subjects of the emperor in comparison to foreigners. However, in practical terms, acquiring subject status meant far less to a foreigner than gaining acceptance into one of Russia's privileged social orders. The entire legal order was based on the idea of separate packages of legal rights and obligations for each individual estate. Nobles had one deal, merchants another. Thus, the key moment in the naturalization process was not acquiring the general rights and obligations of Russian subjecthood—for there were very few such general rights and obligations—but rather in the admission of the individual to a *sostoianie* (legal status group, profession, or way of life). In fact, there were many reasons for people who had entered a *sostoianie* to retain their foreign subjecthood. Not only did it bring exemption from some key obligations (military conscription being the most important), but it also allowed the foreigner to retain diplomatic protection. The latter could be a very significant factor in a land where individual and property rights often were less secure and extensive than would be the case in the individual's country of origin.[46] A foreigner contemplating naturalization might well conclude that diplomatic channels of appeal and bilateral agreements between the Russian Empire and his or her native state might provide greater personal and property protection than he would exercise as a Russian subject (former subjecthood could not be kept upon naturalization in Russia). The 1860s reforms gave foreigners nearly all the rights of subjecthood without the obligations.[47] If the only thing to be gained through naturalization was new obligations, then why naturalize?

In practice, many foreigners never did naturalize. Already in the seventeenth century, the principle had become established that foreigners could serve the tsar (even in the army) without naturalizing. There were separate and unrelated oaths for foreigners entering Russian service, and this distinction remained in Russian law to the end of the imperial period.[48] The only one required for service was an oath of "loyal service" *(Prisiaga na vernost' sluzhby)*.[49] There was a separate, different oath taken to become a subject of the tsar *(Prisiaga na poddanstvo)*. The military archives include numerous examples of foreigners ranging from khans in the Caucasus to German colonist low- rank officers, to foreign nobles of high rank who served the tsar for decades without naturalizing, taking only the former, not the latter oath.[50]

However, by the middle of the nineteenth century, the Russian Empire's rates of naturalization were actually slightly higher than those of Great Britain, the United States, Canada, France, the German Empire, and the Hapsburg Monarchy. According to official statistics from 1839–63, the number of official naturalizations was usually 5–10 percent of the net immigration. In international comparative context, this is quite an impressive number (see Table 5 at the end of the book). There are several possible explanations for the relatively high rates of naturalization in the Russian Empire prior to the 1860s. First, the paramount interest of many European countries (particularly the German states both before and after 1870) was keeping welfare bills as low as possible. Only subjects were eligible for benefits, so these states had a constant strong incentive to hinder and limit naturalization and tolerate large unnaturalized foreign populations.[51] With Russia almost entirely lacking state-funded services for its subjects, there were few corresponding incentives for restrictive naturalization policies. Second, prior to the 1860s reforms, foreign merchants and other foreigners faced significant legal and social disabilities—including the lack of the right to inherit property. Foreign merchants were subjected to a double tax that could be a significant monetary burden, and foreigners did not enjoy equal access to the court system, leaving them potentially more susceptible to lawsuits. They faced many restrictions on participation in retail trade, making deals with other foreigners, and running export operations. They could not get around these restrictions by entering a Russian guild until they naturalized. As a general rule prior to the 1860 reform, foreigners were allowed to invest in factories and enterprises for ten years, at the end of which they had to either naturalize or sell their properties.[52] Third, especially during the conservative reign of Nicholas I (1825–55), the regime imposed substantial new penalties on foreigners who chose not to naturalize, including making inheritance of noble status, titles, and some properties conditional upon naturalization.[53]

One might think that the reforms and liberalization of the 1860s would make the status of Russian subject more attractive to foreigners. Surprisingly, however, the changes had the opposite effect. After the landmark laws of 1864 gave foreigners full equality to subjects under civil law and removed the double tax on merchants, there was no longer much cost to foregoing naturalization. But in an era when dual nationality was difficult to maintain, naturalization would mean giving up the considerable advantage of diplomatic legal protection, something Germany, Britain, and other states defended aggressively on a case-by-case basis. As a result, official statistics suggest that naturalization rates quickly plummeted to a fraction of their previous levels.[54]

A UNIFIED, NATIONAL CITIZENSHIP?

The 1864 decree embodied a conceptual shift toward the creation of a single, generic, unified citizenship to replace other intermediate types. The first of these changes was the abolition of the legal distinction between "temporary" and "permanent" subjecthood. The former status was usually obtained by taking a special oath of loyal service (*prisiaga na vernost' sluzhby*), and brought no political rights; but it usually did bring a set of contractual rights to operate businesses, own or rent homes or factories, and so forth. The status primarily applied to students, merchants, and others who planned to live and work or study in Russia for a certain period of time but wanted to retain permission to leave the country (Russian subjects had no guaranteed freedom to emigrate). Russia was by no means exceptional or particularly late in moving to the fundamental principle of citizenship in international law that naturalization brings full rights in the new country and a full loss of the claims of the old. British citizenship law retained the notion of allegiance (i.e., nonrecognition of the loss of British citizenship through naturalization abroad) until 1870.[55]

A more serious legal distinction related to the status of naturalized foreigners who had taken the oath of permanent subjecthood *(vechnoe poddanstvo)*. A series of rulings in the eighteenth and nineteenth centuries defined the rights and obligations of naturalized foreigners differently from natural-born subjects, thereby giving them an intermediate "denizen" status. Naturalized foreigners most often remained subject to the general restrictions on foreigners, though in some cases could be extended more rights than natural-born subjects.[56] The 1864 law eliminated this intermediary status and naturalized subjects were made equal to natural-born subjects before the law.[57] The 1864 law also recentralized the issuance of final approval of naturalization, both practically and conceptually, making naturalization more an act of gaining membership in the country than one that followed from acceptance into a local *soslovie* body.[58]

The reform era also saw a consolidation of the long-established inclination in Russian law and practice toward *jus soli* principles and increasing the number of subjects of the tsar. This can be discerned from some of the detailed provisions of naturalization law, such as a clause giving governors the power to naturalize children of foreigners in the year following their eighteenth birthday. Likewise, foreigners born on Russian soil could naturalize in expedited fashion simply by taking a job and taking the oath of Russian service.[59]

Vladimir Gessen also stresses another conceptual transition in state membership from "collective" to "individual."[60] He makes an historical argument that naturalization in the eighteenth century (in Russia and Europe) was driven primarily by the policy of expanding the size of the population. Because much international migration in that era involved the resettlement of whole communities, naturalization was often a negotiated aspect of the general process of immigration. Entire migrant communities were naturalized according to special terms and conditions. This type of naturalization could often be better described as "negotiated exemption" of the community from the restrictions that applied to foreigners and obligations that applied to state members.[61] As such, it still fit very much within the paradigm of the separate deals that applied to various migrant and settler groups coming to the empire. Gessen argues that only with the reform of 1864 did naturalization begin to show "concern with the characteristics and character of the individual."[62]

However, several important exceptions to the move toward a combined universalization of norms and individuation of application persisted in citizenship laws after 1864. First, fairly extensive separate rules for the Kingdom of Poland and Grand Duchy of Finland were retained.[63] Finland, for example, was granted the authority to issue *zagranpasporta* both to Russian subjects and to foreigners living in the kingdom.[64] In some matters, the Digest of Russian Laws retained separate sections regulating the acquisition and loss of Russian state membership in these two jurisdictions. According to an 1865 administrative decree, residents of the Kingdom of Poland needed a special "passport to the empire" to cross the border into the remainder of the Russian Empire. The order for entering the Russian Empire for Finns and Poles thus differed little from the legal process for acquiring a visa to cross an international border.[65] An 1867 law granted a set of monetary and legal privileges to Russians from other parts of the empire to enter service in the Polish provinces. These privileges, combined with a set of new restrictions imposed upon the ability of Poles to acquire and inherit land in the region, together moved counter to the general trend of the great reform era toward the creation of a single imperial state membership.[66] For Poland, Finland, and to a lesser degree a few other parts of the empire (the khanates of Bukhara and Khiva, Bessarabia, the Don region, and the Baltic provinces), rules like these maintained at least some local variation in the rights of citizenship.

Second, certain groups of foreigners faced more extensive legal limitations than others—both before and after 1864. Despite much international pressure, foreign Jews were not even allowed to settle in Russia except in individual exceptional cases requiring the approval of the Ministry of Internal Affairs.[67] The exceptional foreign Jews allowed into the country did not enjoy the general rights of foreigners, but were subject to the myriad restrictions on residence and economic activity that applied to Russian-subject Jews. This was not always clearly stated in the law because of major international diplomatic disputes over the issue—especially with the United States, which insisted that all naturalized U.S.-citizen Jews receive equal protections to all other foreigners in Russia.[68] As a result, when providing visas for foreign Jews, Russian consuls were instructed not to write that permission was allowed only for residence within the Jewish Pale of Settlement. For diplomatic reasons, the regime preferred to enforce the restrictions on foreign Jews not in formal laws but rather in unpublished circulars about administrative practice.[69] Conversely, while Jews, Jesuits, dervishes, and Chinese were prohibited from naturalizing, some other categories perceived as desirable received advantages in naturalization. For example, an unpublished circular order of the tsar gave the Ministry of Foreign Affairs the right to waive the five-year residence requirement for naturalization for Turkish-subject Slavs.[70]

Third, while the new rules of 1864 did in principle create a single national naturalization procedure, they did not in practice remove the great differences in the process for different social groups, mainly because they included a prerequisite for those naturalizing to "choose a way of life" *(izbrat' svoi rod zhizni)* and be assigned to or enrolled in a Russian *soslovie* or *sostoianie*.[71] For foreign merchants, entering a Russian merchant organization or guild arguably still remained more important for rights and status under the law than formally acquiring Russian subjecthood.[72] This was even more true for foreign nobles. For both, the real point of access to rights and privileges—the real "naturalization"—remained their induction into a Russian estate or status. For example, foreign merchants and others living in an urban area were required to acquire permission from the city duma and police to enter the status of "city residents" *(gorodskie obyvateli)* before the governor would be allowed to conduct the naturalization ceremony.

Finally, in practice, the great reforms by no means abolished the separate legal status of foreigners. Ironically enough, there were frequent complaints in the decades following the reforms that by equalizing the legal condition of foreigners with Russian subjects under civil law the reforms had removed many of the incentives for foreigners to naturalize. With the granting of full equality under civil law, with diplomatic protection, and with exemption from military service foreigners enjoyed more privileges and fewer obligations than Russian subjects.[73] Victor Dönninghaus provides remarkable evidence of the broad awareness of this privileged position of foreigners in his description of the various foreigner clubs and associations in Moscow, particularly the case of a prolonged 1870s campaign of Russian subjects to gain access to the German Club, an influential and prestigious commercial/social organization that only allowed foreign subjects to join.[74] To a certain degree, the great reforms created a new priveledged social and legal category.

NATIVISM AND COUNTERREFORMS

Russian journalists and politicians quickly spoke out against the new privileges granted to foreigners and the rapid influx of foreign immigrants, merchants, investors, and others that followed. Neither a relatively prominent role for foreigners in the Russian economy nor opposition from the press and Russian merchants was a new phenomenon. In fact, the prominent role of foreigners in commercial affairs in Petersburg, Moscow, and other cities is well documented and was perceived as a problem by Russian merchants long before the great reforms.[75] One of the early focal points of anti-foreign-merchant agitation was Odessa. In 1817 it was declared a free port as a part of the larger set of experiments in the provinces of New Russia aimed at encouraging immigration and foreign trade. As a result, foreigners quickly came to dominate the commercial life of Odessa and much of the Black Sea trade.[76] Odessa is particularly interesting because the foreign merchants there were essentially granted privileges that gave them advantages over Russian-subject merchants. This was in part driven by an attempt to facilitate trade linkages with Christians in the Ottoman Empire, who themselves were a privileged order within that empire.

Odessa was only one example among many of the ways in which the official policy supported a relatively open and inviting policy toward foreigners and non-Russian local commercial diasporas in the development of trade in the borderlands. For example, Armenians were granted extensive tax and commercial privileges throughout the Caucasus, in Astrakhan, and Central Asia. The tsar supported a policy of free trade and intervened often to protect foreign merchants from harassment by local Russian officials. According to Alfred Rieber, in 1847 foreigners controlled an astounding 90 percent of Russian imports and 97 percent of its exports.[77]

There was a long tradition of futile complaints by Russian merchants against this very real domination of foreign trade and commerce by foreign subjects throughout the first half of the nineteenth century. Russian merchants repeatedly argued that foreigners should be forced to naturalize or lose their privileges.[78] The era of the great reforms marked the transformation of sporadic and fairly localized instances of protest against foreigners' role in the economy into a more coherent unified national campaign. Several of the publications that emerged in the 1850s in response to the new press freedoms allowed by Alexander II focused their publishing agenda on issues of economic nationalism and promotion of the interests of the

Russian merchants against foreigners. Fedor Chizhov, editor of *Vestnik promyshlennosti (The Herald of Industry)* and prominent proponent of economic nationalist ideas, developed a comprehensive economic program aimed at reducing the role of foreigners in the economy. He had already come out strongly against the tariff reductions and early liberalization of immigration and naturalization in 1857. He and others, both those of the literary, Slavophile orientation and those who wrote for the Russian merchant community, were very critical of the liberal reforms of citizenship in the 1860s.[79]

However, while their articles and lobbying probably did prevent some liberalizing measures,[80] their critiques were more often simply ignored by the government. Officials pursued a generally favorable and open policy toward immigration until the era of the counterreforms of the 1880s. That said, it should also be noted that international interaction by no means solely pushed Russia to liberalize and open its borders—even in the period of economic boom and international liberalism of the 1860s. Although a series of bilateral agreements greatly expanded the rights and protections of foreigners, different clauses in the same treaties and conventions created much stronger controls on the international migration of deserters, vagrants, Jews, Jesuits, gypsies, revolutionaries, criminals, and political radicals. When one scans the thick files of daily diplomatic correspondence between Russia, Austria, and the Ottoman Empire, it quickly becomes clear how closely these countries cooperated to control the movements of these populations. In this sense, the "long peace" of the nineteenth century not only facilitated international migrations and the "mixing of peoples," but also close cooperation among neighboring powers to restrict migration of undesired groups and individuals into each other's countries.[81]

The nativists were responding to very real and major increases in the volume of immigration to the Russian Empire, which in turn was part of a massive worldwide rise in international migration and travel. Popular nativist reaction to immigration focused on the land question. The late eighteenth-century invitation to immigrants to come and settle broad expanses of available land on the steppe came to an end in the nineteenth century, primarily because in the postemancipation decades rapid population growth led to a serious arable land shortage in many parts of the empire. The rise of the land question to the top of the domestic agenda completely transformed the position of foreign settlers, both in the eyes of the public and the state. Foreign "colonist" farmers bore the brunt of the nativist reaction.[82]

At the same time, the state began to rescind some of the privileges it had granted the colonists to induce them to immigrate to Russia in the first place. The ideology of citizenship in the great reform era combined with these factors to create a powerful argument that colonists should be brought into equality with other subjects in terms of their rights and obligations before the law. This led to the 1871 law abolishing the separate legal-social status of "colonist," and bringing naturalized colonists under all-Russian laws.[83] When the great reform of 1874 declared the principle of universal military conscription, the colonists lost their most important privilege— exemption from military service. This led to a large emigration of German and other colonist settlers.[84] This law is most often portrayed in the context of imperial "Russification" policies. It can also be seen as part of the great reform era shift from the old separate deals paradigm to citizenship. The state was demanding that colonists become Russian citizens, with all the rights and obligations that entailed. For our purposes, one important result of these measures was a sudden increase in the significance of citizenship status. Foreign-subject colonists remained exempt from military service, but naturalized colonists no longer were exempt.

Citizenship laws and practices always include a tension between universalism on the one hand and a tendency toward variegated approaches to different borders and populations on the other. In many ways it is not possible to think of Russian citizenship policy as anything but a set of separate deals for individual populations and groups, further differentiated by border region. Take, for example, the case of policies toward Jewish migration, where the Russian Empire continued its long-standing practice of issuing separate legal clauses for Jews from different border areas. Laws were much more accommodating to the international migration of Central Asian and Karaim Jews along the southern and eastern borders of the empire than they were to the movement of Jews across the European borders.[85]

However, the new great reform era spirit of legality and of the universality of legal and administrative norms challenged the differentiated separate deal approach. In the internal correspondence of Russian officials, there are many instances where proposals for a variegated approach were rejected as being incompatible with national or international legal norms. The oft-repeated principle among Russian jurists and administrators that "laws should be universally applicable, while administrative practices could be differentiated" generally held.[86] Moreover, administrative practices in one region often influenced practices in other regions. The differences and similarities in Russian practices can be seen in two important but very different border regions: Germany and the Far East.

THE GERMAN-RUSSIAN CITIZENSHIP BOUNDARY

The German border was the most important of all Russia's borders and practices there had the greatest influence on general citizenship policies. The perceived need to hold Russian subjects in and to prevent Poles from crossing the border during and after the Polish rebellion of 1831 led to the construction of walls, double-ditches, and guard patrols on the Russian side and comparable measures in Prussia, eventually making the Prussian border with the Russian Empire the most carefully marked and guarded of all Russian borders, and possibly of all borders in Europe.[87] Border officials came to think of the border with Germany as the most modern and scientifically managed of all Russia's borders—a model for the development of imperial migration and citizenship practices in other border regions.[88] The buildup of this border initially was not a result of interstate hostility, but rather it was a chapter in the long history of close cooperation among the Habsburg, Romanov, and Hohenzollern empires on border issues. From the end of the Napoleonic Wars to the 1880s, these powers collaborated on border management, signing and enforcing a series of agreements that created clear and fairly effective means for the direct administrative negotiation of the return of conscription-evaders, vagrants, and political and criminal suspects. While Russian officials paid close attention to these categories, most German-speakers were valued as productive farmers, industrialists, investors, and craftsmen. Decades of relative peace and alliance between the Russian Empire, the Hapsburg Empire and the German states greatly facilitated favorable policies toward German immigration and toward resolving differences over matters of citizenship and naturalization.

Police and local officials were empowered to communicate directly with their counterparts across the border to arrange for individual deportations without the cumbersome and time-consuming process of treating each case as a diplomatic incident. This system was based on a strong set of shared interests among police on both sides of the border in promoting law and order, preventing evasion of tax and military obligations, and, especially, in cooperating to control Polish rebels. In instances when the agreements temporarily expired, the costs of dealing with deserters, draft dodgers, vagrants, political and nationalist radicals, and criminals through internment and internal exile rapidly became apparent. The system of cooperating across borders worked well for all sides.[89]

Thus, it came as an unexpected shock to many Russian officials and outside observers when Chancellor Otto von Bismarck forcibly deported roughly 32,000 Russian subjects in 1883–86 from Germany to the Russian Empire. This act has long been recognized as an important incident in the history of German citizenship—especially for its role in giving birth to the German guest worker system. Bismarck launched the expulsions as part of his demagogic tactic of gaining popular support by whipping up hostility against domestic scapegoat internal enemies of the empire (*Reichsfeinde*). In the 1870s, he had targeted the socialists and Catholics with this tactic of "negative integration." In the 1880s, faced with poor electoral results, he endorsed the nativist screeds of journalists and right-wing politicians against the relatively rapidly growing Polish population in the empire, mixing in an anti-Jewish message that was already gaining traction in the mass press.[90]

Nearly all of the Russian subjects expelled were Poles and Jews, and scholars have stressed the importance of the nationalizing intentions behind these measures.[91] Bismarck, many German officials, and the German right worried that the growth of the Polish and Jewish populations could eventually result in the loss of a German majority in large swathes of East Prussia. The expulsions could help thwart these electoral and demographic challenges by expelling immigrants and at the same time sending a message to potential future immigrants.[92]

Internal negotiations between Bismarck and government officials show that his original proposals for the expulsion of German citizens of Polish and Jewish descent were rejected on international legal grounds (one of the most firmly established principles of international law was the prohibition on the expulsion of one's own citizens to a neighboring country without that country's consent). That principle did not apply to foreign citizens, and in fact even many liberal theorists of international law argued that every state had the right to expel foreign citizens—preferably with the country of origin's consent—but even without such agreement.[93] In 1883, when German police began the selective expulsion of Jews and Poles whose documents were not fully in order, the Russian Ministry of Internal Affairs at first found little objectionable in their actions. The Russian minister of foreign affairs wrote that from an international point of view, "the German government had an 'indisputable right' to conduct such an expulsion and therefore from our side, there was no possibility to counter or stop the fulfillment of this proposal. We need to prepare to settle them and investigate to see if any are criminals."[94] The Russian Ministry of Internal Affairs was perhaps predisposed to be understanding, not only due to decades of cooperation on border issues, but also because the ministry itself was engaged in a comparable effort in the wake of the infamous "May laws" of 1881 to increase police registration and control over foreigners, Jews, and politically suspect individuals throughout the empire. These efforts included occasional expulsions of foreign Jews and other foreigners whose lack of official registration was discovered.[95] Ministry of Internal Affairs correspondence can give the impression that Russian police even sympathized with the common goals and methods of their counterparts in Germany. Moreover, nearly all emigrants from the Russian Empire left illegally, so there was little reason in principle for ministry officials to resent the expulsion of emigrants back to it. Some local officials even appealed to the central authorities to negotiate the forced return of emigrants to their towns and provinces, complaining that they were losing the most valuable members of their communities, young men "in the flower of their youth."[96]

Most of the German mass deportations took place in the summer and fall of 1885. Initially, both internal Ministry of Internal Affairs correspondence and diplomatic notes between the two countries stressed that this was certainly a large-scale operation, but that it fell within the traditions of German–Russian cooperation.[97] Director of the Department of Police P. N. Durnovo stressed that the Poles who had fled the empire to avoid prosecution after the failure of the 1863 Polish rebellion were politically unreliable and that the Russian-subject Jews being rounded up were mostly deserters or draft-dodgers being returned to the empire.[98] The conservative Russian press responded in various ways to the action—not with universal condemnation. In fact, the generally chauvinistic right-wing populist paper *Moskovskie novosti (The Moscow News)* claimed that the Polish and Jewish presses were exaggerating the importance of the action, which the paper claimed was justified on security grounds.[99] The Russian Ministry of Foreign Affairs pointed to three reasons for its reluctance to immediately register a more aggressive reaction to the expulsions. First, it did not find the expulsions of Russian subjects to be outside of the norms of international law.[100] Second, it claimed that during the expulsions, Germany took special efforts to help fight contraband trade and to return deserters and draft-dodgers. The Ministry of Foreign Affairs saw reason to believe that future cooperation in such matters to essentially make a less permeable border would be in Russia's interest. Third, the ministry report noted that Russian law did not allow foreign Jews to settle in the empire, and thus it would be difficult to object to German application of the same principle to Russian-subject Jews in Germany.[101]

But it became increasingly clear that Germany was conducting a population policy of mass expulsion rather than a police action of the old style. Russian officials objected to the "dumping" of vagrants, gypsies, and others without documents at border points and accused Germany of trying to expel German-subject Jews and Poles to the Russian Empire along with Russian subjects. Governors also complained that German- and Austrian-subject Jews were being expelled to the Russian Empire with no notation on their passports or other foreign documents about their Jewish background.[102] In September 1885, the Russian embassy in Berlin sent a formal diplomatic note of protest to Germany against "the application of the expulsions as a general measure against certain categories of Russian and Austro-Hungarian subjects."[103]

Moreover, Russian officials became convinced that there was a strong economic motive to the expulsions. The Ministry of Foreign Affairs claimed that had political concerns been foremost, young males would have been the primary targets. Instead, the deportations focused on "individuals who hardly posed any political danger, such as underage orphans, those who could not work due to illness or age, impoverished widows, and wives of Russian subjects separate from their husbands."[104]

Russian governors reported the appearance of hundreds of undocumented immigrants expelled from Germany but not checked at the border. They expressed concern that political radicals and participants in the 1863 Polish rebellion may be among them and proposed that expellees be gathered at one point at the border so that their backgrounds could be checked and a more orderly process of resettlement could be managed.[105] As a result of their demands, an agreement with Germany was concluded in January 1886, with the intent of bringing greater oversight and control over the process.[106] Special committees were established on both sides of the border to negotiate and examine the documents and political records of the deportees. But Germany continued to push for as complete an expulsion of the Polish and Jewish foreign-subject populations as possible, and was most keen to get rid of precisely the types that Russia did not want to accept.

Russian officials accused Germany of systematically undermining both the letter and the spirit of old cooperative border agreements. For example, German, Russian, and Austrian governors and police were empowered to issue a special type of passport that allowed merchants and others to cross the border in expedited fashion for business or family reasons. First it was a multiple-entry visa with up to ten connected talons that would be taken for each crossing. Then it became a renewable card allowing unlimited crossings. During the expulsions, Russian officials complained that Prussian officials were systematically abusing this system by issuing these documents to the Russian subjects they were expelling as well as to German-subject Poles and Jews who lived far from the border. By October 1886, the Russian Ministry of Foreign Affairs stopped accepting these border-crossing cards because of the repeated failure of Germany to heed its protests against abuse of the system to expel Poles and Jews from interior provinces.[107]

German claims that the action was grounded in old security concerns about deserters and politically unreliable Poles and Jews lost credibility. The scale—along with the formation of a state-sponsored effort among German landowners to purchase Polish landholdings—made it appear that Prussian elites were attempting a broader population policy of trying to alter the demographic balance of the region.[108] In January 1886 Bismarck declared in the Prussian lower elected house that "it was the policy of the government to increase the number of those loyal to the Prussian state . . . to achieve the last purpose we have no other legal means than the expulsion of those Poles who do not belong to the country and who have no right to be tolerated here. We were convinced that we had enough of our own Poles and that we had to reduce the number of Polish agitators by the number of the foreigners who are found here."[109] Along with the expulsions, Germany essentially put a freeze on all new labor immigration from the Russian Empire.

When the Germans began to think and act as though nationality population politics was a zero-sum game, it had a palpable, immediate effect upon the approach of policymakers on the Russian side of the border, encouraging them to tighten controls on immigrants from Germany, particularly those of Polish descent. The first formal note of diplomatic protest from Russia in September 1885 included a detailed addendum explaining the statistics of Polish population growth and landownership in Russia's western provinces.[110] In its 1886 yearly report to the tsar, the Ministry of Foreign Affairs claimed that the German program to buy up Polish estates in Prussia was leading Polish nationalists to promote the idea of taking the money from such sales and purchasing land across the border in Russian Poland. The ministry concluded that this was a good reason to think seriously about further limits on the ability of foreigners to acquire land in Russia.[111] Tsar Alexander III made clear that he wanted retaliatory actions against German-subject immigrants in the western regions. When the governor of Estland reported to the tsar in 1885 that landlords wanted to recruit German subjects to work in their factories and on their estates, the tsar scrawled on the report: "this positively cannot be allowed!"[112] He responded similarly to the governor of Vitebsk's reporting in the same year that "of the 1,625 foreigners in my province, 769 are in Minsk. They do little for the local population; they are foreign to all things Russian, and [their presence] cannot be considered commensurate with the sovereign's will to increase Russian landownership in the region."[113] The tsar's support for such sentiments led to the creation of an interdepartmental "committee to prevent the influx of foreigners into the western provinces" under Senator Viacheslav Pleve.[114]

Germany gradually slowed the pace of expulsions, but only brought them to an end on July 1, 1887. Labor migration from Russia remained suspended for three more years. During that time, opposition to the policy swelled in Germany. Industrialists and Prussian landlords alike found no replacement source of cheap labor and suffered the economic consequences. The shortage of cheap labor even led landlords near Danzig to seriously consider a mass importation of Chinese laborers.[115] Local governments complained of the welfare costs of supporting the families of deported men. After years of contentious debate and behind-the-scenes lobbying, agreement was finally reached on a compromise system only after the intransigent Bismarck was forced to retire in March 1890.

Germany then proceeded to set up the world's first guest-worker system based on modern border and passport controls. It was a grand compromise between the desire of agrarians and industrialists for cheap labor on the one hand and the nativist and nationalist goals of Germanization and prevention of permanent settlement of Poles and Jews in Germany on the other. It reopened Germany to seasonal agrarian labor migration, but created an imposing set of safeguards against permanent settlement and naturalization of these workers. Only unmarried workers could participate, for up to a maximum of three years. They could only work and stay in the country from April 1 to November 15. Nearly all the seasonal laborers were single men. According to international practice, in mixed-citizenship marriages, the woman automatically was ascribed to the citizenship of her husband. Thus, marriage to a German citizen would not be a way out. In practice, local officials and employers applied even more draconian controls over movement through such practices as holding worker passports and documents to prevent them from departing to other employers offering better wages and work conditions.

The expansion of this strict new guest worker system was postponed by the great international cholera epidemic of 1891–92, which led to even stricter bans on both Russian labor migration and overseas migration through German ports. In 1892, Germany even temporarily imposed a categorical ban on the entry of Russian-subject Jews. The ban was not applied to non-Jewish Russian-subject émigrés, and was only lifted once a new medical inspection regime was established at the border and quarantine facilities were constructed in Bremen.[116] Once the epidemic passed and the depression of the late 1880s turned into a period of rapid industrial growth in Germany, German officials allowed foreign seasonal labor migration to expand massively within the new system of controls from 25,000 in 1894 to 454,000 in 1905 and 901,000 in 1914.[117] The number of seasonal migrants from Russia in Germany grew steadily from 17,000 in 1890 to 138,000 in 1910.[118] While most were forced to leave by November 15 each year, substantial numbers (10–15 percent) found ways to stay in Germany legally or illegally. Combined with strict controls on naturalization, this led to a steady increase in the size of the Russian-subject population of Germany. In 1907, the total number of foreign-born workers from the Russian Empire in Germany reached 212,326 (156,847 in agricultural work; 45,439 in industry; and 10,040 in commerce and transport).[119] In short, after a harsh initial population policy of expulsion and restriction, Germany greatly expanded its oversight, documentary requirements, and police controls, enabling the creation of a new system that allowed it to import cheap labor while limiting ethnic demographic effects. Russia and the world took note.

Retaliation against the German expulsions of Russian subjects initially took the form of paying increased attention to enforcing already existing rules. For example, in 1886 Russian officials launched a concerted effort to crack down on evasions of the ban on foreign Jewish immigration. However, retaliation could hardly take the form of reciprocal countermeasures against German subjects in Russia, if only because the role of foreigners was so different. There were very few agrarian or industrial low-wage laborers, but there were substantial numbers of German subjects working in Russian industry as skilled laborers or managers, playing valued roles in the imperial economy. As the Pleve committee discussed possible actions, the key to ruling strategy in the western borderlands quickly rose to the top of the agenda, and it can be summarized in one word: land.[120]

The cornerstone of land policy in the aftermath of the 1863 Polish rebellion was the ordinance of December 10, 1865, which prohibited individuals "of Polish origins" from acquiring land outside cities by any means other than inheritance.[121] Decades of administrative decisions gradually refined exactly what was meant by "Polish origins." The definition came to rest neither upon Catholicism, nor upon place of birth, but rather, upon a subjective determination of whether the individual in question was culturally Polish. In order to prevent insincere conversions to Orthodoxy to get around the regulations, it was determined that conversion did not suffice to free a Polish Catholic from the restrictions. At the same time, the government launched an aggressive program of subsidies to "Russian" purchasers of Polish lands, giving out 22 million rubles in discount loans from 1866 to 1891.[122]

How did foreign subjects fit into these restrictive measures? Ironically, the Russian Ruling Senate issued a legal decision that the great reforms of the 1860s protected foreign subjects from the restrictive laws! Thus, one unintended consequence of the combination of the great reforms and the campaign against Polish landholding was an influx of foreign immigrants into the western provinces, above all into Volynia. Their number grew rapidly, from 90,000 owning 350,000 desiatin (380,000 hectares) and leasing 87,000 (95,000 hectares) in the early 1880s to over 200,000 by 1890. They came predominantly from Germany, but also from Austria-Hungary, and from Russian Poland. In 1890 the foreign-subject population was roughly 72 percent German, 13 percent Czech, 9 percent Polish, and 5 percent Ukrainian.[123] Concerns about the strategic and social implications of these rapidly growing agrarian immigrant communities were exacerbated by the general conditions of an intensifying land shortage in the empire as a whole, and by the disproportionately rapid growth of German colonist land purchases from Slavs in Western Ukraine. The Pleve committee justified specifically targeting policies toward this region by contrasting the nature of the Prussian border with other borders: "that which may be completely harmless and may be allowable in central Russia or on its vast, still unsettled eastern expanses, is fundamentally harmful in our western borderlands, on the border with powerful, first class, foreign states of the same ethnicity as our settlers."[124]

The Russian reaction to the German expulsions of 1884–86 came in this longer-term context. A decree of November 1, 1886 (at the height of the German expulsions) gave governors in the western provinces the power to decide on a case-by-case basis whether individuals should be authorized to purchase land in their region, giving them a means to deny foreign Poles (or the Russian-subject Poles arriving from Germany) the ability to purchase land. Then an edict of March 14, 1887, banned foreign subjects from buying, leasing, or acquiring landed property in Kiev, Podolia, and Volynia in any other way except through inheritance.[125] Although directed in major part against German colonists, it is important to keep the broader perspective in mind. The law was not—as sometimes portrayed—simply an anti-German measure. Had it been, then it would have imposed similar limitations in the provinces of Southern Ukraine, where German landholding was a much bigger issue than in Kiev, Podolia, and Volynia. It was as much a general nativist anti-immigrant measure as a specifically anti-German one, as the refusal to exempt the otherwise favored Czechs from the limits on foreign subjects illustrates.[126] But it was also very specifically targeted toward the land issue. Although military and Ministry of Internal Affairs officials several times proposed restricting the influx of foreigners into urban areas, the Ministry of Finance effectively blocked such an extension of the rules due to the economic disruption such acts could cause.[127] The Ministry of Finance was able to prevail with its strategy of the time, which involved the selective imposition of tariffs on imported products while continuing to encourage the extensive use of skilled foreign workers and managers.[128]

The law effectively slowed immigration of foreign subjects to the indicated provinces. It also caused an increase in naturalization rates as immigrants rushed to naturalize to avoid the restrictions (by 1895, 166,000 of

199,000 "colonists" in Volynia were Russian subjects).[129] The governor of Volynia was appalled to find that immigration to his province continued, but now, rather than from abroad, naturalized immigrants were moving from the Kingdom of Poland to his province. Increasingly tense relations with Germany in the international sphere contributed to the passionate arguments of the ministers of war and internal affairs on the need for restrictions on this immigration. The result was a March 1892 decree banning "non-Russian immigrants even if they were Russian subjects" from settling in rural areas of Volynia, Kiev, or Podolia provinces, and from acquiring land by purchase or lease there.

These decrees and regulations were met with wide resistance and innovative means of evasion. Many Poles and immigrants found and paid legal "straw men" to maintain formal ownership for them. Naturalized relatives signed title deeds for their foreign relatives. Officials were aware of such tactics but had great difficulty uncovering or stopping them.[130] But most importantly, Russian landlords did not want to lose their reliable leaseholder settlers and the governor of Volynia began to realize the potential for economic disruption if the 1892 decree were enforced. So in 1895, the regime backed off, exempting all Russian subjects resident in the province prior to the 1892 decree. The ban on new land acquisition and immigration by foreigners or residents of the Kingdom of Poland was maintained. However, the Council of Ministers rejected the request of the governor of Volynia, to deport those of the 26,000 immigrants who had not yet naturalized if they refused to do so by a set date.[131] In the long run, the attempts to limit the "influx of foreigners" into the western regions resulted in serious limits on German immigration to rural areas in Kiev, Volynia, and Podolia provinces, enforced more through limits on their ability to acquire land than border or visa regulations.

None of these restrictions proved effective at stopping illegal immigration by those willing to take some risk. Often, German officials facilitated illegal immigration through abuses of the existing system. Most notable of these abuses continued to be the multientry visa/border card system for residents of the immediate border areas. In 1889, the governor-general of Warsaw complained that Prussian authorities were continuing to issue such documents—supposedly reserved for people living within three kilometers of the border—to residents of interior provinces, and that the limits of eight days for Prussians and four weeks for Austrians to live in Russia on such documents were not being enforced.[132] His attempts to conduct periodic document checks for illegal immigrants at factories were opposed by Russian factory owners and the Ministry of Finance, and do not seem to have had much effect.[133]

The 1887 decree was an important counterreform and event in the history of Russian citizenship for several reasons. First, after two decades of movement toward the creation of a uniform status bifurcation between citizen and foreigner, the decree reverted to the notion of the denizen, taking landholding rights away from naturalized Poles and Germans in the western borderlands. Second, after over a century of encouraging immigration from Western Europe, the 1887 decree marked a sharp turn toward restriction. Third, a long-standing policy of cooperation with Germany and Austria on border matters came to an end. With the conclusion of a formal alliance with France in 1894, the Russian–German and Russian–Austrian borders increasingly became sites of zero-sum population politics, as both sides tried to restrict the immigration of Poles, Jews, and other "unreliable" populations to their countries.[134]

However, despite all these changes, immigration to urban centers remained easy and was even encouraged. Toward this end, it was in the regime's interest to support international conventions that Russia had signed with foreign powers in the 1860s that explicitly protected the rights of foreigners to own and use property "in cities and ports."[135] Most importantly, Russia continued to make a priority of importing expertise and capital from abroad for its industrialization effort.

Attempts to extend nativist policies from the German border regime to other parts of the empire faltered as the priorities of the empire shifted further toward rapid modernization in the 1890s. One example among many came in an 1898 Committee of Ministers discussion of a proposal from the viceroy of the Caucasus to export the 1887 restrictions on foreign subject land acquisition in three western provinces to border areas in the Caucasus. He wanted to limit land acquisition by Ottoman-subject immigrants (primarily Armenians and Greeks). Minister of Finance Sergei Witte countered that such a measure would hurt his efforts to draw foreign investment in the region and the proposal became one of many nativist initiatives that were quashed in the 1890s in favor of rapid modernization with extensive foreign participation.[136] In the decades of relative peace prior to World War I, workers, employers, rentiers, and proponents of rapid economic development won many more battles with nativists than they lost.

THE FAR EAST

The difficulties in generalizing about a single subjecthood policy for the Russian Empire are apparent when one turns from the modern border between Russia and Germany to the sparsely populated, unguarded, and often even unmarked borders of the Russian Far East. The regions and their problems were not only separated by ten time zones, but were in many other ways a world apart. However, the basic tension between national population policies and goals of economic development was comparable in both border zones and imperial administrators brought some of the techniques and policies from the German border to the Far East.

In the decades following the 1858 annexation of the Far East, the administration, desperate to populate the region by any and all means, resettled Cossacks from Western Siberia to areas along the Far East border and continued to settle convicts and to attract religious dissenters and others with generous grants of free land, and exemptions from taxes and other obligations to the state. At first, this overwhelming need for people combined with the generally open policies of the great reform era to result in fairly tolerant policies toward immigrants from China and Korea. A March 26, 1861, law allowed both foreigners and Russians to get free land from the treasury plus exemption from taxes for twenty years.[137] In 1862, Governor-general Dondukov-Korsakov even allowed Chinese laborers who had been allowed into the country to bring their wives so that "this hardworking element could settle permanently."[138] Administrators in the 1860s vetoed several efforts of Russian merchants and industrialists to restrict immigration, mining, and commercial activities of Chinese, standing strongly in favor of an open, free trade approach.[139]

However, a number of factors combined to convince the authorities in the Far East that immigration needed to be restricted. First, the rapid growth of both Chinese and Korean populations combined with the frustratingly slow progress in recruiting Russians and Ukrainians to migrate to the Far East, raising concerns about the present and future demographic balance of the region.[140] Second, the remarkable success of Chinese in commerce and trade in the region was increasingly seen as a barrier to the goal of making the region an integral part of the Russian Empire and economy and it led some competitors and merchants to call for restrictions on their activity.[141] The Chinese populations in the Far East included both low-wage seasonal laborers and a successful commercial class, with numerous examples along the entire spectrum, from marginal petty traders to wealthy entrepreneurs. Chinese were so numerous and successful in commerce that local newspapers and bureaucrats alike often referred to the "yellow dominance" *(zheltaia zasil'e)* of the commercial sector in ways that paralleled discourses about "German, Jewish and foreign dominance" in other regions.[142] This was not entirely a chimera, as Chinese presence was large and growing in the commercial sector. For example, in 1912 there were more Chinese-operated businesses in Vladivostok than businesses operated by Russians and European foreigners combined.[143] Third, racist attitudes among Russian officials mixed with condescending and exaggerated fears of Asian immigrants as unclean carriers of disease to produce a strong set of arguments for tightening the border and restricting immigration.[144] The great cholera epidemic of 1891–92 led to new documentary, port, and border controls throughout the world, and outbreaks in those and other years in the Far East were important forces toward restriction.[145] Fourth, police and officials in the Far East became increasingly frustrated with their lack of control over Chinese-immigrant activities. Examples include the huge illicit import of impure cheap moonshine *(khanshchina)* which caused many health problems; extensive abuses of the native population; a vibrant network of customs-evading junks conducting import and export operations along the Pacific coast and along the rivers; massive opium plantations with armed guards; illicit cutting of valuable mature trees for timber export; destruction of the oak population through the practice of cutting and infusing the felled trunks with shitake mushroom spores for harvest.[146] Fifth, military officials raised alarms that trading networks gave the Chinese and Japanese intelligence services a ready-made network for spying to prepare for war. This concern grew in significance as the military-strategic importance of the region expanded in the era of the Russo-Japanese War and World War I. Last, but by no means least, the international context proved significant. The land of immigration, the United States, banned all Chinese immigration through the Exclusion Acts of 1882.[147] While it is difficult to prove a direct causal relationship, Russian officials often made reference to U.S. and other international measures in justifying their proposals for action. For example, in the late 1890s, the Ministry of Justice objected to a proposal to single out Chinese for higher taxes and fees than were applied to others because it contradicted commonly accepted international legal principles. The governor-general of Priamur won the argument by pointing out that the United States and European colonial powers both did the same thing in much more extreme fashion, but were not seen as violators of international norms.[148]

Curiously, although there was still plenty of available land, and while the Chinese role in commercial affairs received the most condemnation in the regional press, the first restrictive measures were directed against foreign ownership of land. One likely explanation for the focus on land is the influence of policies toward foreigners unfolding on the other side of the empire, where land was the most important issue. The first step in this direction came in 1882, when a new administrative regulation required foreign subjects to obtain special permission from the governor-general to purchase land in the Far East. After a flurry of memos and projects to move toward more extensive measures, the decisive moment came in 1885, when Tsar Alexander III indicated his support for restrictions on foreign land ownership in the region. As a result, a June 22, 1886, statute of the Committee of Ministers banned immigrants from Chinese and Korean territory from settling in border areas.[149]

In 1888, all Korean immigration without special documented permission was banned. Given that its own government strictly banned emigration from Korea, this in effect forced all new immigrants to come illegally.[150] On June 18, 1892 (again at roughly the same time as an analogous law restricting foreigners in the western provinces of the country), the Committee of Ministers banned the acquisition of land in the entire expanse of the Far East (Amur and Primor'e) by individuals not holding Russian subjecthood.[151] Along with this, Russian authorities declared a series of border zones off-limits to settlement by Chinese and Koreans.[152]

The June 18, 1892, law in principle created a strong incentive for Chinese subjects to naturalize. However, probably mostly because of administrative barriers at the local level, Chinese naturalization seems to have remained extremely rare. The mass departure of the trans-Zeia population in 1900 by no means marked the end of Chinese presence in the region. In fact, the numbers exploded upward in the next two decades as railroad construction, gold mining, and general economic development created an insatiable demand for cheap labor. However, none of the Chinese who stayed, returned, or newly arrived in the region fell under the protections of the Treaty of Aigun. Local officials in the Far East seem to have felt empowered to impose quite wide-ranging new restrictions on Asian foreigners in the years following. For example, on July 26, 1902, the military governor issued a decree banning all Chinese and Korean residence out-side of their defined quarter in the city of Khabarovsk.[153] In 1908, the governor-general of Priamur banned giving state lands to Chinese and Koreans in lease. At first this only affected foreign subjects, but a decree of July 25, 1909, extended it to Russian-subject Chinese and Koreans as well. In practice, such measures proved very difficult to enforce.[154]

The Boxer Rebellion proved to be the first in a series of dramatic events in the history of immigration and citizenship in the Far East linked to mili-tary and security concerns. The second came in 1904–5, when most of the Japanese subjects in the Far East regions of the empire were gathered up for expulsion from the country. The operation began in February 1904, with diplomatic and monetary support from the neutral U.S. government. Although it affected only about one thousand Japanese subjects, it set an important precedent as the first systematic round-up and deportation of civilian enemy subjects during wartime in Russian history.[155] After hostili-ties ended, Japanese subjects were allowed to return to Russia.

But the security concerns of the military and police about the presence of foreigners hardly receded. The end of censorship and the introduc-tion of electoral politics as a result of the 1905 revolution added to the volume and stridency of nativist public discourse about the "yellow peril." At the same time, Russia resumed rapid economic growth and development in the Far East, creating an insatiable demand for labor. A volatile situation resulted in increasingly powerful countervailing forces arrayed against each other.

One of the major citizenship issues of the period involved the legal and policy consequences of the formal annexation of Korea by Japan in Au-gust 1910. Over several months, Russian officials wrote a flurry of memos trying to decide how to deal with the situation. Basically, the dilemma arose from the legal fact that Japan was suddenly empowered to demand all the rights and obligations of Japanese subjects for tens of thousands of Korean subjects in the Russian Empire. This was problematic for Russia for several reasons. First, Korea had not enjoyed most-favored-nation status with Russia, but Japan had. Therefore, all administrative and legal restrictions imposed upon Korean subjects (such as a ban on Korean la-borers in the gold industry imposed by the governor-general of Amur) now conflicted with international treaty obligations, and, in principle, only restrictions applied to all foreigners could henceforth be applied to Koreans.

In discussing this situation, Russian officials took a fairly pragmatic point of view. Facing the prospect of this large population falling under the protection of Japanese consuls (and potentially subject to Japanese military recruitment in the future), officials considered various options. During the exchanges of opinion, nearly all officials expressed a favorable impression of Koreans as orderly, efficient, hard-working, and above all obedient workers who accepted substantially lower wages without complaint. Perhaps because their numbers in commerce were far fewer and less prominent than the Chinese, there was no discussion of their "dominance" in any sector of the Far East economy. In the end, the Koreans were deemed too useful in the Far East economy, and because of their extreme hostility toward Japan, were not considered to be much of a security risk. While the regime continued to apply various special restrictions to Koreans such as the special passport regime and the higher fees that also applied to Chinese subjects, no new restrictions on naturalization or immigration were imposed. Thus, the annexation of Korea by Japan had only a marginal impact on naturalization and immigration rates, both of which continued to grow substantially, in response to both the demand for labor in the Russian Far East and Japanese repression and colonization in Korea.[156]

This incident is indicative of the relatively minor impact of political events on the steady growth of the Asian presence in the Far East workforce (see Table 2 at the end of the book). Russia faced an intractable dilemma in the Far East. On the one hand, the administration wanted to maximize the number of Slavic settlers and minimize the number of Asians. This was considered a matter of national security and—as the events of 1900 showed—a matter of establishing firm control over the region and the border. Russian journalists railed about the "yellow peril" and the need for a stronger ethnic Russian presence. Nearly every possible approach was taken to increase the ratio of "white" to "yellow" populations of the Far East.[157]

The administration used citizenship policy to pursue this overriding policy aim. First, from 1886–88, influenced by the dispute with Germany on the other side of the continent, Baron Korf introduced a new guest worker passport system for Chinese and Korean workers. He imposed special higher passport fees than other immigrants paid, and required a visa that had to be renewed every month for a fee of thirty kopecks. Asian immigrant workers also had to pay a special additional tax of 1.2 rubles per year, plus a 1.5 ruble fee for a special work document. Altogether, the fees and taxes came to roughly five rubles. Korf hoped that the system would create greater administrative control over the foreign workers, slow the influx of these groups, and reduce their economic influence.[158] In practice, the system was farmed out to mine and factory owners, who were made responsible for holding the guest workers' passports and collecting the fees. On the Chinese side, labor recruiters tacked on additional fees and were periodically caught forging passports.[159] Despite the corruption, the system did serve the purpose of all guest worker systems. It got cheap labor and prevented the foreigners from settling permanently in the country. The degree to which the Chinese workforce was limited to seasonal labor is reflected in the astounding gender imbalance reported in 1901—there were only 453 women out of a total 29,284 foreign Chinese in the Priamur region.[160]

The government tried giving free railway passage, five-year tax holidays, five-year exemptions from military service, free land, higher wages, and other inducements to draw Slavic settlers to the Far East. The Ministry of Internal Affairs mapped areas of high unemployment in European Russia and sent agents to recruit labor migration to the Far East. Special rules allowed the descendants of Old Believers and religious sectarians who had emigrated to Bulgaria and other countries to settle in the Far East and naturalize without the typical five-year waiting period. While these measures did bring some Slavic workers, and some stayed, their numbers were never close to enough to meet the massive demands for labor in the gold mines, railroads, and even the construction of defense installations.[161]

Governor-general Nikolai L. Gondatti deployed highly charged racial arguments as he lobbied hard within the government and in the popular press for more restrictions on the employment of Asians. The gold industry in particular relied heavily on Chinese guest worker labor, and was unable to attract Slavs to work the dangerous mines for anywhere near the low wages paid to Chinese and Korean workers. Private firms were able to resist pressures to forego cheap foreign labor. However, on June 21, 1910, the Council of Ministers was persuaded to pass a law requiring state institutions to hire Russians. Immediately, a flood of petitions for exemption came in from the railway administration, various branches of the military in charge of construction, and from other administrative entities. Some were granted, some denied, but overall the attempt to switch to Russian labor had meager results. In 1911, of 31,566 workers in state enterprises in the Priamur region, 46 percent were Asian (mostly Chinese). The numerous exemptions granted to state and military institutions undermined the June 21 law, essentially sending a message that the regime saw rapid economic development as a priority over changing the ethnic balance of the population.[162]

With the outbreak of World War I, the balance tilted briefly but dramatically toward restriction and expulsion of Asians. With little evidence, the army high command claimed that Germany was using its influence in Manchuria to recruit Chinese spies. As a prophylactic measure, army headquarters ordered the internment and deportation of Chinese traders from all areas under military rule.[163] The Ministry of Internal Affairs instructed governors throughout the country to establish close oversight over Chinese in their regions, claiming that the Japanese were using them for spying, and ordered the deportation of any Chinese raising the smallest suspicions.[164] Governors throughout the country responded in August 1914 with clean sweeps of Chinese traders from their jurisdictions.[165] However, China was officially neutral in the war, and its protests led the Ministry of Foreign Affairs to insist that governors restrict their deportations to only those "suspected of spying." Nonetheless, thousands of Chinese subjects were deported from areas throughout the empire. In October 1914, the government categorically banned the entry of Chinese into the Russian Empire. Although China entered the war on Russia's side later in the same month, this ban was not lifted until 1916.[166]

While the conviction that Chinese were prone to spying did not weaken in the army and police leadership, by 1916 economic forces regained the upper hand. Military call-ups and the pressures of defense production created a severe labor shortage in the armament industry, railroad construction, and agriculture. Petitions flowed into the Ministry of Internal Affairs requesting permission to import Asian workers. Already in August 1915, a few contingents of Chinese and Koreans were allowed to enter Russia to work on railroad construction projects.

Once the decision was taken in March 1916 to allow Chinese and Korean subjects to enter the empire, they were imported in huge numbers. The Ministry of Transport requested over 100,000 Chinese workers for its railroad construction projects, including 22,000 for the vital Murmansk railroad. The Ministry of Agriculture proposed a massive program of importing 200,000 Korean and Chinese to work as agricultural laborers in central Russia. The main limiting factor to the inflow of Asian workers quickly became the transportation capacity of the Siberian railroad (approximately 15,000 per month).[167]

Police and army officials remained suspicious of Chinese spying.[168] Their arguments were mostly overruled in 1916, but by fall 1917, economic conditions had begun to change drastically. Labor shortages eased considerably. In some areas, Asian laborers became unemployed, as in Petrograd, which reported 6,000 unemployed Chinese in the city.[169] In September 1917, the Ministry of Labor banned further import of Asian guest workers.[170]

This remarkable swing in policy illustrates the tension between the goals of rapid economic development and exaggerated national security concerns. The guest worker system, dating back to the 1880s, made it possible to have cheap labor without permanent immigration and naturalization. As a precondition for the 1916 mass import of Asian workers, the government tightened the guest worker system with more stringent regulations on documentation and oversight. Police officials played a much more prominent role in the process. They were assigned to each contingent of incoming workers and continued to oversee them after arrival.

The German policies toward Russian-subject guest workers and Russian policies toward Asians in the Russian Far East mirrored each other. The German government resolved the tension between ethnonational goals and the need for cheap labor through citizenship policy by creating a new guest worker system. Russia did not retaliate against German workers in Russian industries in the western part of the country, but did impose a remarkably similar system upon Chinese in the Far East. As in the German case, Russian officials in the Far East were very concerned about the demographic balance in a region with a relatively small ethnic Russian population and a rapidly growing Asian population. Junker and industrial demand for cheap labor led to the imposition of the new documentary and strict seasonal labor controls in Germany. Likewise, in the Russian Far East, the demand of mining companies and the ministries of transport and war for cheap labor helped tip the scales from outright restriction on immigration to a comparable program of strict passport and seasonal labor movement controls. While I have not found explicit statements by Russian officials proving that they borrowed their policies directly from Germany, there is no doubt that they were aware of the conflict in Germany, and it can hardly be a coincidence that Baron Korf introduced the basic passport rules for Chinese seasonal laborers in

1885–86—at the same time Germany was imposing its new rules upon Russian subjects.[171]

While Russia imposed draconian new restrictions on the ability of Asian workers to naturalize and settle permanently in the Russian Empire, and restricted the ability of foreigners and denizens to acquire land in the western border regions, it is important to remember that these restrictive citizenship policies did not halt the exponential growth of cross-border movement. The number of foreigners in the Russian Empire continued to grow, and in many ways, the restrictions on naturalization and ability to purchase land represent the regime's attempt to facilitate a continuation of immigration by limiting the demographic effects on the permanent population of its citizens. The guest worker system proved to be an attractive compromise and means to get cheap labor while neutralizing the threat of naturalized Asian populations overwhelming Slavic populations.

Likewise, even while imposing restrictions on land use and acquisition by foreigners and denizens, the regime continued to encourage immigration to urban areas. Despite all the new concern with population demographics and the generally suspicious attitude toward foreigners during the 1880s, modernization remained priority number one and the Ministry of Finance had a strong mandate that it used often to thwart Ministry of Internal Affairs attempts to restrict urban immigration. Russia continued to make a priority of importing expertise and capital from abroad for its industrialization effort. A kind of international competition for cheap industrial labor and for skilled workers and managers drove Russia to bifurcate its immigration policies. On the one hand, it discouraged migrants looking for land, but on the other it encouraged migrants looking for industrial jobs or urban entrepreneurial opportunities. This bifurcation had strong analogs in Germany and elsewhere. Again, Russian policy cannot be explained by domestic factors alone.

For most of Russian history, immigration and naturalization were encouraged and desired strongly by the regime, but the scale of both was relatively small. When immigration rates rose in the Far East, the regime sharply restricted naturalization as a means to continue to allow cheap labor into the country. On the whole, the "attract and hold" tradition continued to characterize the broad sweep of Russian policy even through the restrictive turn of the late nineteenth century.

During the great reform era, Russia transformed the position of foreigners, granting them many new rights and protections in an attempt to attract foreign participation in Russia's modernization and industrialization. These reforms powerfully linked immigration policy with Russia's modernization and industrialization strategies. This potent connection usually trumped domestic opposition to immigrants and foreigners. The policies of "attract" had some measure of success. Emigration policy basically aimed to "hold" the population in—but its record of success was decidedly more mixed.

FOUR

Emigration and Denaturalization

Few countries have had such a deep tradition of opposition to emigration or denaturalization as Russia. For most of Russian history the fundamental problem was a shortage of people. The most basic institutions of the country were shaped by the overriding goal of keeping serfs, soldiers, servitors, and merchants bound in servitude or service to the tsar. Serfdom evolved as a means to hold labor in place so the noble service class could exploit it. Until emancipation, emigration was unthinkable for the vast bulk of the enserfed population. The tsars also held tightly to their noble service elites. Elaborate systems of collective responsibility, hostage-taking, and monetary penalty and reward were devised to keep nobles from defecting to other states. Departure from the empire without the tsar's permission was strictly prohibited and exceptions were rarely granted. Foreigners in foreign ships coming to Russian ports conducted most trade. Even foreigners who came to Russia to serve the tsar were sometimes refused permission to leave.

Of course, official policies did not entirely stop departure from the empire. First, there was a constant flow of runaway serfs to the Cossack communities of the steppe, and in the seventeenth century defections of nobles to neighboring states were common. Runaway serfs and noble servitors alike were legally classified not as emigrants but as criminals guilty of the serious crime of desertion *(pobeg)*. Their point of departure was not the border, but the breaking of their bonds to their landlords or their sovereign. Russia had agreements with neighboring countries on the return of runaways from the obligations of military service and serfdom. While neighboring countries sometimes welcomed runaways from the Russian Empire, the tsars certainly did not recognize their act as emigration and continued to consider such individuals as Russian subjects. Among the penalties was the confiscation of estates and properties of nobles who spent time abroad without permission. For the lower classes, punishments ranged from corporal punishment and return to prior masters to exile to Siberia. Even after the emancipation of the serfs, absence from the country for more than five years without specific permission was considered a crime equal to *pobeg,* bringing criminal penalties or, for the middle and upper classes, the loss of social status.[1]

The second major means of departure was mass, group flight. Many of these mass migrations occurred after Russian annexation of a new territory, though some occurred decades or more after annexation. The most important and large-scale cases involved the emigrations of Tatar, Nogai, Adyg (Circassian), and several other groups from the Caucasus to the Ottoman Empire, both shortly after annexation in the eighteenth century, then again in 1860–61. The mass departures after annexation share some of the traits of an emigration decision, but also can be seen as part of the process of voluntary and coerced separation of subjects in the wake of territorial changes. In short, "emigration," "post-annexation state optation," "population exchange," "forced expulsion," and "deportation" are not mutually exclusive concepts or practices. Each postannexation mass departure involved several of these elements.

Formal, legal emigration was extremely difficult, requiring approval of the tsar in most cases, and very high-level officials in all cases. Legal departure from the country—whether for a short-term trip or for emigration—required a "foreign passport" *(zagranpasport),* a document dating back to a law of 1649.[2] Those attempting to wade through the thicket of regulations to acquire a *zagranpasport* and travel abroad legally were required to pay fees, acquire permissions from several layers of the bureaucracy, and to publish three notices of the planned departure in the press (to inform creditors and give them a chance to block the departure). Passports usually declare to foreign governments that the bearer enjoys the diplomatic protection and support of his native government. In contrast, the Russian *zagranpasport* served an internal Russian police function as a document required for an individual to leave the country. The *zagranpasport* was not a permanent document, but—like a visa—was valid for one trip only and was permanently retained by border officials upon return to the country. It expired after a set period of time (in 1890, it had a three-month period of validity) and then a new passport had to be acquired.[3] The Russian internal passport *(vnutrennii pasport)* had even less in common with what we think of as a passport. It was a document issued to peasants and lower classes that defined a circumscribed area of their residence, beyond which they were banned from traveling.[4] Neither passport served to facilitate travel or verify individual identity, but rather to limit movement.[5]

A long list of categories such as Poles, merchants, inhabitants of the western provinces or the Caucasus, most minorities, pilgrims, and others required additional fees, stamps, and approval forms.[6] All these factors combined to make legal "emigration" (in the sense that we think of it today) practically nonexistent as a regular yearly phenomenon prior to the 1860s (see Tables 3 and 4 at the end of the book).

The emancipation of the serfs in 1861 did not transform this situation overnight. The emancipation edict maintained a strict system of collective responsibility and internal passports to hold peasants to their villages and to keep them paying their dues to the state in the form of redemption payments over a forty-nine-year amortization schedule. From emancipation through the early twentieth century, internal passports were required for anyone leaving his district *(uezd)* or traveling more than fifty versts from his place of residence.[7] However, the emancipation set in motion a series of domestic changes that contributed to the sudden emergence of emigration as an important yearly phenomenon.

The causes of the large-scale emigrations varied. Identifying and ranking the causal variables explaining the emigration of various groups from the Russian Empire is a task in its own right and one that scholars have yet to systematically undertake. In each case, there were important "push" factors that stimulated emigration. In the case of over 200,000 Nogai and Tatars that went from Crimea to the Ottoman Empire in 1860 and 1861, rumors and fears of government repression following the Crimean War and a movement among Muslim clerics in favor of departure for the Ottoman Empire led to the exodus. For German colonists, Mennonites, and Dukhobors, the introduction of universal military service in 1874 was a key event. For the Jews, the pogroms of 1881 and 1902–7 played an important role. Shortages of land, economic difficulties, and lack of opportunities in education drove members of all groups to migrate. Another major factor was rapid population growth in the decades after emancipation, leading to declining plot sizes and overpopulation. The idea that Russia is overpopulated has often been dismissed because of its vast size. But the areas with reasonably good soils comprise only a small portion of the country, and by 1900 those regions were overpopulated by almost any measure. The resultant downward pressures on plot sizes and wages became key sources of socio-economic tension in the revolutionary era. The institutional constraints of the peasant commune (for Slavs) and the restriction of Jewish residence to the towns and cities of the Pale of Settlement both exacerbated the problem.[8]

However, scholars have begun to revise the picture of emigration as primarily a result of domestic "push" factors. "Pull" factors were probably more important. Economic opportunities in the United States, Canada, and elsewhere correlate more closely with emigration than waves of pogroms or conscription policies. As students of emigration throughout the world have found, on the local level the creation of networks abroad and proximity to transportation routes are often crucial to explaining emigration patterns. For example, scholars have found that emigration from centers of pogrom violence in the southwest did not match rates of emigration from the relatively less violent northwest, where proximity to railways, ports, and emigration agents established patterns of emigration much earlier.[9] Also hugely important is the simple fact that cheap rail and steamship travel made the journey overseas to unsettled prairies of the Americas affordable and feasible for the first time.

THE ETHNIC IMBALANCE OF EMIGRATION PATTERNS

One of the most remarkable aspects of emigration from the great reforms to the revolution is the fact that only 1–4 percent of all emigrants were ethnic Russians (depending on how one defines Russian) from 1861–1914. The United States had the largest number of ethnic Russian immigrants at an estimated 40,000 out of 1,732,000 natives of the Russian Empire in the United States in 1910 (see Tables 8 and 9 at the end of the book).[10] Emigration was just about entirely a phenomenon of non-Russian minorities leaving the empire. The sense that emigration was not a core Russian phenomenon is further highlighted by the fact that many of this tiny number of Russians were members of the Molokane, Dukhobor, or Old Believer sects.

Considered on a per capita basis, this imbalance is simply astounding. Jews were 184 times more likely to emigrate than Russians, Germans 55 times and Poles 57 times more likely. German, Lithuanian, Finnish, and Polish emigrants were all predominantly agrarian and tended to emigrate to parts of the world where land was freely available. The puzzle then is why Russians, Ukrainians, and Belarusians from the Russian Empire did not emigrate in numbers at all comparable to them. The shortage of land was if anything worse among these populations than it was among those who chose to emigrate.

A big part of the answer lies in inheritance and land tenure systems. Russians, Ukrainians, and Belarusians almost entirely practiced communal agriculture with partible inheritance. In systems of primogeniture, landless younger sons provided a constant stream of migrants to the cities and emigrants to other continents in search of land.[11] In the partible inheritance systems of the Russian Empire, younger sons were not forced out of the village. Many chose to stay, even though land allotments were shrinking rapidly. Many made their living on the smaller plot by supplementing their income with seasonal work in the cities or in their homes doing piecework. What they didn't do was emigrate abroad. Interestingly, when territorial expansion in Central Asia and then the Trans-Siberian Railway opened up new lands for settlement within the empire, Russian and Ukrainian peasants willingly took government subsidies to settle there. More than four million Russian subjects made their way to Siberian settlement in the years 1880–1914. However, for the most part, this settlement was often a matter of entire communes traveling to Siberia together rather than individuals or families making their way as migrants. This practice was encouraged by the regime, especially during the conservative reign of Alexander III, who briefly even banned individual emigration to Siberia.[12] Regardless of official policy, peasants practicing communal agriculture with partible inheritance simply did not emigrate as individuals.

The contrast with groups practicing primogeniture could not be stronger. This was clearest in the case of the Russian-Germans. While many of the German communities in the Volga region assimilated the full communal system with partible inheritance, most other German communities did not. Especially in the large communities of Southern Ukraine, Germans developed efficient forms of agriculture and a network of credit unions and financial mutual assistance that was unrivaled in the empire. This helped families and villages to buy land from their Russian and Ukrainian neighbors. As a result, the total amount of land held by Germans grew rapidly in the Black Sea region and Bessarabia. Even so, the land acquisitions could not keep pace with the high birth rates in German families, and landholding size declined. While this process was under way, emigration agents from railroad companies and steamship lines began to appear in Odessa. They quickly found that Germans in Russia were far easier to recruit than Russians or Ukrainians, leading to a large German emigration from the region. Second, third, and fourth sons in the German communities without a land inheritance often chose to emigrate. The operation was so successful that for a decade or so in the 1880s and 1890s, the bulk of the population of the territory of South Dakota was comprised of Russian-Germans.[13]

Differences in land tenure systems proved crucial to differential rates of emigration, but there were other important factors as well. One was the threat (perceived or real) that group exemptions from conscription and other obligations of subjecthood would be lost as a result of the 1874 military reforms.[14] This was of particular concern to the Germans and other "colonists." The separate legal status of "colonist" was eliminated in 1871 and the new settler-landholders *(poselian-sobstvenniki)* became citizens of the empire, losing nearly all the special privileges that had drawn them or their ancestors to the empire in the first place. Most important was the abolition in 1874 of the exemption from conscription that not only Mennonites but nearly all "colonists" had enjoyed as a privilege guaranteed in the charters and statutes defining their "separate" subjecthood deals. In the 1870s, as rumors of the impending abolition of exemptions from military service spread through the empire, so did rumors of mass emigrations. If the report of one observer of an early call-up of recruits in a Bulgarian colony is indicative, then there was probably not a great deal of enthusiasm on the village level for the concepts of citizenship as equalized rights and obligations. An elder of the village reported that "an official came to the colony, read a document and demanded recruits. Our colonists then spoke about a return migration to Bulgaria." The observer told the elder that "it was the tsar's will to make people out of Bulgarians," that he wanted to give them equal rights and obligations, but the elder insisted that "bureaucrats are doing this and the tsar knows nothing about it."[15] The actual outcome in terms of emigration was not so dramatic in this case as it was for the pacifist Mennonites, who sent a delegation of twelve leaders to the United States and Canada to negotiate a mass emigration in 1873, prior to the introduction of the 1874 reforms. When, in contrast to the United States, Canada guaranteed exemption from a draft in the event of a war (there was no peacetime draft in the United States), the Mennonite leaders chose Canada as their primary destination.[16]

The 1874 reform led to a quick rise in the number of reports of young men emigrating illegally to evade conscription. For example, in the two years after the introduction of universal conscription in 1874, a single district in Lomzha province on the border with Prussia lost 282 young men who were liable for military call-up to illegal emigration, none of whom were caught and returned from Prussia.[17] Subsequently, with Russian encouragement, Austria and Prussia introduced a number of policing and documentary initiatives that proved quite efficient in catching and deporting draft evaders back to Russia.[18] The guiding principle for Russia was that young men should not be able to escape their military and other obligations through emigration or denaturalization. Russia's neighbors agreed and cooperated fully in enforcing this principle.

However, it seems that many men were able to slip across the border and continue their journey overseas as part of a rapid rise of illegal emigration without documents. Likewise, many Muslim groups in the Caucasus felt new pressures as a result of the military reforms. Adygs, for example, found that their traditional right to buy their way out of conscription was effectively abolished when the government raised the fee in 1872 to 800 rubles, a level that only the extremely wealthy could even consider.[19] By universalizing and equalizing the obligation of military service to all subjects, the 1874 reform became a key moment in the creation of modern Russian citizenship. However, centuries of successful empire-building and immigration policy were grounded in the reverse—the notion of separate deals, and for many groups nothing was more valued than an exemption from military service. In short, citizenship challenged a key empire-building policy.

OFFICIAL EMIGRATION POLICIES

Official responses to the rise of emigration were largely negative. The general policy tradition of "attract and hold" seems to have retained a great deal of power even when population growth was outstripping land and job availability and emigration could have provided relief to social and economic pressures. Russia's persistently negative policy toward emigration increasingly distinguished it from other countries. While mercantilist notions that population was the source of wealth led most states to ban emigration or make it extremely difficult and expensive in the eighteenth century, many states changed their approach in the nineteenth century.

According to Andreas Fahrmeir, "the right to emigrate ranks high in the canon of fundamental liberties" and it "was already generally recognized as basic by the nineteenth century" in German states and through much of Europe.[20] It was a powerful concept that gradually came to be ensconced in constitutions and statutes throughout the world. The principle was incorporated into comprehensive emigration laws starting with England in 1803, then Holland in 1837, Belgium in 1843, Italy in 1888, Germany in 1897, and Hungary in 1909.[21] While the Austrian half of the Habsburg monarchy failed to pass a comprehensive emigration reform bill, it did declare emigration a basic right in the 1867 constitution (limited only by the requirement that young men fulfill military obligations first).[22] It allowed emigration agents and companies to operate legally in 1897 and established institutions to oversee and protect the interests of emigrants outside the country.[23] The impact of these policies could be huge. For example, Ukrainian rates of emigration from Hapsburg Galicia were many times higher than those of Ukrainians from the Russian Empire. In 1893, even China renounced a ban on emigration grounded in centuries of practice by abolishing all laws punishing emigration or return migration.[24]

The legalization of emigration was probably driven more by pragmatic considerations than the expanding recognition of a new right of man. If the key to wealth and power in the eighteenth century was population growth, by the mid-nineteenth century, overpopulation in rural areas was creating social tensions and keeping the rural economy from improving its per capita economic position. The growth of the welfare state in nineteenth-century Europe made it a priority for some countries to legalize both emigration and denaturalization in order to avoid the return of destitute emigrants who would stake a claim to state support based on their citizenship status. Conversely, remittances from successful emigrants (temporary or permanent) proved to be a substantial source of income. For Germany in particular, the emigrant shipping industry proved to be very profitable and a powerful political lobby in favor of fully legalized emigration.[25]

Although each of these factors applied to the Russian Empire as well, its basic policies contrasted sharply. Legal emigration remained extremely difficult and expensive. Why? It is a bit of a puzzle. In fact, the continued sharp restriction of emigration was in part an aspect of its attempt to filter emigration in pursuit of its broader population policies. A close look at the details of policy and administration reveals that the regime pursued a fairly aggressive differentiated population policy aimed at holding certain groups of the population in while allowing or even encouraging others to leave, and then discouraging or banning their return.

One of the most dramatic policies (at least on paper) was the administrative procedure of allowing emigration only on the condition that the individual be eternally banned from returning to the Russian Empire. Most famously, Crimean Tatars were allowed to emigrate en masse in the time of Catherine the Great, and then again in the decade following the end of the Crimean War in 1855, but only if they renounced their Russian subjecthood and signed a pledge never to return to the empire. As a result of this procedure, their names were inscribed in lists of individuals to be denied entry at the borders.[26] German colonists were also required to relinquish Russian subjecthood upon departure from the country and in principle were not allowed to return, although in a number of cases they did receive special permission to return.[27] By international standards, this was a fairly rare practice, and it continued to be selectively applied in some cases long after the great reforms.[28] There is little reason to doubt that one of the motives for this policy was population management. It was applied only to Muslims, Jews, and in some instances German colonists, but not to Slavs and other favored groups.

The policy of allowing emigration on condition of a ban on return had other iterations. For example, especially in the wake of the 1863 Polish rebellion, hundreds of individual émigrés were sentenced in absentia for "leaving the fatherland" without permission. While they were not strictly banned from returning, the penalties they faced upon return included measures [such as deprivation of the rights of their legal status group *(sostoianie)* and deprivation of the right to live in the Kingdom of Poland] that were harsh enough to deter nearly anyone considering a return.[29]

The eternal bans on return proved very difficult to enforce. The Ministry of Internal Affairs tried to create a system that could get comprehensive lists of such individuals to Russian consulates around the world so that they could prevent the issuance of visas to members of this category.[30] In 1892, the Ministry of Internal Affairs tried to improve the system by issuing an amnesty to anyone expelled in this manner prior to 1881, introducing a new system of record-keeping, and requiring prominent notations on the *zagranpasporta* of departing individuals subject to this rule.[31] Whether these rules were widely or effectively enforced is difficult to determine. James Meyer suggests that there were plenty of ways around the regime. He also found many examples of such "eternal bans" on Muslim emigrants to the Ottoman Empire being overturned.[32]

Moreover, given that most emigrants from the Russian Empire left illegally, without following official documentary requirements, it is logical to conclude that the vast majority of émigrés had no documentation of an "eternal ban" on return. I found no evidence of communication within the Russian bureaucracy that attempted to compile lists of undocumented illegal emigrants and add their names to the lists of individuals "eternally banned" from return. In its 1891 annual report to the tsar, the Ministry of Foreign Affairs noted that because most emigrants left without the appropriate *zagranpasporta*, in practice officials were simply unable to verify the subject status of returnees.[33]

For these reasons, it is possible to conclude that the policy of eternal bans on return only applied to a small minority of Muslims, colonists, and other emigrants.[34] None of this means that the policies were irrelevant, however. Return migration is a major factor in nearly all countries' migration history. By almost any measure, return migration to the Russian Empire was made much more difficult and complex by the official strictures on the practice.[35] Even emigrants who filled out all the forms and paid all the fees to leave legally could face punitive fees if they decided to go back. Emigrants typically had to pay a fifteen-ruble renewal fee every six months for their *zagranpasport*. An expired multientry visa brought fines of sixty rubles per month—a level that few could afford.[36]

The differential application of the bans on return show how the regime attempted to channel emigration in ways that shaped the population according to its ethnonational and confessional priorities. The underlying principle of these practices was that departure was almost entirely an affair of non-core populations. Whether they chose to leave illegally or through a negotiated agreement with the authorities, their departure was conceived as something akin to treason, and they were not to be allowed to return. Thus, it follows that the regime did not consider the fate of emigrants to be of interest to the state.

The Ministry of Foreign Affairs noted this disinterest in its yearly report for 1887, which included a summary of its first major review of emigration policy.[37] The report laid out the results in stark fashion. Consulates and embassies abroad seemed to not even consider tending to the needs and interests of Russian-subject emigrants abroad to be within the scope of their concerns. When the minister of foreign affairs asked each to provide lists of Russian subjects within their jurisdictions and report on their activities to support them, in many cases they could not even provide estimates of their numbers, much less their needs. The Ministry of Foreign Affairs called for changes in consular practice to address the problem, but with continuing strong opposition to providing services to people who had left the country illegally from the Ministry of Internal Affairs, progress was slow.[38]

But, tellingly, it was only with the first major emigration of ethnic Russians and Ukrainians—to Brazil and Argentina in 1890–93—that the two ministries began to show a serious concern for the fate of emigrants after they emigrated.[39] As the correspondence of both ministries consistently pointed out, this emigration was different from previous ones in that it included many Russians and others "from the core peasant population." Several thousand ethnic Ukrainian, Lithuanian, Polish, and Russian peasants departed for South America, enticed by the promise of free land and government-subsidized travel. Unscrupulous shipping companies coerced them to give up their *zagranpasporta,* then dumped them in the countries of destination where the land they had been promised turned out to be completely unsuitable for farming. The majority failed at subtropical farming, lacked money for needed investments, and succumbed to disease and other problems. The impoverished emigrants appealed to the Russian consulates in the region for financial assistance to return to Russia. This spurred a bitter dispute within the Russian government. The minister of internal affairs strongly opposed granting any assistance, arguing that the vast majority of these emigrants had left illegally, and thus should be arrested and treated as criminals, not given money to return. But given the scale of the tragedy and the fact that in this case Russians were also affected, the Ministry of Internal Affairs relented—but allowed no assistance to be given to Jews.[40] The decision to pay Slavs to return but to deny assistance to returning Jews is just one small example of what appears to have been a fairly consistent general emigration policy of encouraging the return of Slavs, but discouraging or even banning the return of other emigrants. The Ministry of Internal Affairs also blocked the return of German colonists, arguing that they had been allowed to denaturalize and leave the country only on the condition of an eternal ban on return to the Russian Empire.

Policies such as these made legal emigration extremely expensive, time-consuming, and logistically difficult, giving a strong incentive for illegal-emigrant smuggling networks to spring up to meet the demand. By the mid-nineteenth century, acquiring a *zagranpasport* had become an expensive ordeal. In 1840, Nicholas I raised the fees for *zagranpasporta* from a nominal level of twenty-five kopecks to 10.5 rubles. Then in the crackdown on travel after the 1848 revolutions in Europe, he raised the fee to 250 rubles, a rate prohibitive to all but wealthy elites.[41] During the great reform era, the fee was reduced to five rubles, but rose in the ensuing decades to stand in 1910 at 17.25 rubles (nine dollars).[42] This amount was roughly equivalent to the average monthly earnings of a Russian farm laborer.[43] The requirement that an applicant receive a document from the regional gendarme administration indicating a "lack of objection to travel abroad" and another verifying that he had no outstanding debts or taxes both added much time and expense to the application process. Each of these documents required stamps, the expense of travel to offices in provincial capitals, and time spent waiting for each step in the process. Altogether, the process could often take three months at an expense of thirty to forty rubles.[44] In addition, if a potential emigrant wanted to formally denaturalize (or if he was required to do so by Russian law) then there were substantial additional fees and bureaucratic hurdles, clearing which could cost as much as one hundred rubles.[45] By the turn of the century, this had become a highly unusual situation. In England, a foreign passport cost the equivalent of one ruble; in Germany 3.25 rubles, and in Spain it was free of charge. Nowhere did the process take so long as in Russia. In Italy, the document was issued within twenty-four hours, and in Spain within three days.[46]

In addition, the Department of Police periodically launched campaigns against illegal emigration. Steamship company representatives who traveled through the empire and the agents they hired to find emigrants were sometimes arrested. Emigration agents had to operate underground, and when they were caught—at least in theory—the penalty for foreign subjects was expulsion from the country without right of return.[47] Russian subjects working as agents and recruiters for emigration were most commonly expelled from border regions to internal provinces and subjected to fines.

Along with arrests and expulsions, governors tried to spread information about misleading claims of emigration agents regarding conditions in emigration. These kind of efforts peaked in intensity when reports of abuses came in from abroad, as in the case of Brazil in 1890. In that case, the governor-general of Warsaw ordered strict additional measures such as temporary bans on the sale of property at auction, confiscation of steamship tickets held by people without *zagranpasporta*, and heightened border patrols.[48] But even after such crises passed, police attitudes remained negative toward emigration agents, and as late as 1913 the Ministry of

Internal Affairs launched an operation to round up agents and root out their networks.[49]

Policies of this nature clearly reduced the number of legal emigrants. But illegal emigration expanded rapidly. By the turn of the century, Russian officials estimated that somewhere between half and 90 percent of all emigrants left illegally, without *zagranpasporta*.[50] Department of Police archives are full of reports from governors and border officials about bribery and collaboration of local officials and border guards in illicit emigration. Letters intercepted from successful illegal emigrants to their friends describe in detail the complicated, but fairly efficient system of moving underground from point to point with an emigrant-smuggler as a guide, paying bribes to specific officials along the way.[51] In 1906, one such letter even described a sliding price scale, depending on the speed of travel and degree of comfort.[52] The smuggling operations grew in efficiency as they grew in scale, and became an attractive option not only for categories that would be banned from emigration (such as young men of service age), but for others as well. The cost was similar and the procedures less time-consuming.[53]

However, crossing the border illegally was not without risk. Some of the agents led nighttime crossings by foot. Though rare, border guards did sometimes exercise their authority to use force to stop illegal crossings. There were also risks involving dishonest emigrant-smugglers who swindled their helpless customers through the extortion of unexpected extra payments and even gave counterfeit tickets, knowing that the law-breaking emigrants could not turn to the police. Furthermore, the illicit emigration system at times failed to screen out emigrants who were denied entry at Ellis Island and other ports due to illness, physical disability, or other criteria. Such individuals were often then forced to pay for the return journey or in the frequent cases when the individuals could not pay for the return trip, became a cost the Russian government was asked to bear.[54]

ARGUMENTS FOR COMPREHENSIVE EMIGRATION REFORM

A serious debate about the legalization of emigration began to emerge in the late nineteenth century; it became more heated in 1906–9 when the Ministry of Trade and Industry led the creation of an interdepartmental committee that worked with the State Duma to draw up a proposal for comprehensive emigration reform.[55] In addition to the problems already mentioned, reform proponents put forth several other arguments. They pointed out that the restrictions on emigration were widely ignored and openly flaunted. The governor of Plotsk reported to the Ministry of Internal Affairs in 1890 about a group of a hundred emigrants caught at the border who "declared brazenly that they would just try again tomorrow," concluding that it was "nearly impossible to stop or affect the flow of people."[56] Another problem was the system of multiexit visas or border-crossing cards, known as "legitimation tickets" *(legitimizatsionnye bilety)*. These were issued free of charge to residents living within about thirty kilometers of the border and were meant to expedite crossing for those whose work required them to cross the border frequently. In practice, the issuance of these documents to individuals from interior provinces in return for a bribe turned into a lucrative business for provincial officials.[57]

By the turn of the century, the emigrant-smuggling operations were increasingly sophisticated and combined with contraband import and export operations. For example, in January 1904, a police investigation uncovered a major emigrant-smuggling ring in the Warsaw district founded by David Tempovskii, a notorious figure at the time who had paid off customs and border officials, as well as the district police, to run both people and goods across the border.[58] Despite the fact that everyone in the region knew of his activities, he continued to operate for years, with only occasional fines and penalties. Another remarkable indication of the culture of corruption was the case of Rotmister Ekimov, an army captain in Lomzha province. Ekimov was widely known to be working closely with an emigrant-smuggling ring, but higher officials only intervened when he went a step too far, freeing ninety illegal emigrants who had been arrested by a naive lower-rank officer, and then firing the officer for insubordination. A subsequent investigation found that Ekimov had been receiving 150 rubles per month from the smuggling ring.[59] A governor-general in Ukraine added that the system made it difficult to fight against large and growing export of women by abusive prostitution rings.[60] At times, violent turf wars broke out among emigration and contraband gangs.[61] In short, there were many parallels to other legalization debates, from alcohol to drugs.

Not only did the costs and delays of the requirement of a new *zagranpasport* for each trip abroad encourage corruption, but also, as the Ministry of Finance pointed out, it often hurt Russian-subject merchants in their competition with foreign merchants along the Prussian, Chinese, and other borders.[62] The Ministry of Foreign Affairs also frequently heard appeals for legalization from its consuls and from communities of emigrants abroad. Clerics, emigrant associations, and consular officials in Canada went so far as to propose eliminating *zagranpasporta* altogether and replacing them with a simple, cheap emigration permit to be issued by local officials in Russia.[63]

Another set of forceful arguments for legalization came from the strong upsurge in foreign travel to and from Russia. Officials everywhere received angry complaints from both Russian-subject travelers to Europe and foreign travelers to Russia. All complained about the red tape and expense of the visa and passport systems. A Russian noble in Britain complained that "revolutionaries, Jews and other undesirables" could easily slip through the many tolerated illegal routes into and out of Russia while honest people suffered delays, expense, and indignities. The governor of Petrokov claimed in 1913 that he was issuing 10,000 or more foreign passports per year. He complained that one of the most time-consuming requirements—the statement from the gendarme administration of "no objections to departure"— was a huge burden, but had become a pointless bureaucratic hurdle; he claimed not to know of a single case of denial in his time as governor. For law-abiding citizens, it was terribly unpopular because this step alone took a minimum of two weeks. It also created a huge incentive for people to turn to illegal means in order to travel or emigrate.[64]

By the early twentieth century, emigration and travel abroad had become big business, but it was run almost entirely by German shipping companies. The idea of creating a Russian shipping industry to compete with the Germans and win some of the lucrative emigration trade for Russian companies had strong support in the popular press, State Duma, and parts of the government. In fact, an interdepartmental committee chaired by the Ministry of Trade and Industry's section for merchant trade developed the most important proposals for legalization of emigration.[65]

According to the system in place, German shipping companies accepted illegal Russian emigrants without documents and gained additional revenue from German railroads and from hostels in Hamburg and Bremen. The Ministry of Foreign Affairs complained that the "passport complications" and the cost of legal migration and return pushed most Russians to shun Russian shipping lines, preferring instead to take a railway to the border, then enter the efficient German system of travel by rail to a German port city, stay at a hostel, then take a German steamship overseas. Besides the waste of time and money for the individual, this system pushed emigration out of state control, accentuated the influence of emigrant-smuggling rings, and lost potential revenues for Russian companies and the state.

Legalizing and simplifying emigration could in theory bring some of those revenues to Russian companies, aiding the development of port cities like Libava on the Baltic Sea, and would keep more money in the pockets of Russian emigrants, seasonal workers, and travelers. Moreover, in the era of the noisy nationalistic campaigns of the German Navy League and the patriotic fervor surrounding naval and military budgets in Russia, building up an independent Russian merchant marine and breaking the long-standing reliance on German and other foreign shipping was a popular issue with national security implications.

Another major factor pushing toward emigration reform was the rise of seasonal labor migration. The rapidly growing industrial sector in Russia could not absorb all the labor from the countryside, much less drive wages up to a level at all comparable to the much more mature industrial economies of Germany, the United States, and elsewhere. The movement of workers from Russia began in the 1860s, at first from the Polish provinces, later drawing from different regions of the empire and growing to a very large scale. By 1910, in a few Polish districts up to 10 percent of the local population was going abroad yearly, most to Germany but with a rapidly increasing share to the United States.[66] Most workers in the United States went to cities or mines, while in Germany landowners employed most of the seasonal migrants as field workers. The committee proposing a new emigration law concluded that the most important factor was relative wages. In 1910, the average yearly wage in the United States was 468 dollars, with average emigration, travel, and living expenses estimated at 144 dollars, meaning that the average labor migrant could save 324 dollars per year (more than 600 rubles).[67] The committee found that this was several times what a worker could save in Russia, and that he not only sent back remittances, but he also typically came back with stronger work discipline and skills.[68]

Moreover, the biggest threat to social stability in late imperial Russia was arguably the shortage of land in the black earth zone, and the regime went to great lengths to ease the pressure on the land by heavily subsidizing a mass migration to Siberia and launching a radical and risky attempt to transform property ownership in the countryside under the Stolypin reforms of 1906. Still, this pressure was unrelenting; although three million peasants resettled in Siberia from 1906–14, net population growth in the central parts of the country averaged two million per year. Land hunger in continental Europe from Germany to Ireland to Galicia was primarily relieved through migration to cities and emigration overseas. Emigration was a logical policy for Russia at the turn of the century. Most governors responding to a 1909 Ministry of Internal Affairs circular requesting comments on the phenomenon of emigration from their provinces argued as much. They claimed that emigration brought little economic damage because most emigrants were landless and those with property usually gave it to relatives or leased it until they returned. At the same time, it gave some relief to the ever-increasing pressure on plot sizes.[69]

The failure to legalize and normalize this rapidly increasing yearly flow of temporary workers and permanent emigrants contributed to all kinds of abuses and problems. Many of these abuses could be traced to the misleading claims of emigration agents; because their activities were illegal, there were few disincentives to dishonesty. Russian consulates around the world received many complaints about cheated and abused workers who had been misled by their agents. For example, 10,000 Russian workers ended up impoverished and stranded in Hawaii working on plantations and suffering from tropical diseases.[70] A group of seasonal workers in Germany in 1900 were fired and expelled before the end of their contract because they complained about wages. Another contingent of workers arrived in Germany to learn that they had been hired as scabs to replace striking German workers. The undocumented status of many workers left them particularly vulnerable. But there were also many problems for legal emigrants with passports or multientry visas. German officials, for example, often seized the passports or multientry visas of workers and held them until the end of the season, using them to keep workers from leaving or striking for better pay or work conditions.[71]

The Ministry of Foreign Affairs also pointed out that the lack of clear policy on this category of temporary migrant left consuls in a weak position to help them when problems arose. Proponents of legalizing emigration pointed out that this was not only a human tragedy for many Russian subjects, but also impeded a more rational and profitable management of the process of emigration and travel for temporary work abroad and put the Russian Empire in an increasingly anomalous position in a rapidly changing world.

DENATURALIZATION

There was a related but distinct debate over the loss of Russian subject-hood (denaturalization or expatriation). Russia's ban on denaturalization was deeply rooted in Russian law and administrative practice. Article 325 of the Criminal Statute on Punishments (Ulozhenie o nakazaniiakh) defined it as a serious crime: "Anyone who is absent from the fatherland, enters into foreign service without permission of the government, or enters into the subjectood of a foreign power thereby violates his sworn subject-hood duties and is subject to: the deprivation of all rights of his legal status group [*sostoianie*] and eternal banishment from the territory of the state, or in the case of voluntary return to Russia, exile to a Siberian settlement."[72]

This was a somewhat more harsh variant of what was a fairly universally accepted principle in eighteenth-century global practice, that denatural-ization could only occur with the permission of the state to which the subject initially belonged. The Russian variant was particularly strong in part as a legacy of the pre-emancipation bonded society where everyone was bound to a master and no one was free to leave. The oath of subjecthood was religious in tone and was often referred to as the oath of *eternal (vech-noe)* subjecthood—illustrating that the tie was never meant to be broken.

The principle that individuals should be free to leave the subjecthood of one country upon naturalizing elsewhere spread through the world more slowly and less completely than the principle of freedom to emigrate. How-ever, in the nineteenth century things began to change. The French Revo-lution moved toward a new principle, that any citizen of the republic who became a naturalized citizen in another country automatically lost his French citizenship as a consequence.[73] Other countries were much slower to move in the same direction than was the case with emigration policy. Britain was surprisingly recalcitrant on this score, retaining its juridical doctrine of "perpetual allegiance" and practices of denying the validity of unsanctioned naturalizations abroad until as late as 1870. The United States emerged in the nineteenth century as a powerful proponent of the princi-ple of freedom to denaturalize. From its revolutionary origins, the United States had fought Britain for the right of its citizens to renounce their for-mer British citizenship. British practices of treating Americans as retaining the status and obligations of British citizenship, and among other things, impressing them into British naval service, were among the causes of the war of 1812. As a country of growing international trade, the United States wanted its citizens to have the freedom to travel abroad.[74]

Given these global shifts and the small but significant beginnings of emigration as a yearly phenomenon in the Russian Empire, one might expect that Russia would have moved in the same direction during the era of the great reforms. We have already seen how the liberalization of immigration and naturalization policy explicitly intended to stimulate international trade and intensify Russian interaction with the world. In fact, a great reform of emigration and denaturalization policy was seriously discussed and nearly passed.

The spur for the first serious discussion of a reform of the denaturalization law came from the United States. In 1868, that country removed the last vestiges of perpetual allegiance from its own laws regarding denaturalization,[75] and began correspondence with many countries, including Russia, requesting bilateral agreements on naturalization and denationalization.

It quickly became apparent that the United States' request could not be granted without the elimination of article 325. In response, in June 1869 Tsar Alexander II ordered the formation of an interministerial committee to propose reforms of the laws relating to the loss or removal of Russian subjecthood. From the start, the committee agreed that "there could not be any advantage to forcibly holding individuals who clearly preferred to belong to another state in our subjecthood."[76] The committee worked out a quite radical reform to replace the old article 325 with a limited but clearly delineated set of rules that amounted essentially to a legalization of denaturalization for all Russian subjects.[77]

The Ministry of Internal Affairs led a successful effort to block the reform and periodic attempts to pass a new law in the following decades were not successful.[78] The failed reform of denaturalization law spurred a long-running "legalization debate" that paralleled the debate over legalization of emigration in general, but had its own distinct domestic and international dynamics.

In the most general sense, the 1868 interministerial committee recognized the similarity of goals between the 1860–64 reforms of immigration and the proposals to reform denaturalization. The goal of the former was to increase Russian integration in the world economy and to spur investment and innovation. The draconian provisions of article 325 sharply limited possibilities for return travel and interaction. The reformers did not have the benefit of modern research showing the remarkable importance of emigrant diasporas as conduits for flows of ideas, capital, entrepreneurs, and labor back to the country of origin, and they do not seem to have been nearly as cognizant of such possible benefits as they were of the benefits of immigration. However, as both permanent overseas and regional seasonal labor migration grew to become mass phenomena in the 1890s and after, successive committees compiled detailed statistics and memos quantifying the potential economic benefits to the Russian economy.

Pointing to the fact that nearly all emigrants were Jews, Germans, and other non-Russian minorities, proponents of legalizing denaturalization occasionally argued that it was in Russia's interest to rapidly, decisively, and legally cut its ties to emigrants by abolishing article 325. The leading jurist Nikolai Mikhailovich Korkunov stated baldly that most Russian emigration was comprised of "those elements whose retention in the composition of the Russian population cannot in any way be considered desirable."[79]

The Ministry of Foreign Affairs made a case for a law on denationalization in its 1890 yearly report to the tsar by referring to the fact that other governments routinely expelled vagrants, criminals, and foreign-subject workers from regions where unemployment became a temporary problem. The ministry claimed that Germany and other countries with laws on denaturalization often denied entry to their former citizens who had lost their subjecthood due to continuous residence abroad for a set number of years. Lacking a Russian law on denaturalization, it was impossible to respond in kind. A law would make it possible to refuse at least some of the Russian subjects that Germany had been deporting to Russia, and would give Russian diplomats some grounds for pressure on Germany to stop its deportations of unwanted elements of the Russian population (Poles and Jews).[80]

A frequently raised objection to the laws on denaturalization had to do with women and divorce. According to Russian law (which was in line with most international practice), any change in subjecthood by a man brought an automatic change in the subjecthood of his wife. Liberals saw this as a completely unacceptable denial of the right of the woman to choose her own nationality. Why, they asked, would the Russian state force a woman who wanted to remain a Russian subject to become a foreigner against her will? Even the far-from-liberal Ministry of Justice opposed the law as inconsistent, ineffective, and unfair.[81] However, the procurator of the Holy Synod and *éminence grise* of the last two tsars, Konstantin Pobedonostsev, intervened several times to block reform, arguing that divorce was much easier in other countries. If this law were removed, a man could denaturalize and change his religion abroad in order to divorce his wife, who would thus, as a Russian subject, get around the strict ban on divorce within the Russian Empire.[82]

There were few issues in the new field of international law that garnered such consensus as the principle that each individual should have only one citizenship. One of the results of the shift of Russia and much of Europe to reserve-based armies was a strong desire to avoid dual nationality. In case of war, all countries wanted to avoid split loyalties or military obligations. Likewise, as states expanded the benefits of membership, including social insurance, health care, and education to the populace, they put greater stress on ensuring that only their citizens should be eligible.[83]

These principles came into constant conflict with unilaterally decreed national citizenship laws—particularly in the realm of denaturalization. After the failed 1868 reform effort, the next major attempt came at the initiative of the Ministry of Internal Affairs in the 1890s. The ministry was particularly keen to follow Germany's policy of automatic denaturalization of any subject who spent ten uninterrupted years abroad. Germany's rule was in large part aimed at giving the state the power to deny the right of return to impoverished emigrants who had not been successful in their new land. After ten years, they would be denaturalized and thus could be denied entry at the border.[84] It also had something to do with a nationalist notion of affective ties being a necessary part of German subjecthood. Those who did not show loyalty by staying should not be allowed to retain a loose and equivocal tie to the fatherland. Other countries denaturalized their citizens abroad even more rapidly. The United States required renewal of a passport at a U.S. consulate after two years, and denaturalized anyone who did not return to the United States within three years of departing. The Russian Ministry of Internal Affairs saw merit in these kinds of policies and proposed a variant for Russia in the 1890s. However, not only international lawyers, but also the ministries of foreign affairs and justice found that such policies would create many undesirable instances of statelessness.[85] The ministries of internal affairs and justice, and liberal jurists all agreed this was highly undesirable.[86]

Finally, the proponents of both international law and domestic rule of law argued for a consistent and clear legal definition of the procedures for denaturalization. Nearly everyone recognized that the old procedures requiring discussion by the State Council (later the Committee of Ministers) and then formal approval of the tsar for each and every case of denaturalization were excessively difficult, bureaucratic, and arbitrary. Vladimir Gessen argued that the existing system undermined the rule of law because it was so cumbersome and unrealistic that many Russian subjects went ahead and naturalized abroad anyway. This often led to undesirable cases of dual nationality. Likewise, the preemptive denaturalizations upon departure, with bans on return, that the authorities often imposed on individuals and certain groups created a strong possibility of creating large numbers of stateless individuals. The only solution, according to Gessen, was to treat citizenship as a subject not of domestic law, but rather of international law.[87] The Ministry of Foreign Affairs agreed strongly, concluding that "laws on naturalization and loss of subjecthood are by nature aspects of international exchange," and that any law on subjecthood must put the elimination of dual subjecthood and statelessness at the center of its concerns.[88] Korkunov argued for a simple solution: change the legal concept from "naturalization" and "denaturalization" to "change of subjecthood." The operating principle, in his view, should be that denaturalization should always and only be allowed at the moment of naturalization in another country.[89]

The lack of a denaturalization law caused particular problems with the Ottoman Empire. According to the capitulations treaties, Russian subjects in the Ottoman Empire exercised substantial extraterritorial rights, including exemption from many local obligations and laws and the important ability to appeal to Russian consulates for legal and diplomatic protection. A contemporary expert, S. Tukholka, found that many Russian-subject emigrants from the Caucasus lived in the Ottoman Empire for generations without returning to the Russian Empire, yet claimed the privileges of Russian subjecthood "even though they had nothing in common with Russia" and only wanted diplomatic protection.[90] He reported numerous cases of Armenian and Greek Ottoman subjects acquiring Russian subjecthood either through consulates in the Ottoman Empire (most often with substantial bribes as part of the deal) or by traveling briefly to Russia, naturalizing, then returning to permanent residence in the Ottoman Empire with all the rights of Russian subjects. Although the law on foreign passports stated that five years of continuous residence abroad brought big fines and expiry of the passport, the law did not clarify whether denaturalization was to automatically follow. In practice, Russian policy was clear. Expiry of a passport did not bring denaturalization. The latter required an official act of the tsar. Tukholka angrily claimed that the instrumental use of Russian subjecthood by Ottoman subjects was spoiling the reputation of good Russian subjects abroad and undermining the ability of the diplomatic corps to defend its true subjects abroad.[91] A series of legal rulings that allowed the children of Russian subjects born abroad to be granted Russian subjecthood compounded the problem. Even though these individuals spent their whole lives abroad without any of the obligations of subjecthood (most notably, military service), they were able to enjoy all the fruits of diplomatic protection and other privileges defined by treaty.[92]

ARGUMENTS AGAINST LEGALIZING EMIGRATION AND DENATURALIZATION

Given the domestic and international forces arrayed in favor of legalizing emigration and expatriation, why didn't it happen? Changes in the late nineteenth and early twentieth centuries did not necessarily all point in the direction of liberalization. From the introduction of universal military conscription in 1874 and beyond, the Ministry of War became a strong opponent of any liberalization of denaturalization law. In the first year of universal conscription, there were several reports of Russian subjects traveling abroad and returning with foreign passports, claiming to be foreign subjects and thus exempt from conscription. The Ministry of War responded by successfully pushing for a ban on departure from the empire or denaturalization for all males from age fifteen (two years before they were inducted into the military) until both active duty and reserve duty were completed (usually age thirty-seven). To implement this, the application for a *zagranpasport* added the time-consuming and expensive requirement of a signed statement of "no objections" by a military official or governor. These were among the more burdensome requirements that must have pushed many emigrants to choose the illegal path (or the path of bribery to get the necessary legal documents). Evasion was indeed a motive for emigration for some young men, and the ministries of war and internal affairs implemented new, even tighter restrictions and oversight over the process to stop it.[93] In 1877, a Department of Police circular banned the entry into the Russian Empire of any former Russian subject for five years from the date of their denaturalization.[94]

While the massive scale of Russian seasonal labor migration was an argument in favor of legalization of emigration, it was also, perhaps decisively, seen by government officials as a reason to make denaturalization difficult. Governors and Ministry of Internal Affairs officials in Petersburg both frequently expressed their dismay that there was a sort of Darwinian process by which the best workers left and succeeded abroad, while the least successful, the impoverished, orphans, widows, infirm, diseased, ruined, all came back to Russia. Officials often complained that emigrants were mostly young men in their prime working years, while families stayed behind.[95] They even at times expressed an affinity for the German police's position that Russian subjects must not be allowed to permanently emigrate to Germany or succeed in gaining German subjecthood. The German guest worker system forced Russian subject workers to leave Germany every fall so they would not become anything more than temporary residents. Thus a kind of symbiosis persisted and even expanded between German exclusionary population politics and the Russian desire to hold onto its healthy working subjects. In addition to these factors, Russian police and military officials occasionally argued that it was preferable not to allow denaturalization of emigrants because it would be much more difficult to extradite or punish illegal emigrants if they returned to the empire as foreign subjects. They cited this as important in its struggles against contraband, spying, and the revolutionary movement.

Official opposition also received some support from the conservative press. *Novoe vremia (New Times)*—consistently one of the top papers in the empire in terms of circulation and influence—led the conservative press with a steady stream of articles denouncing emigration, denaturalization, and any attempts at legalization. *Novoe vremia* opposed all emigration, comparing the supposed cure of emigration for Russian overpopulation to the seventeenth-century belief in "bleeding" to bring relief to patients.[96] According to the paper, Jews and sectarians were leaving to avoid their obligations and their departure should not be allowed except with an eternal ban on return.

Papers of Russian nationalist orientation from the multiethnic western regions like *Kievlianin (The Kievan)* often pointed out that the departure of Jews, Germans, and Poles could help the Russian Orthodox population improve its demographic position.[97] The biggest concern for all these papers was the possibility that Russian Orthodox peasants might begin to emigrate. That would undermine the hopes for consolidation of national and religious control over multiethnic spaces. Moreover, from the late nineteenth century into the twentieth, the nationalist press took a strong interest in the attempts to settle reliable populations (preferably Orthodox and Russian) in the Far East. Overseas migration was portrayed (not inaccurately) as a competing destination for these migrants. While some of the proponents of legalization claimed that return migrants brought back new knowledge, sobriety, and a good work ethic, the conservative press saw them bringing consumerism, revolutionary ideas and connections, and generally undermining the idyllic image of a communal, religious rural world untainted by outside influences. The papers railed against the abuses of foreign steamship lines and emigration agents (especially Jewish agents). These abuses were sometimes very real, but the press exaggerated their scale and the role of Jews in the system. The aim of antiemigration publicists was clear: they saw any liberalization of the laws against emigration, the operation of emigration agents, or denaturalization of core populations as a serious threat to their goal of keeping core populations in the empire.[98]

For the regime too, as long as emigration was predominantly a phenomenon of Jews, Germans, Poles, and other minorities, it was not seen as a matter of great alarm and steps were even taken to facilitate emigration of these groups. When emigration was just becoming a mass phenomenon, the Department of Police circulated a memo in 1881 arguing that despite "all the improvements in the rights of Jews" over the past twenty years, they continued in all ways possible to "avoid carrying the burdens of state life," and that all the efforts to facilitate the assimilation *(sliianie)* of Jews with the rest of the population had failed. The memo concluded that "there was no reason to stop emigration, but that it wanted to be sure that state interests did not suffer as a result."[99] Among other things, in 1881 the Ministry of Internal Affairs proposed allowing emigration of Jews only as full families, in part to avoid having young wage-earning males go abroad while the old and infirm stayed behind, but also perhaps to ensure that the workers going abroad were permanently emigrating rather than just seeking temporary work.

The Ministry of Internal Affairs led the way toward *de facto* legalization of emigration for some groups. From an early stage, the regime was relatively accommodating of the requests of Germans to emigrate—probably most importantly because of the rising perception that the German colonists were acquiring too much land at the expense of Slavs.[100] The biggest step toward legalization of emigration for a minority group was the decision in May 1892 to allow the Jewish Colonization Association (JCA) to open branches throughout the country and to provide information and assistance to Jewish emigrants. A highly successful organization with over 400 offices by 1910, it spread news about emigration, gave assistance in purchasing tickets, arranged cheap lodging en route, and helped Jews plan for life in the new country. Those leaving through the offices of the JCA did not have to pay the expensive passport fees, and the organization took care of the complex and time-consuming paperwork for the emigrants. The state even gave a discounted train fare to the border. Tolerance of this organization's activities could be read as an indirect endorsement of Jewish emigration.[101] By 1910, an official government committee went so far as to propose exempting Jews from the expensive and bureaucratically complex requirement of acquiring a *zagranpasport* and allowing them to exit the country based solely on documents prepared by the JCA.[102]

The policy that emigrants departing through the JCA had to denaturalize and were to be placed on the lists of individuals eternally banned from returning to the Russian Empire suggests that lurking behind the opening of the door to Jewish emigration was population policy.[103] In addition to being placed on these lists, governors added a line to the exit documents (*vykhodnye svidetel'stva*) issued to the emigrants that the individuals were considered to have left Russia forever.[104]

This procedure continued to be applied to other groups as well, including the several thousand Dukhobors championed by Leo Tolstoy. Nearly 8,000 emigrated to Canada in 1899, but were forced to renounce their subjecthood and submit to an eternal ban on return to the empire. The addition of required denaturalization and eternal bans on return to these "legal" emigrations turned them into something akin to permanent exile, and clearly marked them as directed toward the empire's population-management priorities. The practice continued into the twentieth century. In 1902, a decree allowed Crimean Tatars to emigrate to the Ottoman Empire without hindrance, with the condition that they be subject to a ban on return to the empire. This spurred another wave of Crimean emigration. In May 1905, the tsar gave an order allowing 3,600 Muslim mountain people from the Kuban to emigrate on the condition of no return.[105]

While denaturalization was thus a required part of the emigration process for many, the regime generally proved unwilling to allow it without an accompanying eternal ban on reentry into the empire. The most important reason came from a long-running dispute with the United States over recognition of the validity of naturalization in that country. This dispute began in the 1860s and became arguably the biggest issue in U.S.–Russian relations over the next fifty years, culminating in an acrimonious 1913 abrogation of the commercial treaty between the two countries.[106]

The origins of the dispute reach back to the 1845 declaration of Secretary of State James Buchanan that freedom to emigrate and to change citizenship was "an inalienable right of the individual."[107] In the mid-nineteenth century, when the United States abandoned the concept of perpetual allegiance and embraced the principles of the unequivocal and universal freedom to denaturalize, it joined France and helped push a number of other countries to embrace the same concept (at least in their bilateral relations with the United States). However, Russia was not alone in its insistence on retaining control over the denaturalization of its citizens.[108] In 1864, the first case of conflict with Russia over the issue occurred when Bernard Bernshtein, a naturalized U.S. citizen, was arrested in Russia for draft-dodging and leaving Russian subjecthood without permission. In 1868, the U.S. Congress, mostly in response to British arrests of naturalized U.S.-citizen Irish nationalists, passed an act declaring the right to denaturalize to be a "natural and inherent right" and that naturalized American citizens were to be accorded the same rights abroad as native-born citizens. But for this to take effect, individual agreements had to be negotiated with countries which did not recognize the right of denaturalization. This led the United States to open negotiations on the topic with Russia. Although internal records suggest that Russia came close to drafting a new law on denaturalization, the effort ultimately failed, setting the stage for decades of conflict over the issue.[109]

The basic problem was straightforward. Russia did not recognize the right of denaturalization in its laws. Thus any emigrant who had left without permission was treated as a Russian subject upon return. He had to fulfill military and other obligations that may have been missed while illegally absent from the country and pay any fines and criminal penalties. Since the vast majority of Russian emigrants had left without permission, nearly all were subject to these rules. Moreover, if Jews had left legally and had been officially allowed to denaturalize, they had almost invariably done so under the condition of an eternal ban on return. If that was not enough, there was a centuries-old provision in Russian law that foreign-subject Jews were banned from immigration into the empire with exceptions only granted to investors, craftsmen, medics, or rabbis after a lengthy review that would be likely to discover whether the petitioner was formerly a Russian subject.[110] Thus, even in the unlikely event that a Jewish emigrant managed to denaturalize legally, as a foreign subject, he could not return. According to Russian law, it was thus nearly impossible for naturalized American Jews to return to the Russian Empire.

The United States continued to insist that naturalized and natural-born citizens should all be treated the same. The issue rose to the top of the agenda between 1902 and 1907 due to agitation in the United States against the horrific wave of pogrom violence against Jews in the Russian Empire. Frustrated by the inability to do anything about the pogroms, Jewish organizations in the United States embarked upon a remarkable campaign to force the abrogation of the 1832 commercial treaty with Russia.[111]

The first clause of the treaty guaranteed that foreigners visiting each other's countries would be free to reside and travel freely throughout the country: "The inhabitants of their respective States shall mutually have liberty to enter the ports, places, and rivers of the territories of each party, wherever foreign commerce is permitted. They shall be at liberty to sojourn and reside in all parts whatsoever of said territories, in order to attend to their affairs, and they shall enjoy, to that effect the same security and protection as natives of the country wherein they reside, on condition of their submitting to the laws and ordinances there prevailing, and particularly to the regulations in force concerning commerce." However, the tenth article of the treaty arguably gave Russia the right to enforce its existing restrictions on Jews: "But this law shall not derogate in any manner from the force of the laws already published, or which may hereafter be published by His Majesty the Emperor of all the Russias, to prevent the emigration of his subjects."[112]

By 1911, the issue had gone far beyond the legalities and details of the treaty. It became the means for the United States to express its deep disapproval of the pogroms, for politicians to respond to a strong and increasingly powerful domestic constituency, and not least, for the country to defend its principle that it would defend the rights of naturalized American citizens to be treated the same as natural-born citizens. The United States renounced the commercial treaty in December 1911, allowed it to lapse on January 1, 1913, and did not renegotiate a new one before World War I intervened.[113]

The dispute highlights the interconnections between domestic concepts of citizenship and international negotiations of naturalization and denaturalization policy. Jewish emigration to America expanded rapidly along with the great global expansion in international trade during the last decades of the nineteenth and early twentieth centuries. Many former Russian-subject Jews returned to Russia with business plans and ideas. But they continually came up against the fact that they could not operate with the rights of foreigners, but remained subject to the restrictions imposed on Russian-subject Jews.[114] Even after the 1905 revolution expanded rights and freedoms to all citizens, the regime insisted on retaining the welter of restrictions and limitations on the rights of its Jewish subjects. As long as Russian-subject Jews had far fewer rights of citizenship than others, it was impossible for the regime to allow Jews to denaturalize. It would have created a massive loophole in the restrictions on Russian-subject Jews. This is one of the most powerful explanations for the failure of all attempts to legalize emigration and denaturalization in general (not just for Jews) until the February 1917 revolution created a single unified domestic citizenship by sweeping away the myriad of limitations on the rights and obligations of various domestic groups.

There also was a strong desire to maintain ties with "Russian" emigrants from the presumed "core" parts of the imperial population. Retaining control over denaturalization was a means to that end. The traditional lack of interest or concern in the fate of Russian subjects abroad came to an end in the late nineteenth century, largely because the regime began to take note of the rising number of emigrants from the core population.[115]

International lawyers and diplomats pushed hard to eliminate instances of dual citizenship. The best way to accomplish this was to introduce rules that made the loss of subjecthood automatic upon the acquisition of another subjecthood. France and the United States generally held to the principle that naturalization abroad should automatically bring denaturalization, but several states opposed this principle. For example, the Ottoman Empire pointed to cases of its subjects (most commonly Christian minorities) naturalizing in another country then returning to claim all the privileges and protections guaranteed by the capitulations treaties. It responded with a law of 1869 that banned any act of denaturalization without explicit approval.[116] From its founding, the German Empire had rules on the automatic loss of subjecthood after ten years. However, pushed hard by irredentist nationalists, the government introduced a controversial new citizenship law in 1913 that allowed emigrants to retain their subjecthood abroad for ten years, and then to renew it for another ten years by filling in a simple form at a consulate abroad. Russia was not alone in its opposition to denaturalization. In fact, the Russian Ministry of Internal Affairs even seemed to sympathize with the Ottoman approach. In the 1880s, the ministry sent a secret circular to the governors, informing them that former Ottoman subjects who naturalized in the Russian Empire must be told that if they returned to the Ottoman Empire, they would be denied consular services and diplomatic protection because the Ottoman government had not authorized their change of citizenship.[117]

Along with policies making denaturalization of favored "core" populations difficult and rare, the regime actively sought to draw these same populations back to the empire by giving them an expedited naturalization procedure. This was generally done on a case-by-case basis. For example, in 1899, 500 descendants of Old Believers who had emigrated to Prussia in the early nineteenth century were allowed to immigrate, naturalize immediately, and purchase land in Siberia at discount rates.[118]

This procedure was formalized in April 1908, when a group of Old Believer families, descendants of communities that had emigrated from the Russian Empire to Romania in search of greater religious freedom, petitioned for the right to settle in the Russian Empire. This group, once persecuted and driven from the empire as heretics, was welcomed back with great enthusiasm by the entire administration of the Far East and the Ministry of Internal Affairs. The Far East governors and the Ministry of Agriculture heartily agreed that Old Believers were precisely the ethnic stock that they desperately sought for the region. Because all foreign subjects were banned from acquiring land in the Amur and Primor'e regions, the government issued a set of "temporary rules" that allowed for rapid naturalization without the normal five-year wait required of all other petitioners for naturalization.

These temporary rules were then applied to other groups and were incorporated into the general strategy of aggressive recruitment of any "core" Slavic population groups that were willing to settle in the Far East. A few months later, the Council of Ministers determined that the temporary rules devised for the Old Believers could be applied to a group of 600 Ukrainian families from Romania who wanted to settle in Siberia and return to Russian subjecthood.[119] During the discussions, Minister of Agriculture Krivoshein asserted that these descendants of Zaporozhian Cossacks had preserved their nationality and Orthodox faith abroad. He and others noted that while there were times in Russian history when Old

Believers and Little Russian (Ukrainian) Cossacks may not have been considered fully desirable elements of the population, they were "completely desirable for the colonization of the Far East."[120]

Germany's almost automatic practice of allowing descendants of denaturalized subjects to regain German subjecthood upon return to the empire on a *jus sanguinis* basis has been portrayed as exceptional. These cases and others suggest that the Russian Empire was moving toward similar practices in the early twentieth century. In fact, in its 1908 decision, the Council of Ministers specifically concluded that "they were to be considered not as foreigners, but as individuals restoring their connections to their former fatherland."[121]

In sum, Russian denaturalization practices that seem on the surface to be riddled with contradictions actually display an inner consistency. One of the most important practices was compulsory denaturalization as part of the process of emigration with an eternal ban on return. It was applied on a group-by-group basis and categorically to the emigration of Jews through the intermediation of the JCA. Vastly more people denaturalized through this procedure than through the cumbersome official process for individual petitioners.

The highly restrictive Russian policies on emigration and denaturalization trace their origins deep in Russian history as an integral part of the "attract and hold" population policy that persisted through the centuries. However, Russia and the world changed enormously in the half-century after 1860. Emancipation of the serfs, cheap long-distance travel by railway and steamship, and other changes caused emigration to rise from insignificant levels to yearly phenomena of hundreds of thousands per year. Despite an increasingly long list of good reasons to reform emigration and denaturalization law, the restrictive approach proved remarkably persistent. In part, this illustrates a general point about citizenship and migration history—-that countries evolve their distinct national traditions of law and practice which prove to have lasting impact. Article 325 and many of the key components of the Russian tradition were deeply embedded in the legal system and in long traditions of administrative practice. As the dispute with the United States over denaturalization shows, if article 325 had been removed, it would have created a loophole in the myriad restrictions on Jews within the empire. That said, the regime selectively abandoned the restrictive approach in the 1890s, when it allowed Jewish emigration through the offices of the JCA. But the restrictive approach remained strong for other groups right up to 1914. The one unifying theme in both emigration policy and denaturalization policy was population filtering: holding on to favored populations while allowing others to leave. Denaturalized Jews could not return due to the preexisting bans on foreign Jewish immigration. The eternal bans on return were applied to them and to other minorities. The maintenance of strong restrictions on emigration and denaturalization aimed to keep "core" populations in the country, or if they left, to keep them in the body of Russian subjects in the hopes that they would someday return.

FIVE

Citizenship in War and Revolution

By the turn of the century, the future seemed to lie with the forces pushing toward a liberalization of Russian subjecthood policies. The counterreforms had rolled back some of the reforms of the 1860s, but Russia's historic industrialization drive was in full swing, led by Minister of Finance Sergei Witte, a powerful advocate of integration in the global economy and an open door to foreign labor, investment, and talent. Steam and rail travel facilitated an unprecedented globalization of international economic activity, a process in which the Russian Empire was a full participant. A rapidly expanding seasonal labor migration was bringing back significant sums in repatriated earnings and new Russian steamship companies were leading a push to legalize emigration and gain a bigger share of the proceeds. Outside the government, a vibrant liberal political movement was emerging and its ideas centered on creating modern citizenship based on equal rights and obligations for each individual member of the state. Within the government, 1890s laws on residence permits and Jewish emigration moved in a relatively liberal direction. Even within the Department of Police, committees were at work drawing up deeper reforms. The 1905 revolution brought a new semiconstitutional order.

As in other liberal revolutions, freedom of movement was considered to be among the more important revolutionary freedoms. Among other things, the opposition proposals for a new constitution in the summer of 1905 prominently included the abolition of all internal passport restrictions on movement within the country. However, neither the tsar's October 1905 Manifesto, nor the 1906 Fundamental Laws included freedom of movement in their extensive lists of civil rights and freedoms.[1] As long as the government viewed the communal system as a source of social control and stability, it proved impossible to really change the passport system, which was seen as a very important lever of social control over peasants who left their village. Major changes in policy came only when Stolypin decided to embark on a radical reform of peasant landholding, issuing a landmark law on October 5, 1906, "on the elimination of a few limits in the rights of rural inhabitants and individuals of former tax-paying legal status groups [*podatnykh sostoianii*]." It took a big step toward abolishing the separate civil legal status of peasants and other lower orders and toward granting them full civil rights. It removed the old principle of the passport as tying the holder to a place of residence, but it did not abolish or fully transform the role of the passport. A permanent passport book replaced the old five-year document. The reform brought a big conceptual change from a document holding individuals in place to a document of individual identity. Former tax-paying legal status groups (most importantly, peasants) were given the freedom to choose their place of permanent residence on the same basis as individuals of other *sostoianii*. "Place of residence" was no longer defined as the place of registration in their *sostoianie*, but rather the place of work or residence. This was a concrete change meant to facilitate movement of peasants into the urban workforce.[2] From an instrument of control, the passport was transformed into a document giving rights and verifying identity.[3] This transformation was made possible by the elimination of the principle of collective responsibility for fiscal and military obligations in 1903, the abolition of remaining "redemption payments" owed to the state by peasants in November 1905, and by the determination of the government to embark upon a comprehensive attempt to transform the agrarian systems of land ownership and communal organization. But the process was ongoing and by no means complete for peasants, and it left several major groups out entirely. All the complicated and onerous restrictions on Jewish residence and movement throughout the empire were retained and continued to be enforced through the documentary regime, and *inorodtsy* (aliens), gypsies, and convicts were all denied the right to hold a passport in the new system.[4] The reforms were grounded in the same motives that had underpinned the great reform era changes—liberalizing movement to facilitate industrial development. This time, the reforms aimed to facilitate the Stolypin agricultural reforms, and to recognize new levels of civic equality and freedom for previously restricted lower classes in the empire. The changing role of the internal passport reflected a deep underlying and rapid set of changes that was transforming the old-regime world of separate deals and group subjecthood relationships to the state into a new world of more clearly defined and registered individuals who were more "face to face with the state" than ever before.[5] These changes heightened the significance of the external boundary around the empire. Freedom of internal movement made it harder to control individual departures at the local level. Better control of identities made it easier to attempt to enforce controls at the external borders. Along with the freeing up of movement within the territory of the country, the police pursued ambitious new projects to use the revamped documentary system to document each individual and put each into a new system of registration and oversight.[6]

The newly freed press produced a surge of publications calling for the replacement of old-regime subjecthood with a new modern citizenship in all its aspects. Publications ranged widely from mass-circulation instructive pamphlets explaining the differences between a "subject" and a "citizen" to a massive compilation of the laws that would need to be changed in order to move to a system of equal rights and obligations under the law.[7] Liberals in the Duma pressed hard after 1905 for a modern citizenship law, pointedly demanding language in the oath which would reflect their idea of citizenship as based on shared rights and obligations and loyalty to the state and its laws rather than to the person of the tsar. Various proposals were taken seriously not only in the Duma, but also within the Ministry of Internal Affairs. But it proved difficult for all sides to compromise on matters as fundamental as whether the oath of citizenship should be to the state or to the tsar, and the proposals were never enacted.[8]

However, powerful as the forces of liberalization were, World War I trumped everything. The total-war experience not only thwarted liberal reforms, but was also a transformative force of its own that crushed the tendrils of liberal rights-based citizenship and reversed the globalizing trends of the previous fifty years.

When World War I broke out, Russia was more fully integrated in the global economy than at any point in its history. Nearly half of its yearly gross capital formation came from abroad, and by any measure the goal of drawing labor and expertise from abroad had succeeded on a large scale. From the great reforms to the outbreak of World War I, there was a net immigration of approximately 2 million individuals from Russia's three main adversaries during the war. Many naturalized, but foreign subjects lived and flourished in Russia with rights equal to Russian subjects under civil law, so many did not. At the beginning of the war, there were over a million permanent resident foreigners in Russia, approximately 600,000 of whom were from enemy countries, plus visitors to the country, who did not take up permanent residence within the Russian Empire. The number of visitors was large and contributed significantly to the foreign presence in Russia at any given moment. In 1912, for example, 2.5 million German subjects traveled to Russia for short-term visits.[9] Russian workers were traveling abroad for seasonal work in unprecedented numbers, while cheap seasonal labor flowed into the Russian Empire from Asia and the Middle East. While there were still legal uncertainties and barriers to the free flow of people both ways across the border, there were plenty of legal, quasi-legal and illegal options. Flows of people, capital, and goods all increased in volume right up to 1914. All this was exactly what the great reforms of the 1860s had intended to achieve—rapid modernization through intensive interaction with the world economy. This pattern was hardly exceptional. Nearly every modern rapidly industrializing country except Japan witnessed a more or less comparable globalization as it modernized.

Immediately after the declaration of war, it looked as though the status quo might not be overturned. In the wars of the preceding half century, neither Russia nor most other countries had taken actions against the enemy subjects on their soil.[10] Other than the expulsion and internment of around one thousand Japanese subjects during the 1904–5 war,[11] there were few other recorded instances in Russian history where the legal rights of enemy subjects within Russia had been affected by the state of war.[12]

When war broke out, the Ministry of Internal Affairs sent a circular to all governors promising that "peacefully occupied Austrians and Germans who are outside any suspicion may remain in their places [of residence] and retain the protection of our laws, or they may leave the country."[13] Minister of Foreign Affairs Sergei D. Sazonov declared that the norms of international law would apply to all enemy subjects and that "no measures which would harm their person or property are to be allowed: they are protected by the law as in peacetime."[14] However, Russia abandoned this approach within months, partly in response to the actions of other powers. In a series of measures from August to November 1914, which became known as the Trading with the Enemy Acts, Britain banned transactions with persons residing in enemy states and appointed inspectors who had the power to oversee the financial dealings of enemy-subject-owned firms to ensure that they were not making payments to enemy states. Most of the other powers followed Britain's lead and imposed similar restrictions, including Russia.[15]

Pushed by a jingoistic press calling for radical measures and by several army commanders who used a remarkably extensive set of war powers to overcome civil government resistance, Russia quickly embarked on a set of radical measures that amounted to a reversal of the course of citizenship policy over the preceding half century.

In September 1914, the Russian government voided all international agreements and conventions protecting enemy subjects and deprived them of the right to court defense in civil cases.[16] With this hasty decision, one of the fundamental principles of the great reforms was swept away. It would not be fully restored until the late 1980s. Deprived of domestic or international legal recourse, the path was cleared for more extensive administrative measures against enemy subjects.

BANS ON DEPARTURE AND DENATURALIZATION

Some German and Austrian subjects were able to flee the country during the days before and after the declaration of war. But within days, Russia banned the departure of enemy subjects and imposed control on their movement within the country. On September 21, 1914, the Ministry of Internal Affairs banned local officials from granting any enemy subject the right to leave the area of his or her residence.[17] As hostilities commenced, most of the country's borders turned into impassable armed fronts.[18]

Thenceforth, the only possibility for civilian enemy subjects to leave was by bilateral agreement. On August 24, 1914, the Russian Ministry of Foreign Affairs concluded the first such agreement with Germany and Austria. However, under the wartime Military Statute, the army had gained control over administration of the borders and it effectively blocked implementation of this agreement. After two months, on October 14, 1914, the army chief of staff simply informed Chairman of the Council of Ministers Goremykin that enemy subjects would not be allowed to leave the country.[19]

The Russian government rightly saw this as a radical step, and worried about retaliation against Russian subjects in Germany and Austria, as well as the large financial holdings of Russian subjects in German banks, stocks, and real estate. The Vatican, diplomats from neutral countries, and the Red Cross also pressed Russia to allow the departure of enemy subjects.[20] The

United States and other neutral intermediaries negotiated a new agreement in late January 1915 that allowed all enemy subjects (except military-obligated males) to leave the country.[21]

However, the army again thwarted implementation by imposing extensive bureaucratic hurdles and allowing individual commanders to simply ignore the agreement. For example, in January 1915 the commander of the Southwest Front, Ivanov, banned the exit from the country of all enemy subjects from the entire Southwest region.[22] This order was still in effect when the head of the Kiev Military District posted a declaration that all enemy subjects, regardless of age or sex, had to leave the empire by February 28, 1915, or face deportation to the Russian interior.[23] Based on incomplete data, it does not appear that the number of civilian enemy subjects who were able to leave the country according to the negotiated agreements with the Central Powers was very large—probably less than 10,000—with nearly all leaving in the first six months of the war.[24] This amounted to only about 2 percent of the total number of enemy subjects residing in Russia before the war.[25] In practice, after April 1915 departures were only allowed as bilateral negotiated exchanges, according to the same stringent and cumbersome process used for prisoner-of-war (POW) exchanges.[26] The ban on enemy-subject departure stayed in effect for the remainder of the war, and was not lifted under the Provisional Government.[27]

Chapter 4 showed that the freedom to emigrate was not established as a legal principle for Russian subjects prior to 1914. Therefore, no special laws or decrees were necessary to abolish the freedom of Russian subjects to emigrate. Official permission had been required prior to the war; during the war it was exceedingly rarely granted. Most emigration prior to the war was unofficial: the war stopped this type of emigration by turning porous borders into impassable front lines. However, the great reforms had established the right of *foreign citizens* to leave the country at any time, a freedom that became firmly established in the half century prior to 1914. These wartime actions eliminated that right for a large part of foreigners on Russian soil. The Soviet Union never fully restored the freedom of foreigners to leave in the 1920s and seriously restricted it in the 1930s, expanding the wartime principle to all foreigners and applying it even in peacetime.

Finally, the already strong bias against denaturalization increased during the war. A multifaceted "war on spying" made officials even more reluctant to recognize the denaturalization of former Russian subjects and their transfer to a new citizenship. The fear was that they could use their intimate knowledge of the country to return on foreign passports as spies.[28] The regime tried to establish contact with and encourage the return of Russian-subject men abroad to serve in the army. Many problems were revealed. For example, the Russian consul in Pittsburgh, responsible for 387,000 immigrants in Pennsylvania, claimed that most were Ukrainians and Poles "infected with nationalist, democratic, and revolutionary ideas." He thought their return would be worse than leaving them in the United States. In any event, few were registered with the consulate, so he could not contact them directly. Moreover, few of the lower-class immigrants could afford the expense of return, and nearly all of the very small percent of Russian-subject men who responded to the call to arms asked for financial assistance to pay for the trip (which was quite logistically difficult and expensive). These types of arguments seem to have convinced the Russian government not to press for the return of Russian emigrants abroad during the war.[29]

DEPORTATION AND INTERNMENT OF ENEMY SUBJECTS

The army and the Ministry of Internal Affairs quickly escalated their measures against enemy subjects far beyond the bans on departure and denaturalization, embarking upon a radical set of measures to arrest and intern all enemy subjects from a large swath of the empire. On July 26, 1914, the minister of internal affairs ordered the arrest of all enemy subjects on Russian soil who were either enlisted in enemy armies or in their reserves. They were sent to four internal Russian provinces for internment as POWs.[30] On July 29, the Ministry of Internal Affairs expanded the definition of those to be interned to include all German and Austrian males aged eighteen to forty-five capable of carrying a weapon.[31] These groups were designated as "civilian deportees" and as such fell outside protections granted by treaty to POWs.[32] The deportation of this category affected only a small part (about 50,000) of the roughly 600,000 enemy subjects with permanent residency in the Russian Empire.[33]

However, as early as September 1914 the army began to order the deportation of civilian enemy aliens from regions near the front, starting with 7,000 enemy subjects from Riga.[34] On December 13, 1914, the army ordered the deportation of all Austro-Hungarian, German, and Ottoman subjects (including women and children) from the ten provinces of the former Kingdom of Poland.[35] In the course of the next three months, similar orders targeted Volynia and parts of the Baltic region.[36]

At a special meeting of the Council of Ministers in October 1914, the minister of war proposed arresting and interning enemy subjects not only in the front-zone areas under military rule, but throughout the entire empire. The civilian ministers opposed this proposal, arguing that it would undo decades of interconnected economic relationships, causing both temporary and permanent damage to the economy, as well as spurring costly retaliations against Russian subjects abroad. In the end, the ministers limited deportation and internment of enemy subjects from areas under civilian rule to retaliations against specific new German and Austrian measures against Russian subjects abroad, and proposed a series of exemptions for Slavs, continuous residents of the empire for twenty-five years or more, and those with relatives in the army.[37] The army command was disappointed that the civilian authorities were unwilling to arrest and deport all enemy subjects, but proceeded with a sweeping program of mass deportations not only in the theatre of military operations, but throughout much of the vast area that had been declared under military rule.[38]

The Russian internment of enemy subjects was not unique; however, several features distinguished it from comparable measures in other countries. First, the scale and speed of the operation exceeded that in nearly every other country by a substantial margin. Estimates fall in the range of 250,000–300,000 enemy subjects interned during the war—roughly half of the entire registered population of enemy citizens when the war began.[39] France interned 32,000 civilian enemy aliens within the first weeks of the war and 60,000 by 1918.[40] Britain did not turn to internment until June 1915, but in the course of the war it deported and interned approximately 30,000 civilians.[41] Germany turned to large-scale internment in late 1915 and had interned approximately 112,000 civilians by November 1918.[42] Second, in contrast to most countries (with the exception of the Ottoman Empire), once the deportations were under way, Russia applied the policy to hundreds of thousands of its own subjects, forcibly expelling at least half a million Jews and a quarter million Russian-subject German farmers from the zones under military rule to interior Russian provinces.[43] These mass expulsions had an unanticipated outcome. Army orders forcing Jews to leave areas under military rule put enormous pressure on the few provinces that were both outside this area but still within the Pale. In an emergency response, the government took the historic step in August 1915 of abolishing many restrictions on Jewish settlement in the interior of the country. Thus, ironically, one of the most violent acts against a group of Russian subjects during the war led to their emancipation from one of the most potent symbols of their lack of full citizenship rights and took a major step toward equalizing freedom of movement for all citizens within the country.[44] Finally, while in most countries, enemy subjects were relatively unassimilated recent migrants, predominantly from the working class, in Russia many were relatively integrated long-term residents, including many members of the middle-class entrepreneurial, managerial, and technical professions.

NATIONALIZATION OF ENEMY SUBJECT PROPERTY

The key aim of the great reforms of citizenship in the 1860s had been to pave the way for rapid Russian modernization and integration into the global economy. A few statistics from the eve of 1914 show the resounding success of this policy. Russian industrialization from the 1890s on depended very heavily on direct foreign investment and import of managers, entrepreneurs, and technicians, especially from Germany. Foreign investment accounted for nearly half of all new capital formation in industrial corporations, and by 1914 foreigners held over 40 percent of the nominal capital of corporations operating in Russia. At the turn of the century, a third of all technicians in Russian industry and a tenth of all administrative personnel were foreign subjects. This was an intentional result of the long-range industrialization strategy supported by a succession of ministers of finance, and it was very much facilitated by the citizenship policies of the great reform era.[45]

The 1860s reforms granted full equality under civil law to foreign subjects, leaving little incentive for these increasingly numerous foreigners to naturalize. However, after the revolution of 1905, there is some evidence that rates of naturalization began to rise and that foreign-owned firms were beginning to replace foreign technical and managerial staff with Russian subjects.[46] Thomas Owen's database of Russian corporations shows a sharp relative decline in the share of foreigners among corporate managers, from over 10 percent in 1905 to less than 6 percent in 1914.[47] Much of this statistical "replacement" was a result of foreign subjects' naturalization. A recent study of the Germans in St. Petersburg, the area with the largest number of German and foreign entrepreneurs and businesses, finds that rates of naturalization, Russian-language facility, and cultural assimilation among these communities were very high.[48] In short, it seems that the dreams of the great reforms were being realized. There were groups who strongly supported this vision well into the war years. For example, the influential main organization of Russian entrepreneurs in the relatively cosmopolitan Petrograd region, the Association of Industry and Trade (AIT), strongly supported free trade and opposed restrictions on foreign economic activity throughout the war.[49]

For decades prior to the war, many individuals and groups denounced the prominent role of foreigners and supported Russian economic nationalist ideas and the promotion of Russians into entrepreneurial and managerial professions. The scholarly consensus holds that they were not very successful in influencing policy.[50] However, the war transformed the situation. Most of the foreign subjects in the economic sphere were from Germany or Austria. When war broke out, mass circulation papers like *Novoe vremia* (*New Times*) and *Moskovskie vedomosti* (the *Moscow News*) unleashed a torrent of articles demanding radical action to reduce German influence in the economy. Groups like the Moscow Merchant Society, the "Society of 1914," a special Duma committee "for the war against German dominance," and other organizations led boycotts against businesses owned by foreigners and naturalized ethnic Germans and lobbied for restrictive legislation.[51] In the context of the general wartime mobilization against the external German enemy, this mobilization at times transcended class boundaries as well. Workers seem to have taken the campaign quite seriously and one of the biggest worker actions of the war took the form of a violent three-day riot and strike against German and foreign businesses in Moscow in May 1915.[52] Some rioters carried lists compiled by a Russian nationalist organization with addresses of enemy subjects and immigrants from Germany and Austria who had acquired Russian subjecthood less than three generations earlier. In terms of monetary damages, the riot ranks among the most damaging of any in Russian history and was the biggest ever to take place in either of the two capital cities of the empire.[53] The popular pressures to act did not just come in the form of the riot; workers throughout the country engaged in a series of strikes, protests, and incidents directed primarily against alien managers, owners, and foremen.[54]

The government's response to the wave of popular and military mobilization was at first cautious. According to a Russian legal expert, Russia had not sequestered the properties of enemy subjects in the recorded history of its wars over the previous century.[55] Moreover, a contemporary expert argued that the protection of the private property rights of enemy citizens was one of the most firmly established principles and practices in international law by the early twentieth century.[56] The Council of Ministers was keenly aware of the crucial role enemy subjects played in many spheres of the Russian economy and was leery of embarking on a potentially costly and disruptive set of measures in the midst of its unprecedented mobilization for total war.

But pressure from the army and society led to a series of measures that became increasingly radical and broad-ranging as the war continued. On September 22, 1914, the tsar signed a decree banning the acquisition of land or any property owned or leased by enemy subjects throughout the empire for the duration of the war.[57] This decree marked a massive expansion of all such prewar limits, which had only applied to a few provinces. Then, in January 1915 a decree forced the liquidation of firms owned entirely by enemy subjects, partnerships in which one or more of the partners was an enemy subject, and stock corporations deemed to be of "enemy nationality." The country in which a stock company was incorporated defined its "nationality."[58] In remarkably quick order, 3,054 firms were identified. About half were exempted upon appeal, mostly on the grounds of the Slavic, French, or Italian ethnicity of the enemy subjects in these businesses. By July 1, 1915, a total of 1,839 firms had been liquidated. The process required enemy subjects to sell their share of the property, either to Russian subjects or to the state at a hugely discounted price. Payments could not go directly to the enemy subject, but rather went to special frozen accounts in the State Bank, to be released at the end of the war.

In December 1915, a new decree expanded the liquidations to large industrial firms. On the eve of the February 1917 revolution, another decree forced the liquidation of enemy-subject-owned shares in corporations chartered under Russian law. The February revolution did not stop the implementation of these laws, and by November 1917 fifty-nine major industrial firms had been liquidated, with proceedings under way for another seventy-five. "Liquidation committees" forced the liquidation of 50 million rubles' worth of enemy-subject-owned stocks in Russian corporations. The entire operation was extremely complex. Hundreds of officials delved deep into the internal structure of firms in an attempt to disentangle the rich layers of interconnection between native and enemy-subject employees, owners, managers, and suppliers.[59]

A parallel set of measures was enacted in the countryside. A decree of February 2, 1915 forced the expiry of all land leases held by enemy subjects within one year and forced enemy subjects living within a broad zone roughly incorporating the territories of modern Ukraine, Belarus, Poland, Finland, the Baltic region, and the Caucasus to sell their properties by certain deadlines or face expropriation without compensation. These measures were also applied to Russian-subject German descendants of immigrants from the enemy states living in rural farming communities within the ten Polish provinces and a 160-kilometer band to the interior of the empire's western and southern borders from Finland to the Caspian Sea.[60]

While the liquidations of businesses focused on enemy subjects, the land laws included the following: members of a *volost*, agricultural village, or communal institution formed by former Austrian, Hungarian, or German subjects or by immigrants of German origin (ethnicity); individuals registered in villages or colonies in Kholm or the regions overseen by the governor-general of Warsaw; and individuals entering Russian subjecthood after January 1, 1880.[61] This essentially recreated the long-defunct "colonist" legal category as a denizen subset within the body of Russian subjects, literally reversing the inclusion of colonists into the great reform era concept of unified subjecthood. So in some very significant ways, the wartime mobilization undermined modern Russian citizenship and reestablished old separate legal status categories.

A series of important decisions during the implementation of the various wartime measures also undermined the citizenship boundary by establishing that ethnicity could trump citizenship when decisions were taken on categories of people to include in or exempt from sanctions. Russian-subject Germans were included in several of the measures initially applied only to enemy subjects. Conversely, a substantial list of "enemy subjects" claimed that they should be exempt from all sanctions and treated like allies.

Czechs, Slovaks, Poles, Serbs, Christians from the Ottoman Empire (Armenians, Greeks, Bulgarians), and a few other smaller groups were able to negotiate more or less complete exemptions from the sanctions applied to enemy subjects, which ranged from deportations to expropriation of land and liquidation of businesses. Enemy soldiers of these backgrounds were given preferable treatment in POW camps, where some of them were allowed to form ethnic units to fight in the Russian army.[62]

WARTIME NATURALIZATION POLICY

In many other ways, however, the war greatly strengthened the citizenship boundary. Russia took large strides in the direction of instituting a new and tighter regime of controls over citizenship, entry into the country, and exit from it.[63] Mass deportations and liquidations of properties put a premium on defining the subjecthood status of people and even of businesses and stocks. Various committees received floods of petitions and requests for expedited naturalization or simply for exemption from the rules. The first response was to tighten up requirements that foreign males naturalized during the war immediately enter military service.[64] On June 14, 1915, two weeks after the riot in Moscow against enemy subjects, the tsar presided over a special meeting at army headquarters with Grand Duke Nikolai Nikolaevich all the major army commanders, and the entire Council of Ministers. It was the first such gathering of all the country's top leaders during the war, and the fate of civilian enemy subjects and naturalization policy was a major part of the agenda. The conference drew up a set of rules that the tsar quickly decreed into law, including an outright ban on all naturalization of enemy subjects and neutral subjects who entered the country after the declaration of war. With this ruling, Russia became the only major power to ban naturalization during the war. Exceptions were allowed only with the approval of the tsar. The report ordered the expulsion of all enemy subjects from Moscow (with exceptions for Slavs and a few other categories). The rules also granted broad powers to governors and police to intern individual immigrants who had been naturalized after January 1, 1880, and encouraged the deportation of any "undesirable foreigners" from the country if international agreements allowed.[65]

The wartime innovation of tighter documentation, registration, identification, and control over foreigners was applied not only to enemy subjects, but to other foreigners as well. For example, in the first year of the war, the military came to suspect the large number of Chinese and Korean temporary laborers in the empire of espionage and disloyalty. As a result, the army and police conducted a series of mass expulsions of Asian workers from the country. However, both countries were neutral in the war, and the resulting dire shortages of labor for agricultural fieldwork and railroad construction convinced the government not only to reverse these policies, but also to expand the number of temporary workers brought into the empire. This episode also illustrates the impact of World War I on state institutions' control over immigrants and foreigners in general. As a condition for the importation of Asians in 1916, a whole set of new controls and passport regulations were developed. Wartime rules tightened the requirements for both Asians and any other temporary workers to possess passports and register, while employers had to sign papers making them responsible for maintaining control over their workers' places of residence. Police officials were assigned to each contingent of incoming Asians. These measures were part of the general wartime innovation of tighter controls over foreigners, an important long-term development both in Russia and throughout the world.[66]

Thus, by 1917, under the pressures of war, the old regime had moved radically and rapidly to undermine a half century of citizenship policy. Ostensibly temporary security measures like the internment of enemy subjects were turned into more decisive and permanent measures as they became entwined with policies to liquidate their businesses and landholdings. The campaign against enemy subjects went beyond its original boundaries, targeting naturalized immigrants from enemy countries. It also resulted in some new regulations and laws that affected all foreigners. The war brought a sharp break from the era of internationalization, bringing bans on denaturalization and naturalization along with extremely sharp constraints on emigration and immigration. In short, after a half century of internationalization, Russia veered toward isolationism, but in a way it did so with the encouragement of its international partners, participating fully in an international shift toward tighter documentation and registration of individual identities and a serious hardening of the citizenship boundary. These developments established a powerful context for the revolutions of 1917. While revolutions typically bring a period of openness to naturalization by those who are seen as supporters of the new order, the fact that both revolutions of 1917 occurred in the midst of war limited their revolutionary potential in this respect.

THE FEBRUARY REPUBLIC

There is, nevertheless, no question that the February 1917 revolution brought a revolutionary break in the history of Russian citizenship. The very first declaration of the Provisional Government promised "to provide the country immediately, even prior to the convocation of the Constituent

Assembly, with laws safeguarding civil liberty and equality in order to enable all citizens to apply freely their spiritual forces to creative work for the benefit of the country."[67] Less than two weeks later, it published what might well be considered the most fundamental decree of the revolution: "The Abolition of Restrictions Based on Religion and Nationality."

> Holding the unshakable conviction that in a free country all citizens should be equal before the law and that the conscience of the people cannot accept the limitation in rights of any individual citizens on the grounds of religion or origins, the Provisional Government decrees the abolition of all restrictions in currently existing laws and regulations on the rights of Russian citizens on the basis of their religion or nationality.

The decree elaborated nine different spheres of restrictions that were immediately abolished, including matters of settlement, residence, travel within the country, ownership of property, participation in businesses, state service, admission to educational institutions, participation in the legal system, and in the use of non-Russian languages in education and business. Then, in case there was any doubt, another clause reiterated the sweeping universal nature of the decree, making clear that it eliminated not just restrictive laws and decrees, but also any administrative orders, military commands, and legal interpretations that undermined the general principle: "All administrative orders published by either civil or military authorities prior to the publication of this law that restrict any right on the basis of religion or nationality are invalid."

Article 9 extended the decree to abolish discriminatory laws and regulations on the basis of religion or nationality to all foreign citizens in Russia, with the important exception of the citizens or subjects of enemy states.[68] On March 19, 1917, the largest women's demonstration in Russian history pushed the leaders of the Provisional Government to accept women's suffrage. When the Provisional Government published its new electoral statute on July 20, 1917, Russia formally became the first major country in the world where women had the right to vote and to hold elected office.[69]

The response in society was immediate. Almost overnight, both official documents and common parlance switched from the term *poddanstvo* (subjecthood) to *grazhdanstvo* (citizenship). From the socialist left to the conservative right, papers published long, glowing articles of praise for this decree. For liberals, it was the realization of the disappointed dreams of the 1905 revolution, the creation of a body of citizens with equal rights.

Novoe vremia and other voices on the conservative side pointed to the creation of a body of citizens as key to a renewed war effort. All but the extreme right lauded the end of unfair restrictions on Jews. Along with this decree came announcements of the intention to abolish all legal differences based on *soslovie* (estate) membership. Taken as a whole, the decree was the logical end point of the movement toward the creation of full "citizenship," defined as equal rights and obligations before the law for all individual members of the polity, a process that had taken huge steps forward in the great reforms and again in 1905–6. Of course, implementation of this sweeping directive required the elimination of huge sections of existing laws and regulations.

Treatment of "enemy aliens" shows how the decree heightened the importance of the boundary between citizens and foreigners. The general principle was to immediately repeal all laws restricting the rights of Russian citizens, while keeping many restrictions on foreign citizens in place. As early as March 11, 1917, the government voided fifteen wartime laws restricting the rights of Russian-subject German "colonists." Thousands of Russian-subject Germans and Jews who had been expelled by military order from the front zones and other regions to the interior of the country began to return to their homes.[70] Military officials pushed back on this and succeeded in getting the government to issue a decree on April 21 that required local officials to acquire permission from the military authorities for every individual to return to areas under military rule.[71] However, these orders seem to have been broadly flouted, and many thousands of Russian-subject civilians made their way back to their homes, no doubt emboldened by the declarations of the end of all national and religious discrimination, and the uncertainty of many local officials about their new status. In contrast, officials seem to have had more success holding deported enemy subject civilians in their places of internment, though here too it took strong army intervention to assert the policy.[72]

However, at the same time, the government kept many of the restrictive wartime laws in place for the citizens of enemy states.[73] Both in the countryside and in the urban economy, the Provisional Government continued to press ahead with the programs to liquidate enemy-subject properties and financial holdings. The scale of the liquidations the new government completed during its brief period in power was very significant.[74] Thus, on the whole, there was a fairly consistent policy. Citizens were to be treated equally; foreigners continued to be subjected to restrictions. In short, the citizenship boundary grew in importance.

While the wartime ban on naturalization was not formally lifted, the Ministry of Internal Affairs approved several individual and small-group naturalization requests.[75] The government also expanded the policies of granting exemptions to Slavic enemy subjects. Most significant in this regard was a decision of June 27, 1917, which granted full exemption from all sanctions to Polish enemy subjects, followed by an August 1, 1917, decision extending the same exemption to Czech and Slovak enemy subjects.[76]

The war was a transformative event in the history of Russian citizenship. The blockade and hostilities combined with policies to seal the citizenship boundary in ways not seen for at least a half century. Naturalization and denaturalization were both effectively banned. Officials deported, interned, and nationalized the properties of foreigners from enemy states, effectively ensuring their permanent removal from Russian society. For enemy subjects, the wartime measures reversed the key great reform era principle that gave foreigners equal rights to Russian subjects under the law. They also created categories of the citizenry who were deprived of their most basic rights. These themes and patterns of policy proved to have much more in common with Bolshevik policies than the extraordinary but short-lived revolutionary declarations of the Provisional Government.

SIX

Soviet Citizenship

According to Sergei Kishkin, an early Soviet juridical expert on citizenship law, "the October Revolution sent 'subjecthood,' along with all the other relics of the old regime to the museum of antiquities. . . . Subjecthood of the Russian Empire and subjecthood of the bourgeois provisional republic were replaced by Soviet citizenship [*grazhdanstvo*]."[1] While there indeed were revolutionary elements in Bolshevik citizenship policy—including its class basis and policy toward women—in other ways the new regime went back to pre-reform-era subjecthood practices. If the primary contrast between subjecthood and citizenship is the latter's definition as a polity in which all members exercise more or less equal rights and obligations, then the apogee of citizenship came under the Provisional Government. It was roundly rejected by the Bolsheviks, who created a new regime of separate deals for various subgroups of the population, and relegated millions to the status of *lishentsy* (individuals deprived of the rights of citizenship), an extreme form of "obligations only" subject status not seen since the era of serfdom. The Bolsheviks also revived and enforced old bans on emigration that had been undermined and much less aggressively enforced for decades.

But Bolshevik citizenship policy was far from a simple return to old-regime subjecthood. It was very different in that it abandoned the old populationist aims of growing and holding the population, shaping its ethnic and religious composition, and responding to the ups and downs of the labor market. As Golfo Alexopoulos has argued, "Soviet citizenship policy was not principally guided by economic considerations or concerns about population size, labor shortages, or immigration. Rather, political forces proved central."[2] After briefly pursuing revolutionary internationalist and class-war aims, the guiding principle of citizenship policy for most of the history of the Soviet Union emerged: the creation, preservation, and defense of a largely autarkic unified state. By the late 1920s, the state had developed unprecedented capacity to control its borders and population movements across them, making great strides toward overcoming the traditionally huge gap between policy intentions and actual practices. The state created one of the hardest, most rigorously enforced citizenship boundaries the world has ever seen.

In principle, the initial period of Bolshevik rule saw a relative openness to foreign ideological supporters to travel to the homeland of the revolution and to naturalize as Soviet citizens or enjoy the rights of citizens without naturalizing. A report to the All-Russian Central Executive Committee on the decree on Soviet naturalization stated the theory clearly in April 1918: "As for ourselves, socialists, for a long time past . . . the membership of a man in our socialist world has been determined by his acceptance of the socialist system, and it is immaterial to us what language he speaks, where he lives, where he was born."[3]

According to the first revolutionary decrees on naturalization, members of working or peasant classes could naturalize by showing proof of identity and submitting a simple two-page application to a local provincial, regional, or district-level soviet. The soviet would inform the People's Commissariat of Internal Affairs [Narodnyi kommissariat vnutrennikh del (NKVD)] for registration purposes and the People's Commissariat of Foreign Affairs [Narodnyi kommissariat inostrannykh del (NKID)], which would inform the new citizen's former government (in the hope of avoiding dual citizenship).[4] There was no five-year residence requirement (as was standard in most countries, including pre-1917 Russia), and the small number of naturalizations that occurred in the initial period of the revolution seems to have gotten approval rather quickly. A March 1918 decree issued an open invitation to foreigners to seek asylum in the Soviet Union from political or religious repression in their home countries, promising that the new regime would not grant extradition requests for such individuals.[5] Naturalization was thus in principle quite easy for workers, peasants, socialist activists, and—in an ideological anomaly—for oppressed religious groups.[6]

Seeing themselves as the vanguard of a global proletarian revolution, the Bolsheviks in charge of citizenship policy initially put much less stress on citizenship status than on class. Article 20 of the July 10, 1918, Constitution of the Russian Soviet Federative Socialist Republic (RSFSR) declared that "in support of the solidarity of the workers of all countries, the RSFSR grants all the political rights of Russian citizens to foreigners living on the territory of the Russian Republic and to members of the working class or peasants not using the work of others, and recognizes the right of local soviets to give these foreigners the rights of Russian citizenship without any burdensome formalities."[7] As a result of these class-based policies, foreign workers could hold many more rights of citizenship than native-born citizens who had been deprived of rights according to article 69 of the constitution.[8] The 1860s shift toward treating foreigners and citizens equally under the law continued for foreign and domestic workers and communists, but was rejected for nearly all other classes and political groups.[9]

One of the most revolutionary aspects of Bolshevik citizenship policy was its break with the widely accepted principle of international law that in marriages involving two different citizenships, the wife automatically acquired her husband's citizenship status and lost her old one. According to a law of October 22, 1918, each partner in a mixed marriage could opt for either citizenship status. Upon divorce or death of a partner, the wife or husband was free to return to her or his original citizenship status.[10] This law was unprecedented in international practice; only later was it to become the norm in international law. At the time, it led to many conflicts with other countries and to many *de facto* cases of dual citizenship because of the refusal by other countries to recognize the precedence of Soviet law over their own. During the later debate over a new citizenship law for the Soviet Union, Commissar of Foreign Affairs Georgii V. Chicherin extolled the progressive nature of the principle and argued successfully that international disputes were a price worth paying for the law.[11] The principle of free choice of citizenship was extended to children as well. Children aged fourteen or older whose parents changed their citizenship were given the right to choose which citizenship they would adopt upon reaching adulthood.[12]

Bolshevik citizenship policies continued the revolutionary changes that the Provisional Government had ushered in with its landmark decrees extending the franchise and other basic citizenship rights to women.[13] In early 1918, internal rulings of the Central Committee for Prisoners of War and Refugees (Tsentroplenbezh) and the NKVD allowed female Russian citizens to marry foreign POWs, granting the former the choice of retaining their citizenship or taking that of their spouse.[14]

These early policies were, however, more a matter of theory than practice. In the midst of a horrific civil war, famine, hyperinflation, unemployment, and total economic disarray, there was little reason for workers or peasants to migrate to the RSFSR—and very few did. In part this was due to Bolshevik policies. As early as December 2, 1917, the Bolsheviks required visas for entry into the country and used the visa system as a means to prevent the return or immigration of all but the preferred categories of workers, peasants, and revolutionaries.[15] Moreover, especially initially, the lack of both diplomatic representatives abroad and formal recognition of the Bolshevik government hindered the issuance of visas, thereby making immigration all the more difficult.

While the regime had in theory opened the door for those of the right class backgrounds and political persuasions, the NKVD was suspicious from the start, and legal uncertainties were numerous for the foreigners who were allowed into the country. Secret NKVD instructions to local officials ordered them to provide apartments and jobs, but also to "carefully and fully register them and keep vigilant oversight over anyone who crossed the border without a visa or who might in any way bring harm to the republic."[16] Foreigners were not exempt from criminal prosecution, including capital punishment for a broad range of crimes committed in Russia or abroad. In normal times and a normal regime, this would be unremarkable, but in the midst of the civil war, with the political police empowered to arrest and execute suspected subversives, this put many foreigners in a precarious position. Generally, the regime pushed against many of the traditional protections granted to foreigners under international law.[17] Article 8 of the Civil Code gave the RSFSR broad powers to limit the civil capacity of foreigners in terms of travel, choice of profession, acquisition of property, and in business activities. The regime also made it an explicit policy to restrict the rights of certain foreigners in retaliation for the actions of other states.[18]

The March 1918 Treaty of Brest-Litovsk briefly created a major benefit for foreigners from the Central Powers (the majority of foreigners in the RSFSR) that citizens were denied—an international guarantee of property rights against nationalization by the regime. However, this guarantee was lost with the declaration of the nationalization of all industry on June 28, 1918.[19] When the Central Powers collapsed in November 1918, other protections in the Treaty of Brest-Litovsk also lost effect.

Moreover, the traditional advantage of last resort for foreigners—the ability to tap diplomatic support from their home country—meant much less than it had under the old regime. Few countries had established formal diplomatic recognition of the Soviet Union, and in any event were usually far from energetic in defending the interests of radical workers and activists who found themselves in trouble there. A July 6, 1921, decree gave the All-Russian Extraordinary Commission to Combat Counterrevolution and Sabotage (Cheka) and the courts broad discretion to expel foreigners "who in their way of life, activities and conduct are recognized as not corresponding to the principles and ways of life of the worker-peasant state . . . even if they had previously received permission to live in the republic."[20] International constraints on this practice were far weaker than in the prewar decades, when the expulsion of foreigners was governed extensively by international law and bilateral agreements.

World War I and the civil war played a vital role in the formation of early Soviet citizenship policy. Approximately six million refugees and forced migrants from areas of military activity during World War I had appeared in internal Russian provinces by 1917. The civil war, famine in the countryside, food shortages in the cities, and epidemics pushed somewhere between one and two million to emigrate abroad and millions more to move from one region to another within Soviet territory. Peace treaties with the newly independent Baltic states, Finland, Poland, and Romania created new external borders that left many former Russian subjects outside the territory of the Soviet Union, and raised the question of the status of hundreds of thousands of refugees from these areas within the Soviet Union. The fate of over two million POWs in Russia and more Russian prisoners under the control of the Central Powers needed to be decided. All these extraordinary situations raised a series of important questions about the citizenship of millions of individuals.

FOREIGN POWS ON SOVIET TERRITORY

There were more than two million POWs on Russian territory in November 1917 (roughly two million Austro-Hungarian subjects, 170,000 German subjects, 50,000 Ottoman subjects, and 200 Bulgarians).[21] Shortly after the revolution, their legal position became quite unclear. The Bolshevik government wanted to quickly negotiate a comprehensive exchange of all prisoners from both sides. But the Germans in particular had reason to pause, not least because Germany had vastly more Russian POWs (1.43 million) than Russia had from Germany (167,000).[22] During the war, Germany had come to depend heavily on the labor of these prisoners and was unwilling to exchange them with Russia, especially at a ratio of 9:1. German and Austrian authorities also feared that POWs had been infected with Bolshevik radicalism, nationalism, or epidemic diseases (or a combination of these), and thus tempered their efforts to facilitate POW returns, imposing inspections, quarantines, and other procedures that created barriers to their quick return and reintegration into their home societies.[23]

In June 1918, the Bolsheviks gave way to the Central Powers, signing an agreement that only recognized exchanges of equal numbers of POWs going each way. Suspicions and negative attitudes from the military and government on both sides slowed and restricted the extent of POW repatriation by official channels. Moreover, by the time the agreement was in place, the Russian civil war had gotten well under way. The White armies and governments controlled many areas of POW imprisonment and they all refused to recognize the validity of the Treaty of Brest-Litovsk. Thus, until the Central Powers surrendered in November 1918, the white authorities kept POWs in prison and tried to apprehend POWs moving through areas under their control.[24] For these reasons, officially approved POW repatriation from the former Russian Empire slowed in the second half of 1918. It still amounted to roughly a quarter million individuals.[25]

However, the vast majority of POWs who departed left on their own, making their way home without asking about the legal procedures, often traveling without documents. Alon Rachamimov estimates that 670,508 Austro-Hungarian POWs had managed to return from Russia by October 18, 1918. He estimates that only a quarter of them departed via official channels—the vast majority escaped, were released, or simply left.[26] Refugees and POWs alike often paid bribes to cut through formalities. These individuals had a very tough time getting home because official negotiations dragged on into 1920–21, when most of the peace treaties and separate agreements on the repatriation of prisoners were finally signed.[27]

In the intervening period, Bolshevik authorities pressured POWs to join the Red Army and agitated among them to promote socialism and nationalism against their governments. Germany and Austria responded by forcing the inclusion of a clause in the Treaty of Brest-Litovsk that banned these practices and instructed the Bolsheviks to admit into the Red Army only "volunteers of foreign origins who have become Russian citizens." Nevertheless, many reports of forced conscription of POWs continued to come in during the civil war. In the end, an estimated 50,000 POWs ended up enrolled in the Red Army for one reason or another.[28] There is little question that many of them entered the army without naturalizing as Soviet citizens, despite the Treaty of Brest-Litovsk and many complaints from the German and Austrian sides in the years following the abrogation of the treaty. Recent studies contend that this tiny minority (2.5 percent of the total number of POWs in Russia in late 1917) exerted an outsized impact on the Red Army and the spread of communism in East Central Europe.[29] The most famous POW convert to the communist cause, the Hungarian officer Béla Kun, returned to Hungary and led a communist revolution. However, many of the POWs who chose to naturalize did so for pragmatic or nationalist reasons. For example, a group of Ukrainian and Rusyn POWs in Siberian prisons chose naturalization as a way to gain release and the opportunity to migrate to the Ukrainian Soviet Socialist Republic (SSR) to join their co-ethnics.[30]

One conspicuous exception to the general pattern was the repatriation of Slavic POWs from Russia and Ukraine. In 1917, the Provisional Government accelerated a program begun under the last tsar to form ethnic military units from POWs to fight against the Hapsburg Monarchy. A force of 40,000 Czechs and Slovaks formed the Czech Legion (later to grow to 70,000) and a South Slav Serbian force of 30,000 was also formed.[31] When the Central Powers invaded Ukraine in March 1918, the Czech Legion tried to exit the country via Vladivostok. On the way, it got embroiled in the Russian civil war when a misunderstanding with Leon Trotsky led him to order their disarmament. The legion rebelled, seized much of the Trans-Siberian Railway, fought with the Whites and allies against the Bolsheviks, and finally negotiated a mass departure from Vladivostok in 1920.[32] With the end of the civil war, the last major groups of several thousand POWs were finally able to leave the country in 1921–22.[33]

Another category of wartime prisoners, the roughly 300,000 civilian enemy subjects expelled from front zones, shared a similar fate to the POWs. Most of them were able to make their way out of Russia during the chaos of the revolution and civil war, and although the conditions of the armistice included a provision requiring the return of civilian prisoners, the process of return was slow and incomplete until a formal agreement to allow their departure in April 1920.[34]

SIFTING BY NATIONALITY

Mass movements of refugees and deportees from the front zones to the Russian interior during World War I left millions of people originally from regions that formed new nation-states between 1917 and 1921 in Bolshevik-held territory. Likewise, many former Russian subjects remained in these new countries, and not all of them were willing to become citizens of the new states. Public pronouncements initially gave the impression that refugees of all types would be able to go home, and rumors spread quickly, spurring a wave of emigration.[35] By late 1917/early 1918, reports began to come in that masses of Polish, Jewish, and Lithuanian refugees were piling up at the Western Front, asking for permission to cross the front in order to return to their homes. Leaders of refugee organizations on both sides of the front called for cooperation of the authorities in resettling these populations. But suspicions and restrictions on both sides created a stalemate. Germany did not want an unregulated mass movement of impoverished migrants (many Jews, Poles, and others who might end up in German territory, and among whom epidemics were rife), and the Bolshevik authorities were reluctant to allow unregulated movement for many reasons, not least of which was the possibility of deserters from the Red Army getting away. The regime also worried that young men might cross the border to join the White, Polish, or other armies.[36] The NKVD issued strict orders that any refugee or POW attempting to leave without all requisite documented permission was to be detained. The ability of local officials to demand bribes and impose arbitrary controls over anyone trying to leave enabled many to get around official strictures, but also probably restricted the number who left by raising the unofficial cost of exit.[37] For example, even a group of Lithuanians with all their papers in order and official Bolshevik approval to return to Lithuania ended up bribing various Ukrainian and Russian officials eight times on the journey from Ekaterinoslav to Lithuania.[38] Refugees and POWs without cash or valuables (and this would seem to include most) would have had a hard time making it to and through the border.

Later, Bolshevik wars with the Baltic states and Poland, as well as the Russian civil war, prevented a formal agreement on repatriation and made unsanctioned individual return an even riskier venture. While hundreds of thousands nevertheless made the dangerous and costly trek, officially sanctioned repatriation had to wait for a series of "optation" agreements incorporated into peace treaties and separate agreements, most in 1920. An optation agreement is one that gives individuals a certain period within which they are free to choose between two different citizenships, usually with the requirement that they then relocate to the country of their citizenship choice.

The idea of granting individuals the option of choosing their country of residence and citizenship following a change in international borders spread in international practice through the late nineteenth century.[39] The principle is grounded in democratic notions of contract between the state and its members, and especially in the idea that the citizenry and the national community should be congruent (or at least that individuals should have the opportunity to make them congruent). The prominent role of plebiscites and optation in the postwar settlement marked the pinnacle of these notions in international practice. The Bolsheviks ended up signing a series of optation agreements with newly independent successor states—in part under duress, but also with certain permutations that worked to their favor. Upon closer inspection, the optation agreements appear to be pragmatic responses displaying a surprising range of differences from treaty to treaty, yet are united by the unique Bolshevik approach to nationality as well as the inherited traditions of the Russian Empire.

The first, albeit abortive, instance of an optation agreement came in a decree of July 13, 1918. This gave permanent residents of territories no longer part of the RSFSR or other Soviet republics the right to petition to the NKVD for denaturalization, as well as the right to emigrate from the RSFSR. The decree was reluctantly passed under heavy German pressure, four months after the Treaty of Brest-Litovsk. It allowed individuals only one month from the issuance of the decree to submit their petition and required denaturalized individuals to emigrate from the country immediately upon the granting of the petition. A similar agreement was signed between the RSFSR and Ukraine on June 12, 1918, under heavy German pressure. The agreement guaranteed the right of Russians and Ukrainians to freely depart from one country to the other if they desired. The wording was exceedingly vague, referring to "Russians" and "Ukrainians" without indicating whether they were defined by ethnicity, language, domicile, or religion. It left plenty of room for officials to block departures. These rules were only in place for a few months before the November 1918 collapse of the Central Powers and the subsequent annulment of the Treaty of Brest-Litovsk and other agreements forced upon the Bolshevik state by the Central Powers. George Ginsburgs claims that several tens of thousands of individuals took advantage of the optation agreements in this short time.[40]

With the annulment of the Treaty of Brest-Litovsk and other agreements in November 1918, optation did not resume until the end of the wars of succession in the Baltic region, Ukraine, Poland, and the Caucasus (the optation laws did not technically go off the books, but implementation seems to have halted). In 1920, the RSFSR concluded optation agreements with Estonia, Latvia, Lithuania, Georgia, and Finland, and in March 1921 with Poland and the Ottoman Empire. In contrast to the domestic laws of 1918, these were bilateral agreements, sometimes with separate agreements for the Ukrainian SSR and Belarusian SSR with the same countries. While there was substantial diversity in the details of these agreements, they all shared a few common features. Article 4 of the February 2, 1920, peace treaty between Estonia and the RSFSR was the first, and it set the mold for the rest. Individuals of Estonian origin in the RSFSR were given one year from the date of ratification of the treaty (February 14, 1921) to apply to opt for Estonian citizenship. If their application was approved, they then had one year from the date of approval to leave the RSFSR. In the case of people whose Estonian origins could not be determined, the principle of prior domicile (or that of their parents) in Estonian territory could suffice. Conversely, individuals of non-Estonian origins residing in Estonia had the right to apply to opt for RSFSR citizenship. Although the rules gave individuals broad latitude to choose their citizenship, each government retained the power to reject individual applications. Moreover, there is no mention of the firmly established legal principle that only members of the working class were to be allowed to naturalize as citizens of the RSFSR, but it seems to have been a factor in the decision making of the Bolshevik authorities in charge of the approval process.[41]

What was to happen to individuals who did not exercise their rights of optation, or to those who did but then failed to leave the country by the end of the one-year deadline for departure? The treaty was not clear on these important points. In 1918, some zealous local NKVD officials rounded up and arrested individuals who had opted for another citizenship but had not left by the deadline. As late as November 1922, the NKVD ordered "decisive measures to deport" Lithuanians and Estonians who neither opted for Soviet citizenship nor left the country by the deadline for optation. But these were exceptional orders. More often, it appears that any optant who did not leave by the deadline simply could no longer claim foreign citizenship.[42]

The other optation treaties differed on some important points. For example, the Latvian agreement stated that "to establish Latvian origins, nationality and religion have no significance. Residence in the territory is all that matters." Any refugee who could prove residence in Latvia prior to August 1, 1914, and everyone living in Latvia at the time of ratification of the peace treaty were automatically recognized as Latvian citizens. While the Estonian laws and practices created stateless people (Estonia often refused to admit Jewish and communist optants even after they had been denaturalized by Soviet authorities), the Latvian laws were biased toward creating dual citizens and toward naturalizing people who did not necessarily want to be naturalized.[43]

If the Latvian agreement put the territorial principle first, the one with Poland went furthest toward an ethnic definition. The right to opt for Polish citizenship was given not only to residents and former residents of the Kingdom of Poland, but also to those able to prove they were descendants of people who fought for Polish independence in the insurgencies of the 1830s or 1860s, and to the descendants up to the third generation of former residents of the Polish-Lithuanian Commonwealth (if their language, activities, etc., showed their attachment to the Polish nation).[44] Thus, individuals of Polish descent from Petrograd to Siberia were given the right by treaty to opt for Polish citizenship even if their ancestors had migrated to the Russian Empire over a century earlier. All successful petitions to opt for Polish citizenship were to result in an act of denaturalization by Soviet authorities.[45]

In an attempt to keep ethnic Russians from becoming citizens, the Lithuanian treaty excluded anyone in civil or military service who was not originally from Lithuania even if he lived in Lithuania.[46] Perhaps surprisingly given the nationalizing tenor of politics in most of the new states, Lithuania was the only country to include such a clause. Every other optation agreement granted individuals able to prove permanent residence status in the territory of the new state the right to opt for its citizenship. However, the numerous Russian refugees who ended up in each neighboring state who could not prove prior resident status generally faced barriers to naturalization. Many ended up stateless.

On the other side, the Bolsheviks were generally open to non-Russians opting for citizenship in their republics—with one very big exception. Only members of the working class had the right to opt for RSFSR citizenship. Members of other social classes whose permanent residence was outside RSFSR territory were allowed to opt for RSFSR citizenship only on a very exceptional basis requiring attestations to the loyalty and reliability of the individual at several levels of the bureaucracy. Even if nonworkers were allowed to naturalize and return to the RSFSR or other republics, they could face deprivation of the *rights* of citizenship (see below) and end up with *lishentsy* status and a second-tier, obligations-only citizenship. Another innovation was the recognition of republic-level citizenship in the optation process. Thus, the Ukrainian, Belarusian, and other Soviet republics each had their own optation treaties with each newly independent state, and optants could choose to naturalize in their titular national republic rather than simply in the Soviet Union.[47] This was particularly important for Ukrainian refugees from former Hapsburg lands on Soviet territory and conversely for Ukrainian refugees in Poland. Both were free to opt for Ukrainian SSR (rather than RSFSR) citizenship. Even after the formation of the Soviet Union, an optant could nominally choose Ukrainian SSR citizenship. This approach increased the appeal of Soviet citizenship for many Ukrainians and other nationalities. Finally, all but one of the agreements imposed a requirement on all individuals who opted for a foreign citizenship that they leave Soviet territory within a certain period (usually six months to a year).[48] Any optant remaining beyond the deadline was to be treated as a citizen of the Soviet republic in which he remained.[49] This model of setting a deadline for departure and then ascribing citizenship to all who failed to depart was also applied to smaller groups of foreigners even in the absence of a formal optation treaty.[50]

A special case dealt with the border changes in the Caucasus. The March 16, 1921, treaty between the Ottoman Empire and the RSFSR gave inhabitants of the territories that had been under Russian control prior to 1918 the right to opt out of Turkish citizenship and depart for a Soviet republic. Likewise, inhabitants of the Batumi area (ceded by the Ottoman Empire to the Georgian republic) were free to leave for the Ottoman Empire. The period of free optation by these border populations was extended several times, until a final deadline of March 11, 1928. In practice, however, the Ottoman Empire blocked Armenian attempts to return to Turkish territory, and before the final deadline, moved to categorically denaturalize all former Ottoman or Turkish-subject Armenians outside the country.[51]

Thus, in principle (with all the qualifications discussed above), the optation treaties were quite an innovation aimed at giving populations the ability to vote with their feet for the citizenship of their choice. While optation had been practiced by Russia after the annexation of the Kars, Batumi, and Ardahan regions in 1878, and by other powers after annexation, the Soviet experiment in optation was unprecedented in scope and scale. To a remarkable degree, the treaties were grounded in the principle of the nation-state—that the national and state communities should be congruent. On paper, the treaties pursued these goals in a consistent way. In practice, however, Soviet authorities found ways to obstruct the implementation of the agreements. Because the entire procedure required formal approval of each individual case, officials had broad scope to deny applications to opt out of Soviet citizenship on even the flimsiest of pretexts. Any application for optation from a soldier in the army had to include a certificate releasing the individual from army service. This was not easily acquired.[52] The All-Union State Political Directorate [Ob'edinennoe Gosudarstvennoe Politicheskoe Upravlenie (OGPU)] secretly reviewed each petition and overturned many without providing any explanation for its decisions (or even allowing acknowledgment that it had vetoed the application).[53] Other officials imposed petty bureaucratic barriers that for impoverished refugees could take on major significance, one example being a 1921 requirement that all optants departing the country must provide two photographs per family member—not a minor detail in a land suffering economic disaster and where photographers were few and far between.[54]

Policies regarding the property of refugees from occupied areas and optants were also a barrier to exit. In early 1918, the Tsentroplenbezh promulgated a set of highly restrictive rules on the complex issues of property, restitution, and export and import of property belonging to refugees from occupied areas. It imposed sharp limits on the export of precious stones and metals, money (1,000 rubles per person) and other items. Anything above the norm was to be seized and held in a frozen account for an undefined period. In principle, in the unlikely event that the emigrant were to return to Soviet Russia, he could claim the property or money received and held as a result of its sale. Whether any returning emigrant was actually able to claim such property is uncertain—I found no evidence that the rule was ever applied. Regardless, because return migration was by all accounts very rare, the actual effect of these laws was essentially the nationalization and seizure of all property and money of emigrants and optants beyond the low minimums. These measures amounted to a form of *droit d'aubaine* more extreme than any medieval precedent.[55]

Early results of implementation of the Estonian optation agreement show how effectively the Soviet bureaucracy blocked implementation of the ostensibly liberal agreement. As of September 8, 1921, the NKVD reported that 1,234 applications had been approved, 1,826 denied, 835 returned without starting a file, 357 remained under consideration, and 1,574 files remained to be examined.[56] Rates of approval increased in the following year, and were higher for other countries. For example, a 1922 report on applications from Siberia to opt for Polish citizenship reported 1,940 approved, 79 refused, and 29 sent to Moscow for resolution.[57] These results show a significant difference between the principle of free optation and the realities of official barriers to leaving the country. There are hints in the archives that official obstructionism could be overcome by bribes. However, this became more difficult in the 1920s as the sophistication and staffing for border institutions grew.[58]

REPATRIATION AND THE GREAT DENATURALIZATION

World War I, the civil war, the collapse of urban economies, and famine in the countryside combined to lead around two million Russian subjects to seek refuge in countries throughout the world, but predominantly in Europe and China. These refugees were a diverse group that grew by stages. During the era of the civil war many individuals fled the brutal fighting, epidemics, urban economic collapse, and famine in the countryside (especially intense in 1921). Hundreds of thousands of Poles, Lithuanians, Ukrainians, Latvians, Moldovans, and Estonians left for newly independent states founded by their co-ethnics, but many also found their way to other destinations in Europe or overseas. After the Bolsheviks had won the wars against Poland and the White armies, large numbers of soldiers and civilians retreated and emigrated to escape Bolshevik rule. Included in the emigration were many former government officials as well as the administrations of the White armies (most importantly, that of Piotr Wrangel, the last general to leave the field of battle from the Crimea).

One of the truly exceptional aspects of the situation was the large number of ethnic Russians among the refugee/emigrant populations. This marked the first substantial ethnic-Russian emigration in the country's history.[59] Bolshevik policies toward the new Russian diaspora wavered between the deeply rooted policy tradition of doing all possible to hold Russians in the country or to maintain their citizenship status on the one hand and the desire to permanently cut all ties to individuals whose loyalty was suspect because of the very fact of their departure from the country on the other. Ultimately, the Bolsheviks chose the latter in dramatic fashion.

After the civil war came to an end, the Bolshevik government pursued contradictory policies toward the return of veterans of the White armies. In January 1921, an article in *Pravda* by Aleksandr V. Eiduk, the head of the Tsentroplenbezh, seemed to promise a change in policy toward welcoming soldiers to return. Then, the *Reshid Pasha*, a ship with 3,000 Cossack soldiers from Wrangel's army, returned with much fanfare from the Ottoman Empire to Novorossiisk in Spring 1921.[60] In another important 1921 propaganda coup, the Cheka recruited a high-ranking hero of Wrangel's army, General Iakov A. Slashchov, to return to the RSFSR along with several other officers and associates.[61] However, throughout 1921, the messages were mixed. Right after the *Reshid Pasha*'s arrival, the politburo issued a resolution prohibiting the return of Wrangel's army to the RSFSR. Moreover, for all the propaganda success of the Slashchov return, official policies toward any returning White officer remained severe. They generally faced interrogations, strict oversight and registration, internal exile, and a prison sentence of up to two years. Exceptions to these general rules could be granted, but it took a real leap of faith to believe (as some did) that Slashchov's special treatment would be granted to others.[62]

Finally, in a landmark decree, on November 3, 1921, the All-Russian Central Executive Committee [Vserossiiskii tsentral'nyi ispolnitel'nyi komitet (VTsIK)] declared an amnesty for all low-rank soldiers who had been forcibly impressed into service or "who had been deceived" into serving in the White and Ukrainian national armies.[63] Individuals had three months after the formation of an amnesty committee in their country or until May 1, 1922, in Austria, Germany, and Czechoslovakia, to take advantage of the amnesty. The instructions on resettlement imposed by the Cheka show that the police were very suspicious of these individuals. They could not settle within one hundred versts of the western or Caucasian external borders of the country and each returnee had to go through a thorough "filtration" procedure of up to two weeks of interrogation and background checks by the special sections of the Cheka. The filtration was not a pro forma procedure. The instructions exhorted the Cheka to check carefully for spies posing as wives or parents of the returning veterans. Anyone suspected of disloyalty was subject to arrest, and the two individuals who had verified the loyalty of the individual would be punished as well. Even those who passed were placed under a special regime of registration and oversight. Moreover, according to Maksim M. Litvinov's February 14, 1922, report from Czechoslovakia, implementation was severely hampered by Cheka bureaucratic resistance and a serious lack of funds. Other reports from Europe mention incompetence and disorganization that must have seriously hampered implementation of the decree. In one case, M. A. Strashkevich, a repatriate in a filtration camp in Czechoslovakia, objected to Soviet newspaper reports that he had been shot at the border, pointing out that he was in fact very much alive and upset that he was being portrayed as an active White guard illegally trying to enter the Soviet Union.[64]

Officers, presumably because they were more politically motivated and likely to be of bourgeois or noble-class background, were not granted a blanket amnesty, and instead had to apply through a difficult procedure on a case-by-case basis.[65] Group amnesties were granted to Volga Germans, Kalmyks, Crimean refugees and other groups who had fled to the Ottoman Empire to escape famine.

In 1922, the Soviet Union created the "Union for the return to the Soviet motherland" to try to convince rank-and-file Russian troops abroad to return.[66] These efforts yielded some results, particularly among Cossacks. However, the regime was on the whole extremely suspicious of any citizens who ended up as refugees or émigrés abroad.[67] This was not entirely paranoiac—there were many politically active individuals and groups strongly opposed to the Bolsheviks and dedicated to opposing the regime. However, there were also many more individuals who had left for other nonpolitical reasons. Bureaucratic battles over the policy pitted the NKID (which tended to favor defense of Russian citizens abroad in order to defend the prestige of the state) against the NKVD and OGPU, which wanted to keep the ideologically suspect out of the country.[68] In October 1922, the OGPU decisively gained the upper hand when it was granted final authority over both repatriation decisions and all issuances of visas.[69]

Despite its attempts to attract immigrants and return migrants in early 1920, in November of the same year the regime took a hard line on émigrés who did not return immediately. Decrees of November 3 and 19, 1920, ordered the confiscation of all land, housing, and personal possessions of individuals who had left the territory of the RSFSR.[70] This amounted to a powerful policy against the return of émigrés and refugees, and it established the basic Bolshevik approach to its diaspora: return immediately or never.

This policy was carried further by the landmark VTsIK and Council of People's Commissars [Sovet narodnykh kommissarov (SNK)] RSFSR decree of December 15, 1921, that declared the denaturalization of all

(a) individuals who had been abroad for more than five years and had not received passports from Soviet representatives by June 1, 1922;

(b) individuals who had left Russia after November 7, 1917, without permission from Soviet authorities;

(c) individuals who voluntarily served in the armies fighting against Soviet government or participated in any way in counterrevolutionary organizations;

(d) individuals who had the right to opt for Soviet citizenship but had failed to do so by the set deadline;

(e) individuals other than those in point (a) who resided abroad and failed to register with Soviet representatives by June 1, 1922.[71]

Over the course of the next two years, the other Soviet republics issued similar decrees, concluding with the May 21, 1923, decree of the Transcaucasian Socialist Federative Soviet Republic.[72] With the formation of the Soviet Union in December 1922, and the promulgation of the Soviet constitution in 1924, a single Soviet citizenship was created. A new statute confirmed the mass denaturalizations according to individual Soviet republic laws and added that any individuals who left the territory of the Soviet Union with or without permission who refused to return upon the request of the authorities lost their Soviet citizenship. The statute likewise granted the courts the right to use denaturalization as a punishment.[73]

Few émigrés were willing to apply for Soviet citizenship, and those who did by no means received an automatic acceptance. Officials abroad and at the border were instructed to be vigilant against allowing the naturalization and return of class enemies and any individuals who were in any way suspected of potential disloyalty.[74] The decree amounted to a mass denaturalization of the vast majority of the population of former subjects of the Russian Empire residing outside the empire. In the interwar era, most countries moved toward restrictive policies on immigration and naturalization, making it very difficult for émigrés to acquire citizenship in their countries of residence. The result was roughly 1.5 million stateless individuals.[75] The few who returned were registered with the police and were required to sign a document promising not to leave the territory of the Soviet Union.[76]

The mass denaturalization of Russian refugees was the first act of its kind in the modern era, and the world was not prepared to deal with the resulting situation.[77] The problem was in part addressed in innovative fashion by the League of Nations, which set up a committee under the famous polar explorer Fridtjof Nansen to deal with the problem of the stateless Russian refugees. Nansen tackled the issue by encouraging refugees to return to the Soviet Union. He oversaw the return of roughly a half million individuals, mostly POWs. But many more people refused to return or take Soviet citizenship. For them, on July 5, 1922, he created a new document to verify identity and enable travel through countries that recognized it. The document came to be known simply as the "Nansen passport." Most importantly, he was able to convince twelve countries to recognize the validity of the document in 1922, and fifty-one by the end of the 1920s.[78] Approximately 450,000 Nansen passports were issued in the 1920s.

The Nansen passport allowed its holder to travel through countries that recognized it, though return to the Soviet Union would lead to voidance of the passport. It generally brought all the legal obligations of citizenship in the country of residence, but not necessarily all the privileges. Each country defined its rules of access to welfare and social organizations, and such privileges varied widely from country to country.[79] When Turkey followed the Soviet example by declaring a mass denaturalization of Armenian refugees, Nansen took up the issue of stateless Armenians in a comparable way.[80]

Taking a long view, the great denaturalization was in some ways grounded in traditions of Russian practice. From the eighteenth to the twentieth century, the regime had granted exceptions to the general ban on emigration by requiring that groups choosing to leave be banned forever from returning, often accompanied by denaturalization. However, this type of emigration and denaturalization had always been decreed on a case-by-case basis, never as a general policy toward all emigrants. More characteristic was the extreme reluctance of the old regime to allow its subjects to leave Russian subjecthood—even its ostensibly least-valued Jewish populations.

Perhaps the biggest break with prior emigration policy was the denaturalization and *de facto* recognition of the emigration of millions of ethnic Russians. The old regime had gone to great lengths to prevent emigration and had shown great reluctance to allow or recognize denaturalization of any ethnic Russians. In fact, it strove to promote return migration of its perceived core groups whenever possible. The mass denaturalization was thus an unprecedented event. In a few years, roughly fifteen times more ethnic Russians left the country than during its entire history prior to 1914, and the Soviet response was to make this mass emigration permanent through denaturalization and confiscation of property.

All that said, the great denaturalization did not entirely end the phenomenon of return migration. In fact, efforts to convince émigré groups to return continued sporadically through the following years and decades. Several contingents of Cossacks who had fought with the White armies, some German farmers, Finnish workers, and a few others trickled back to the Soviet Union in the 1920s. However, these return migrations hardly differed in practical or procedural terms from immigrations of foreigners. They had to apply for permission to immigrate through a cumbersome bureaucracy, and each group application was reviewed by the ever-suspicious and increasingly xenophobic OGPU. Under these conditions, and with the generally difficult economic situation, the number of return migrants remained very small—hardly a significant proportion of the former subjects of the tsars scattered around the world. Scholars have estimated that roughly 200,000 lower-rank veterans of the White armies returned to the country after the end of the civil war. There are no reliable estimates for the number of civilians who returned.[81] We have seen that the return of émigrés through official procedures was difficult and risky. Illegal, unregistered return was even more dangerous—even in the chaotic early years of the new regime. There are a few documented cases of small groups returning illegally, including nearly 3,000 officers from Denikin's army in November 1920. But the story of their return—with the help of smugglers, fishermen, bribes, and the like—only emphasizes how dangerous and difficult the illegal route could be. The danger was compounded by the extremely suspicious and hostile attitude of the authorities. For example, in a May 1922 politburo meeting, Lenin proposed executing any émigrés who returned from abroad without permission of the authorities.[82]

The great denaturalization also took an important step toward the economic and social isolation that became a defining feature of the Soviet Union. Ethnic diasporas can be powerful sources of cross-border communication, investment, income, and exchange.[83] In the early 1920s, the Soviet Union decisively broke ties with its large diaspora, making travel and eventually even communication between the diaspora and the Soviet population extremely difficult, if not impossible. This decisive shift played out in an interesting 1922 exchange between Deputy Commissar of the NKID M. M. Litvinov and Deputy Commissar of the State Political Directorate [Gosudarstvennoe Politicheskoe Upravlenie (GPU)] Genrikh

Iagoda. Iagoda, the future head of the secret police during the great purges, responded hotly to a VTsIK proposal to set rules on the readmission to Soviet citizenship of former Russian subjects denaturalized as a result of the December 15, 1921, decree. In grammatically challenged but forceful language, Iadoga argued that the government should welcome back neither white-collar employees for their skills nor the "so-called laboring element," which he claimed was politically unconscious and unaware of what the Soviet Union was all about. He wrote that such gullible people were unreliable, while the white-collar returnees would doubtless include irreconcilable elements that were highly undesirable and even dangerous.[84]

Moreover, once the great denaturalization came to an end, the Soviet Union went back to the old policy of refusing to recognize the validity of naturalizations abroad. By the late 1920s, Soviet citizens who left the country and took another citizenship were not considered free of the bonds of Soviet citizenship. More importantly, the regime turned highly restrictive in its policy toward emigration. As it built up its border institutions, it proved increasingly capable of enforcing this policy. For example, when groups of Germans and Poles tried to use the old methods to slip across the borders surreptitiously in the late 1920s, nearly all of them were stopped at the border. Those who were allowed to leave had to do so by special arrangement. Emigration became a near impossibility in the 1930s as the Soviet Union created one of the most effective border systems in terms of holding its people in that any country had ever constructed.[85]

DEPRIVATION OF THE RIGHTS OF CITIZENSHIP AND MOVEMENT

The great denaturalization of Russians abroad fits into the broader context of the Soviet approach to domestic citizenship, which included a peculiar variant of partial denaturalization that involved deprivation of the rights of citizenship while retaining the obligations and the status of citizen. Soon after the October revolution, the regime moved to reverse the fundamental principle of the February revolution, that all citizens enjoyed full and equal rights. The regime divided the populace into citizens with the full rights of citizenship (*polnopravnye grazhdane*) and those deprived of the rights of citizenship (*lishentsy*).[86] Citizens could be deprived of the rights of citizenship individually or collectively as members of a long list of categories including: private traders, clergy, persons who hired labor, former members of the nobility, former members of the tsarist era police, and the mentally ill. According to Golfo Alexopoulos, *lishentsy* groups were "defined differently at various times. In the eyes of the party leadership, they could represent classes, families, clans, as well as national or ethnic minorities."[87] This could be seen as an innovative element of class war, or as a re-creation of the long tradition in Russian history of different baskets of rights and obligations for different groups of subjects. In this sense, the policies marked another feature of the move of the regime from "citizenship" to a new form of Soviet "subjecthood." The powerful revolutionary ideology of citizenship, with its promise of equal rights for all, was replaced by a class-war ideology that entailed depriving some groups of their rights while extending preferences to other groups (such as poor peasants, workers, and "backward" nationalities). According to Alexopoulos, "the importance of social discrimination in the USSR (both positive and negative) in generating inequalities among citizens and compromising claims to citizenship by certain groups cannot be overstated."[88]

The differentiation of the rights of citizenship according to class, nationality, and other criteria was a key feature of Bolshevik citizenship right from the start. However, its effectiveness was predicated on working systems of registration, documentation, and control of the population. There had been substantial progress under the old regime toward making the internal passport the unified document verifying identity and serving as the means to register the entire population.[89] However, the old passport and residency permit (*vid na zhitel'stvo*) systems were too tied up with the old *soslovie* social orders for the Bolsheviks to simply pick up and expand or alter these systems. Instead, SNK decrees of October 5, 1918, and June 25, 1919, attempted to replace passports and other elements of the internal passport system with "work books" (*trudovye knizhki*). It was a typical "war communism" policy. It pursued the aim of mobilizing labor and identifying and punishing those who did not work. As such it was an example of the increasingly desperate attempts of the state to mobilize production for the war effort in the context of the complete collapse of the market and most industrial production, as well as the decision to replace worker control of management with centralized and coercive managerial control.[90] Introduced with the slogan "He who does not work, neither shall he eat," the policy was more about winning the war than creating socialism. The Bolsheviks set extreme penalties and threatened to apply the policy to anyone of any class who could not prove he was working. Holders of work books were required to register monthly at their local soviet, and no jobs, housing, or ration cards were to be issued without presentation of the books. In theory the system replaced the old residency permits and internal passports with a strict new set of controls on movement within the country, but in practice the state hardly had the capacity to enforce the system during the civil war.

On the other hand, the policy also aimed to promote revolutionary class politics. Everyone was required to register his or her social status in the work books. The books were required to move, migrate, and most importantly, to acquire ration cards. "Non-laboring elements" often found the books to be a means of deprivation of these rights that were so crucial to survival in the years of famine and economic disaster.[91] The policy marked a stunning attempt to expand documentary control over the population and use it to fight class war and mobilize for war. But it faced enormous practical barriers to implementation and enforcement. Indicative of the distance between intentions and realities was an NKVD report to the People's Commissariat of Finance [Narodnyi kommissariat finansov (NKF)] on February 5, 1921, that implementation of the work book decrees was stalled due to a shortage of paper. It requested 28,000 puds (458,640 kilograms) of paper, suggesting that recycled documents be put to use.[92]

The government moved to give the restrictive regime a stronger basis by reintroducing internal passports in February 1922. However, these systems proved incompatible with the turn in spring 1921 toward the New Economic Policy (NEP) and the reestablishment of limited internal markets for grain, consumer goods, and labor. Thus, an SNK decree of June 20, 1923, abandoned the requirement of internal passports and work books.[93] This loosened administrative control over the population and its internal movements, but did not spell the end of it. With the launching of forced industrialization and collectivization, controls on movement progressively tightened, culminating in the 1932 reintroduction of a draconian internal passport system aimed at forcibly asserting control over domestic migration and bonding peasants to their villages and collective farms. Soviet citizens were bound to their localities in powerful new ways that, when combined with greatly reinforced border patrols and barriers, proved remarkably effective in preventing illicit emigration.[94]

Documentation and control of foreigners was also tightened. In 1926, the NKVD had launched a major campaign to "uncover the true citizenship status of all people living on the territory of the RSFSR and to re-register all foreigners in the country." Committees examined the documents and files of all individuals whose "true citizenship" came into question in any way, with the aim of defining clearly once and for all whether the person was a Soviet citizen or foreigner. In the process, thousands of individuals who appealed to keep their foreign citizenship were forced to relinquish it and be recognized as Soviet citizens, or leave the country. Individuals who were recognized as foreigners were much more carefully documented and registered. It became much more difficult for foreigners to remain in the country as foreigners.[95]

CENTRALIZATION OF CITIZENSHIP

During the revolution and civil war, control over citizenship policies in theory resided in the Central Executive Committee (TsIK) of each socialist republic. This was an aspect of Soviet federalism and the revolutionary ideal of the formation and growth of a loose association of communist republics that would grow as revolutions swept through other lands. As a result, separate citizenship laws were issued for the Soviet republics of Ukraine, Russia, the North Caucasus, the Far Eastern Republic, Belarus, the Transcaucasian republic, and Georgia. The content of these laws varied from republic to republic, sometimes on quite significant issues. For example, unlike the RSFSR, the Ukrainian SSR incorporated a strong *jus soli* principle of treating anyone born on Ukrainian soil as a Ukrainian citizen. Deadlines and procedures for the optation process of assigning citizenship to refugees differed by republic. People's Commissar of Foreign Affairs, Georgii V. Chicherin, pointed out that various republics enacted different laws with different deadlines in response to the December 15, 1921, law requiring former Russian subject refugees to return or formally be deprived of their right to Soviet citizenship. Exasperated, Chicherin noted that the Belarusian SSR did not even issue its own law at all. The Ukrainian SSR pursued its own policies regarding naturalization of Ukrainians in Poland and policies toward refugees entering Soviet territory.[96]

However, the NKVD and OGPU limited the degree of decentralization quickly after the revolution. By October 1922, the OGPU secretly centralized and took control over all decisions on repatriation and evacuation of refugees to and from the territory of the Soviet Union.[97] A 1923 statute gave the OGPU control over all border crossings.[98] The OGPU strove to keep its role secret. In response to one petition, the foreign section of the OGPU informed the NKVD that it had refused the request of a Pole to leave the country, but ordered the local administration to keep the OGPU role quiet "in order to preserve the conspiratorial nature of its work."[99]

Formal, open, and more systematic centralization of citizenship came with the statute on a single unified Soviet citizenship *(soiuznoe grazhdanstvo)*, enacted on October 29, 1924 (see The Statute on Soviet Citizenship at the end of the book for the full text). The law was the subject of heated debates in the constitutional committee over several issues—especially the loss of control over citizenship policies at the republic level. Chicherin argued for strong centralization, complaining that early drafts "included so many references to republic citizenship, [that it was] as though the union was formed to publicly show its insignificance. We need to use the words *'sovetskoe grazhdanstvo'*."[100]

Ukrainian SSR Commissar of Education Oleksandr Shumskyi responded angrily, making a broad argument that the Ukrainian republic needed to retain its autonomy on matters of citizenship. Many of his arguments focused on the unique particularities of what Terry Martin has called the Soviet "Piedmont policy" of creating a model Soviet Ukrainian cultural home that would be attractive to Ukrainians outside the Soviet Union (mostly in eastern Poland) and analogous policies for other nationalities divided by Soviet borders.[101] Shumskyi argued that citizenship policies—from granting visas to Galician visitors to the naturalization of Galicians as Soviet citizens—were best handled at the Ukrainian republic level. He claimed that heavy-handed interference by Moscow through the NKVD and OGPU on a daily level in even the smallest cases of naturalization and immigration was undermining these important foreign and national policies. The ability of the Ukrainian authorities to offer a distinct Ukrainian citizenship had, he claimed, huge appeal to Galician and Bukovinian Ukrainians abroad. Shumskyi went on to accuse Chicherin of "forgetting what a Soviet republic is."[102] He also bitterly complained that Chicherin and the NKID were now proposing rules that would make it harder to naturalize Ukrainians abroad and facilitate their migration to the Ukrainian SSR.[103] But another speaker noted that even now, the Ukrainian TsIK must get permission from the Ukrainian branch of the OGPU in each decision on naturalization and a whole line of border and citizenship questions. He claimed that Director of the Cheka Felix E. Dzerzhinskii had long ago required that the Ukrainian OGPU get approval from the Moscow OGPU.

In short, the center already controlled citizenship. No matter what the letter of the new law, the sense of the discussion was that the OGPU had centralized control and was pursuing a policy of very tight border controls and a strongly negative approach to naturalizing Ukrainians, Persians, Chinese, or other ethnic groups residing outside of the Soviet Union.[104]

In the end, Chicherin's argument for simply switching to a single Soviet Union citizenship was amended to retain the concept of republic citizenship: "The citizen of one of the union republics within the composition of the USSR is at the same time a citizen of the USSR and possesses all the rights and carries all the obligations established by the constitution and laws of the USSR as well as by the constitution and laws of the Soviet republic in which he resides."[105] Soviet jurists quickly developed the "principle of dual unity of Soviet citizenship" (*dvuedinstva sovetskogo grazhdanstva*), which essentially meant the clear precedence and universality of union citizenship over the republic level. The official policy still favored every individual taking a republic-level citizenship as well, but allowed some groups and individuals to hold union citizenship without any republic level citizenship.[106] In short, republic citizenship remained the public and *de jure* forms, but the *de facto* secret control over citizenship was very much concentrated in the Soviet center. Since in matters of citizenship the "center" was the OGPU and NKVD, *de facto* citizenship policy leaned much more toward Soviet xenophobia than the Piedmont policy variant of the old "attract and hold" principle that had been so central to the long imperial Russian citizenship tradition.[107]

Another important and contentious issue was article 12, on the loss of Soviet citizenship. Chicherin reported that the committee could not come to agreement on a policy and thus did not include an article on the legal order for denaturalization (other than for a list of exceptions to the rule like optants and refugees). Chicherin and the NKID strongly favored a law on denaturalization in order to reduce the incidence of dual citizenship and to deal with the many international disputes arising over citizenship, but their attempts to raise the issue were blocked by the GPU. He claimed that the simple procedure for denaturalization at the local level was abolished during the time of civil war and economic distress, when many people began to leave the country and its citizenship. Chicherin blamed the Cheka for the reestablishment of a full ban on denaturalization, which he condemned as "quite imperialistic."[108] After a long debate, the committee voted to describe the process as "exit from Soviet citizenship" rather than from "Soviet citizenship and along with it from the citizenship of a republic."

However, in a close vote, it did not eliminate a republic-level TsIK role in denaturalization cases, stating that either the republic or the union level TsIKs could rule on such cases. Given that OGPU approval was secretly required for each case and given the hostility of the OGPU to denaturalization as a matter of principle, it is hard to see a great deal of significance in this article of the law. It would not be a stretch to say that, in practice, individual denaturalization remained banned.[109]

In these two important aspects the police view prevailed. Its impact was also apparent in article 3 ("Every individual on the territory of the USSR is considered to be a citizen of the USSR insofar as it is not proven that he is a foreign citizen"). This clause on the surface appears simply pragmatic. However, it declared a new principle potentially affecting very large numbers of people who would otherwise have been considered to be foreigners or stateless individuals. For example, a very large portion of temporary laborers in Russia—especially those from Korea, China, and Persia—came without documents, or in many cases did not want to renew their documents. They in principle were ascribed Soviet citizenship by this decree. Likewise, article 3 ended the ambiguous position of foreigners or former Russian subjects who had failed to exercise their right to opt for the citizenship of another state by their optation deadlines.

IMMIGRATION AND NATURALIZATION POLICY

"Workers of the world, unite!" had been the rallying cry of Marxist movements since 1848. While it did not prove so easy for the Bolsheviks to bring the revolution to the world, the regime in principle opened the door to workers, communists, and others sympathetic to the cause to migrate to the center of the revolution. Although initial policies after 1917 were favorable for immigrants of these types, the civil war, foreign intervention, the blockade, and severe epidemics, famine, and economic disasters kept the actual numbers very low. Likewise, as we have seen, the secret police imposed controls that limited the ability of foreigners to enter the country. The situation changed with the end of the civil war, the revival of the economy under the NEP, and the end of famines and epidemics in the countryside.

The best-known immigrants to the Soviet Union in the 1920s were politicals—veterans of the failed communist risings in Hungary and Germany, and communist activists from around the world.[110] One of the earliest decrees on citizenship policy declared that "any foreigner, repressed in his homeland for political or religious reasons, can exercise the right of asylum in Russia."[111] But there were many other reasons for immigration. The largest category by far was the return migration of various former subjects of the tsar. POWs and others came back primarily to reunite with family members left behind. However, throughout the 1920s, unemployment and a lack of available land prevented larger numbers of former subjects from returning. One notable exception was about 20,000 Karelian native former Russian subjects, most of Finnish descent, who returned to Karelia both from Finland and from places as far as North America. They were enticed by promises of work and land in the relatively sparsely populated region, as well as promises of substantial cultural autonomy granted as part of the Soviet Piedmont policy.[112] In theory, this had powerful potential to push immigration policy toward openness to cross-border immigration. In practice, however, it does not seem to have had a great deal of impact other than in the exceptional case of Karelia. In large part this is because Soviet policies were intolerant of dual loyalties and cross-border movement. Even in the case of Karelians, the security branches of the administration frequently clashed with the People's Commissariat for Nationalities over the issue.[113]

The end of the civil war, the lifting of the blockade in January 1920, and the declaration of the NEP in March 1921 were all part of an important shift toward a more pragmatic approach to governance. In terms of immigration policy, it cut several ways. During the spring and summer of 1920, a series of meetings at the highest levels discussed quite extensive plans to facilitate mass immigration of industrial and agricultural workers, preferably with skills that could increase productivity in the Soviet economy. Lenin took a personal interest in these discussions and overruled opponents who favored autarkic development or raised security concerns. Three hundred fifty million rubles was allocated to the effort, which centered on negotiations with an association that planned to bring a projected 100,000 German immigrants. These initiatives to promote immigration were aimed as much at return migrants as at foreigners.[114] Correspondence and negotiations with various other groups interested in migrating to the Soviet Union expanded, and the leadership created the Permanent Commission for Immigration and Emigration within the Council of Labor and Defense [Sovet truda i oborony (STO)] and gave it the authority to coordinate immigration policy and negotiate individual and group immigration cases.

On November 20, 1920, Lenin introduced a new policy that—within tight constraints—allowed foreign investors to come to the Soviet market and establish business operations as "concessions" that were governed under the old principle of the "separate deal."[115] Special procedures were established to facilitate visas for those concession employees who were allowed to enter the country. For a few years, the regime had high hopes for the possible contributions of foreign investors to economic recovery and growth through the concession system, though debates within the central committee revealed deep misgivings and distrust right from the start.[116]

Likewise, some members of religious groups who had emigrated abroad in search of greater religious freedom petitioned to return to the Soviet Union. Despite official hostility toward all religions, I found little evidence in internal Soviet correspondence that religion played a role in decisions on group petitions from Dukhobors, Molokane, Tolstoians, and other religious groups. If anything, the status of these groups as previously persecuted under the old regime seems to have helped their cause.[117] The contrast was particularly sharp for Jews. Under the old regime, it was extremely difficult for foreign Jews to migrate to the empire, and naturalization was even more unlikely to be approved. As for Jewish emigrants, the small number who followed legal procedures were sometimes barred from ever returning to the Russian Empire, and those who left illegally faced many barriers to return as well. In contrast, the STO committee resolved not to oppose the return migration of Jews who had gone to Palestine and took steps to inform Jews in the Soviet Union about the hard realities of immigrant life there in an attempt to prevent further Jewish emigration.[118] In short, the early Soviet regime welcomed Jewish immigration and naturalization and discouraged emigration—exactly the opposite of the old regime's policies.

Finally, the STO committee most often responded favorably to petitions from Germans—both former subjects of the tsar and native Germans seeking work or land in the Soviet Union.[119] This was of course a complete reversal of the policies of the World War I era, but the internal discussions about German petitions to immigrate bore an uncanny resemblance to discussions in the eighteenth century. Much was said about their knowledge and skills, and attempts were made to settle them not in compact settlements, but rather to have them spread throughout the country so they could serve as an example of advanced techniques.[120] The generally positive attitude toward German immigrants and return migrants was complemented by vigorous opposition to the German government's attempts to treat ethnic-German former Russian subjects as holding the rights of German citizens. Soviet officials insisted on the policy that such Germans remained the citizens of the Soviet Union alone, and could not receive any privileges or protections from Germany or any other foreign powers.[121]

The new regime likewise pursued a nationality policy in the 1920s that would seem compatible with immigration of various borderland nationalities. Policies of indigenization *(korenizatsiia)* in the Soviet republics tolerated and even promoted the cultural and linguistic consolidation of the titular nationalities in each republic. Until the centralization of citizenship in 1922–24, the leaders of the Soviet republics were allowed a fair degree of latitude in shaping their own citizenship policies. As we have seen, this proved particularly significant for Ukraine and in the Caucasus.

The consolidation of nationalities could logically include a kind of call to return to the motherland, to immigrate to new Soviet national homelands. In principle, immigration of these groups could be seen as "demonstrative evidence that the Soviet Union was attractive to cross-border populations."[122] Soviet budgets allocated extra funds to border regions to make them attractive to cross-border populations and at the same time prevent emigration. There were some cases of ethnic return migration or even first-time immigration. For example, around 20,000 former Russian subjects of Finnish descent returned in the 1920s to Karelia from Finland, the United States, and Canada.[123] Most impressively, at least 300,000 Armenian refugees from Turkey settled in what would later become the Armenian SSR.[124] The STO committee reported that its single biggest expenditure was distribution of a secret allocation of 23,165 rubles to facilitate the settlement of immigrants from eastern Poland in Ukrainian SSR.[125] Tens of thousands of Ukrainians from the eastern regions of interwar Poland ended up in the Ukrainian SSR.

These examples show that the Soviet government opened a few doors to immigration that had been previously closed and was willing to accept significant groups of immigrants from abroad. It would, however, be inaccurate to characterize any part of the 1920s as a time of free and open immigration—even (perhaps especially) for some of the ideologically most favored groups.

There are several reasons for this. First, the NKVD and OGPU retained and even strengthened centralized control over the entire process. The police retained their security-state mentality and generally used their power to block any large-scale new immigration. Second, there were serious ideological contradictions on many levels. Third, whether it was a result of a combination of the previous factors, or simply bureaucratism run amok, the procedures for immigrants were so burdensome and time-consuming that many potential immigrants gave up and others who heard their stories dropped their intentions to immigrate.[126] Fourth, and most importantly, objective economic conditions were not favorable for immigration. Unemployment and underemployment in the industrial sector proved to be a decisive argument against allowing working-class immigration and a shortage of land proved decisive in the countryside. Even at the peak of the NEP, the STO committee was far from a proponent of working-class immigration. In June 1924, it secretly informed the NKID and the OGPU "that because of unemployment in the USSR, the return of Russian emigrants should be limited to the smallest possible scale, and that in the opinion of the STO, it was necessary to take all measures to ensure that their return faced the maximum number of obstacles."[127]

The statistics show that this policy was pursued vigorously. Between 1922 and 1925, the STO claimed that it received 420,000 requests for permission to immigrate and granted only 11,000.[128] Real wages were only 30 percent of the prewar level and work conditions were horrible. Some of the first groups to arrive wrote to their compatriots about the shocking conditions and word spread quickly via embassies, unions, and newspapers. Soviet authorities too made it official policy to warn workers about conditions to avoid embarrassing returns and bad publicity.[129] In 1924, the STO even rejected a proposal to resettle 100,000 mostly ethnic-Russian refugees from Lithuania due to a lack of funds, and for all the other reasons above.[130]

In the countryside, the agrarian revolution and urban economic collapse had drawn millions of workers from the cities back to the village communes. There was little to no land to distribute to immigrant farmers. Moreover, the regime aimed in the long run to move to collectivized agriculture. Drawing substantial numbers of immigrants to the countryside would require recognizing their ownership of land. It was hardly desirable to bring in the complicating factor of foreign populations into the countryside while planning a massive restructuring of property relations. But, primarily for propaganda reasons, the regime did set aside 220,000 desiatin (240,000 hectares) in the Volga region for allocation to agrarian immigrants. Yet, in case after case, the STO imposed so many requirements on potential immigrants and (more often) return migrants that the applicants never came. The most common approach was to insist that potential agrarian migrants finance their own return travel and bring their own implements and machinery. Likewise, the STO often required potential migrants to form their own artels prior to migrating, preferring to deal with groups rather than individuals or families. This proved to be a barrier in many cases for individuals who wanted to return to be reunited with their families and communities in the Soviet Union. Official STO policy did not favor family reunification.[131] By far the most important limitation was the shortage of land. It was such a problem in Ukraine that, despite the acknowledged political importance of welcoming Ukrainian peasant immigrants from Poland, the Ukrainian commissariat of agriculture banned any migration to the Ukrainian countryside. The STO thus had to try to settle Ukrainians in the Volga or Siberia. The Volga region was no panacea, however. Crop failures there in 1924 led to the cancelation of several groups of return migrants that were already en route. The land shortage was considered so important that the STO often refused permission even to groups that wanted to rejoin their families and communities, as in a 1926 case of 148 Germans trying to return to Kharkov; they did not return after they were offered only the chance to settle in Siberia.[132] Thus, overall agrarian immigration was practically nonexistent. The STO committee reported that from 1922 to 1925, it approved only twenty-two groups with 2,300 people for rural settlement, most in populated areas, with the aim of spreading technical knowledge. Settling untilled lands was a secondary consideration and of little interest to potential immigrants.[133]

In the Far East, the long and sparsely populated border regions made it difficult to monitor and control cross-border movement in the early 1920s. One result was a fairly substantial immigration of Korean farmers, many from Manchuria, to border areas within the Soviet Union. In 1926, the drive to register foreigners revealed much larger numbers of Koreans than officials had expected. At the same time, officials were striving to support Slavic agricultural settlers in the region and encourage more to migrate because of the sense that Slavs would better secure it than Koreans and Chinese. This had more to do with prejudice than reality, as Koreans saw the Japanese as their greatest enemy. Soviet planners also much preferred Slavic agricultural practices to Korean rice cultivation and slash and burn techniques. Because the amount of cultivable land in the region was relatively small, officials also felt that they needed to stop Korean immigration to ensure that usable land was available for a planned influx of Slavic settlers and to increase the insufficient plots that Soviet-citizen Koreans had at the time. For these reasons, officials began to implement policies to limit further Korean and Chinese immigration and settlement in the region.

Officials saw settlement near the border as both a security issue and a magnet for further illicit immigration. Thus, various resettlement schemes were devised for the resettlement and distribution of land to Koreans to the north and east, away from the borders. These failed miserably because the land was greatly inferior. Thus, in the Far East a shortage of arable land combined with old-regime-style goals of bringing more Slavs to the region to secure it against Asian demographic dominance. The result was an attempt to seal the border against further immigration and to prevent unnaturalized foreigners from gaining access to land. This changed during collectivization, when the regime decided to simply treat all foreigners as Soviet citizens and subject them equally to collectivization. Roughly 50,000 Asians fled abroad from the Far East during collectivization. The state then proceeded to tighten up its border institutions and stop both emigration and immigration to the degree it was able. It all culminated in the mass deportation of the entire Korean population to Kazakhstan and Uzbekistan in September–October 1937.

Another important case is that of Armenian refugees in Greece, Syria, and many other countries during the 1920s, especially after the failed Greek war with the Ottoman Empire in 1922.[134] Despite the possible propaganda gains from a Piedmont policy of creating an Armenian homeland and place of refuge for hundreds of thousands of refugees, and despite the persistent efforts of Nansen and the League of Nations to negotiate and fund the settlement of the tens of thousands of Armenians who were willing to settle in Soviet Armenia, the Soviet Union refused to fund or allow a full-scale return. The reasons are not entirely clear, but seem to have been primarily economic. A 1923 STO committee discussion resolved that 50,000 Armenians wishing to immigrate to Soviet Armenia should not be allowed to return unless they paid for all expenses.[135] The amounts exceeded the resources of the Armenians and the League of Nations refused to fund the project because some member states did not want to provide assistance to the Soviet Union. Nansen spent several years trying to raise contributions from individual countries and organizations. On the whole, the project did not succeed in settling more than a small percentage of the refugees willing to migrate. According to the 1932 League of Nations report, only 6,000 Armenians were resettled in Soviet Armenia from Greece.[136] Of course the other side of the story was the unwillingness of the Soviet Union to provide funds to the Armenian SSR to prepare land and housing for the resettlement of Armenians. This example shows that there were definite limits to the willingness of the Soviet Union to act as a magnet for national home-lands within its borders.

NATURALIZATION POLICIES

Naturalization policy was also rent with contradictions right from the start. Easy admission to Soviet citizenship served the goals of world revolution and the consolidation of the laboring classes into a single polity. As revolution failed to spread, the communist slogan "The working class has no motherland" morphed into the claim that Russia was the socialist motherland, open to all workers to join. Closer to home, an open policy fit well with the early 1920s Piedmont policy by making it easy for ethnic groups divided by new borders to opt for Soviet citizenship.[137] For example, the Soviet consulate in Romania was instructed to allow natives of the Bessarabian areas previously within the Russian Empire to settle in the Soviet Union and naturalize. To "encourage" their naturalization as Soviet citizens, their Romanian passports were confiscated when they settled in the Soviet Union.[138]

As early as 1918, the NKVD began to push back against the relatively open invitation to foreigners to naturalize by taking the power to naturalize away from local officials and imposing individual background checks that had to run through the capital.[139] A VTsIK decree of August 22, 1921, formalized the power of authorities to deny applications for naturalization to individuals they deemed "undesirable" as Soviet citizens. It also heightened the stress on loyalty by, among other things, requiring an oath to "respect and defend the constitutionally-defined state structure of the RSFSR from any infringement." The decree also essentially announced that the naturalized Soviet citizen could not claim dual citizenship; that any attempt to appeal to his former country of citizenship for diplomatic protection and rights as a foreign citizen would be blocked and deemed invalid by Soviet authorities.[140] Applications for naturalization were often conditionally approved, pending presentation of a document indicating release from prior citizenship from a consulate.[141]

Despite these very significant restrictions, the general line on naturalization remained strongly in favor, and the main limitation was the unwillingness of foreigners to naturalize. Why lose foreign diplomatic protection and become subject to military service and other obligations when foreign workers could acquire the "rights" of citizenship without naturalizing?[142]

There is little evidence of foreigner willingness to naturalize, with one major exception—the Koreans. Unlike the Chinese, substantial numbers of Koreans in the Far East had naturalized prior to 1914. All naturalization was banned during World War I. During the civil war that followed, Admiral Alexander V. Kolchak's White Army and Japanese and American troops occupied the main areas of Korean settlement. An independent buffer state called the Far Eastern Republic was created by agreement of the Bolsheviks with the Whites and Allied forces on April 6, 1920. The state had its own citizenship rules, but does not seem to have actively attempted to naturalize foreign-subject Koreans.[143] When the Japanese troops left in 1922 and Soviet control over the region was established (the region was annexed into the RSFSR on November 15, 1922), the authorities refused to recognize any passports or other documents of identification that had been issued to Koreans after 1917 by White, Japanese, or other foreign authorities. In essence, this meant that all Koreans were treated as either Soviet citizens or as foreigners, depending on their pre-1917 status. As a result, Koreans who had naturalized prior to 1917 could automatically acquire RSFSR citizenship.[144] The majority of Koreans in the RSFSR were, however, unnaturalized foreigners—many with expired passports or simply without documents. Many entered the country after the revolution; by one estimate, their numbers grew from 54,000 in 1917 to 168,000 in 1926.[145] Few Koreans were keen to renew their Japanese citizenship through Japanese consulates and Soviet authorities refused to recognize anyone on Soviet soil as a foreigner without valid documentation. These factors combined to make mass naturalization a logical solution. The government took one step in that direction with a curious program. During the civil war, Korean underground guerilla fighters often found common cause with Bolsheviks in fighting against the Japanese forces in the Far East.[146] The government recognized this by granting free residence permits to about 13,000 active and former Korean guerilla fighters against Japan and for Soviet power.[147] The process came to an end in the midst of the general campaign against foreigners in 1926.

However, while the idea of a broader mass naturalization was discussed, it was not ultimately pursued because ethnic tensions between Russians and Koreans in the region ran high, and also because the NKVD generally opposed mass naturalization, instead favoring individual applications that involved background checks. The Far East section of the NKVD insisted on a screening process to exclude "disloyal elements, collaborators during the time of civil war and foreign occupation."[148] Thus, instead of a mass naturalization, a committee was formed in Vladivostok to screen and filter applications. VTsIK worked out a simplified procedure to facilitate naturalization, but by one estimate only 80,000 of roughly 250,000 Koreans in the Far East had acquired Soviet citizenship by 1922, and well under half had done so by 1926, after which naturalization became much more difficult and infrequent.[149]

The case of Korean naturalization is in a sense the exception that proves the rule. Although it was exceptional in the number of people who willingly naturalized, NKVD and local opposition sharply limited the extent of naturalization even in this atypical case. The reluctance to naturalize had serious ramifications later. In April 1928, in the midst of collectivization and intense ethnic conflict between Korean and Slavic peasants in the Far East, a decree called for the resettlement of all Koreans without Soviet citizenship from the Vladivostok region and other strategic border and coastal areas in the Far East to interior regions north of Khabarovsk. The plan targeted over 80,000 Koreans. Although it was halted in 1931 after the resettlement of 2,500 individuals, it is a powerful reminder that naturalization policies could have very serious consequences.[150]

In sum, while ideologically there was some openness to the idea of immigration and naturalization of certain groups in the NEP period, few people actually migrated to the Soviet Union during this era, and official attitudes were fairly hostile toward immigration and immigrants in general. During an administrative drive to reregister all foreigners residing in the Soviet Union, the NKVD estimated that in 1928 there were only 80,000 foreigners in the Soviet Union (less than one-twelfth the number in 1913).[151]

THE WAR SCARE AND TURN TO ECONOMIC AUTARKY

Increasing state capacity through the 1920s was very important in enforcing the ever-more strict controls over immigration and emigration, but the really definitive shift came with the broad interrelated political and economic turn of the late 1920s. Just as the era of modern Russian citizenship began in the 1860s as part of a comprehensive strategy of rapid economic modernization linked to other great reforms, so too the decisions about economic development in the late 1920s turned citizenship policy in a fundamentally new direction.

Given the broad agreement that the Soviet Union had to industrialize rapidly in order to build socialism and defend the motherland of the revolution from a hostile capitalist world, most of the leadership saw no alternative to concessions, loans, and foreign trade as a means to rapid industrialization. Indeed, the Soviet state faced a dilemma. With world revolution decreasingly likely, the focus switched to maximizing the speed of industrialization in the Soviet Union. Against substantial opposition, Lenin pushed through the NEP, and along with it policies that made attracting foreign investors, stabilizing the ruble, and increasing foreign trade big priorities. Grain exports and foreign trade progressed relatively well, and under Commissar of Finance Grigorii Sokolnikov, inflation was tamed, a semiconvertible currency introduced, and restrictions on precious metal flows across the borders loosened. In 1923–24, just two years after one of the most devastating famines in modern history, grain exports rose to 2.7 million metric tons. Ambitious foreign trade plans were drawn up for the coming years.[152]

In 1925–26, Politburo member Nikolai Bukharin was in alliance with Josef Stalin; his position was strong and his economic ideas influential. He famously called for continuing the NEP, promoting peasant and kulak production, and balancing growth between agriculture and industry. What is much less appreciated is that at the same time he became the most extreme proponent of economic autarky. He let loose a barrage of criticism against concessions, foreign trade, and imports, stressing the need to rely solely upon domestic sources for growth. Stalin fully supported these policies, declaring at the fourteenth party congress the "general line, which starts from the fact that we must exert every effort, so long as the capitalist encirclement exists, to make our country economically independent." The Soviet Union, he claimed, "possesses all that is necessary for the construction of a full socialist society, without so-called 'help' from foreign capital."[153] In 1926, Stalin and Bukharin spoke and wrote frequently on the theme of economic independence, loudly condemning concessions and other ties to the outside world as leading to the "surrender of our industry to international capital."[154]

Leon Trotsky denounced this approach, claiming that Bukharin had become the "architect of the absurd theory of a closed [zamknutnoe] national economy and a closed construction of socialism." More than anything else, Trotsky and others objected that Bukharin's autarky would require the Soviet Union to accept slow industrial growth, what Bukharin himself described at the December 1925 party congress as industrial development "at a snail's pace."[155] Critics warned that the industrial growth of the NEP era had been primarily based on returning existing capital stock to operation, and the next stage of growth world require a more intensive program of new capital investment. The only way to do that was to expand the concessions program, increase trade, attract loans, and generally become *more* engaged with the international economy. The decision to move to an autarkic context for rapid industrialization was predominantly political rather than economic. Autarkic rapid industrialization not only went against Russian historical traditions, but also was unprecedented in the global history of industrialization. It made little economic sense and many at the time thought it simply would not work without massive, unacceptable levels of coercion of the peasants. Yet, this is precisely what happened.[156]

Many of the key decisions were taken in 1926–27 in the midst of an intense "war scare" mobilization. The war scare began with Josef Pilsudski's seizure of power in Poland in May 1926. Pilsudski's anti-Russian views and eastern-oriented vision of Poland's natural borders were viewed in Moscow as a serious threat. For reasons that are still not entirely clear to historians, by fall 1926 a campaign of articles began to appear in the Soviet press pointing to the danger that the British could lead a unified western bloc against the Soviet Union, possibly with Germany to receive Danzig and the Polish corridor, and Lithuania to be granted to Poland, or possibly in a broader attack on the Soviet Union itself.[157] The campaign became intense in early 1927, especially in April, when the Soviet embassy in China was raided, Chiang Kai-Shek began a tough repression of the Communist Party, and the Soviet China policy was revealed as a failure. In May, Great Britain broke off relations. In June, the Soviet ambassador to Poland was assassinated and the OGPU launched a series of arrests and summary executions of dozens of Poles and others with suspicious "foreign ties" within the Soviet Union. This sent a strong signal to lower-level NKVD and OGPU officials, who responded by increasing the intensity of their oversight and outright harassment of foreigners in the Soviet Union. The Soviet Union had been offering a fairly comprehensive compensation agreement to pay French holders of tsarist-era bonds that the Bolsheviks had voided in return for loans, trade, and investment.[158] But in September, French-Soviet economic negotiations broke down and France forced the recall of the Soviet ambassador, Khristian Rakovskii.

There were clearly things to worry about in international affairs, but most scholars agree that the war scare rhetoric went well beyond reality.[159]

Stalin, Bukharin, and Grigorii Zinoviev led the way, whipping up a growing sense of xenophobia and hostility toward the outside world. At the time,
Trotsky was the head of Main Concessions Committee (Glavkontsesskom),
which was charged with attracting foreign concessions, and he vehemently
opposed Stalin and Bukharin's withdrawal from the global economy. In this
way, the expulsion of Trotsky from the Comintern and the party in October
1927 was an important event in the turn toward autarky.

The OGPU gained power and the xenophobic turn continued with such
highly publicized events as the March 1928 arrest of fifty engineers (prominently including three Germans) in the Shakhty region, followed by a May
1928 show trial where accusations of ties to foreign firms and intelligence
services played a key role.[160] The German government responded quickly
by breaking off trade talks. "Elsewhere, the arrest of the German engineers was regarded as proof that one could not do business with Communists" and the political and economic isolation of the Soviet Union deepened.[161] While there were some attempts to come to terms with individual
countries (especially the United States), the general line of rapid industrialization in economic isolation was pretty well set by late 1928.

The policy of attracting concessions had been a lynchpin of the NEP
policy of relative engagement with the world. Not only were efforts to conclude new agreements dropped, but also most existing agreements were
unilaterally voided by the Soviet regime. Many of the agreements covered
periods from ten to fifty years, but in case after case, officials imposed arbitrary tax increases and other requirements—even when in clear violation
of the original agreement—in order to prevent the repatriation of profits.
Moreover, in the context of a public campaign against "bourgeois specialists," local communist groups and OGPU units stepped up their harassment of concessionaires and their employees.[162] The U.S. State Department's file on the Lena Goldfields concession, the largest in terms of capital
invested and labor employed in the 1920s, provides a detailed record of the
methods used in this campaign.[163] In 1928, the concession had completed
its major investments and mining reconstruction projects, and was set to
begin the production and export of gold (which had been the whole point
of its contract). However, the OGPU conducted systematic raids on
Lena offices and a press campaign accused the company of all sorts of
breaches of contract and espionage. A show trial was launched, at which
four Lena employees were convicted of treason. An arbitrage court in
London awarded sixty-five million dollars in damages, but the Soviet side

refused to appear at court or pay the fees. Such heavy-handed methods were applied in many other cases as well.[164] The underlying nature of the legal statute for each concession made it particularly susceptible: each was a "separate deal" operating outside the general protections of either Soviet or international law.[165] The concessions policy formally came to an end with a resolution of December 27, 1930, which repealed all former concession legislation and truncated the functions of the Glavkontsesskom. A purge of the committee resulted in the arrest and execution of several pro-concessions members. By 1933 all but a few minor concessions had been liquidated, and the committee itself was formally dissolved in 1937.[166]

The elimination of concessions did not mean the end of foreign involvement in the Soviet economy, however. To acquire technical expertise, the Soviet leadership instead turned to "technical assistance contracts" (TACs). This was typically a consulting agreement where a firm or individual provided advice and services in return for fees. It was much less risky for both sides and provided needed expertise without the political problems of foreign ownership. Thousands of engineers and skilled employees came to the Soviet Union and contributed to industrialization through these contracts. They were much more expensive for the regime, which had to pay substantial fees in desperately scarce foreign currency—quite a difference from concessions, which brought capital and investment from abroad. Economists have argued that TACs brought much less to the economy in terms of entrepreneurship, managerial skills, efficiency, and ability to respond to the global market. Whether that is true or not, everything about the TACs was more temporary, conditional, and revocable. The special rules to facilitate visas and to give special protections to the employees of concessions were not extended to the employees of TACs. Cost, the expansion of police oversight and control over foreigners, and the further erosion of their protections from the state, proved to be a serious barrier to a large-scale expansion of the TACs, even in the 1930s when qualified workers were cheap and available on the labor market due to the global depression.[167] With the elimination of concessions and the victory of the isolationist path of industrialization, the powerful synergy between modernization and citizenship policy that had prevailed from the 1860s to 1914 was decisively and comprehensively rejected.

SOVIET AUTARKY

From 1926 to 1930, nearly all aspects of the citizenship boundary became more firm and restrictive. Immigration, emigration, naturalization, and denaturalization all became much more difficult. There were several motives for the restrictive turn—xenophobia, security-mania, ideological zeal, and an all-consuming desire to prevent the loss of hard currency, precious metals, and other valuables through illicit export.[168] The growing power of the OGPU during the war scare directly translated into stricter enforcement of the boundaries on all types of citizenship issues. For example, in one file, the NKVD, itself far from liberal on case-by-case decisions, frequently asked the OGPU why it had vetoed individual applications of Soviet citizens for foreign passports, but received only laconic answers like "it was denied for political reasons" or "it was denied by the local OGPU." NKVD officials complained constantly about OGPU foot-dragging (*volokita*) on these cases.[169]

Some of the oldest laws in the imperial Russian citizenship tradition were those that banned the immigration of Jesuits, rabbis, and certain Muslim clerics. An October 2, 1926, decree revived those strictures and expanded them to ban all foreign clergy.[170] The consular statute of January 8, 1926, gave consuls the power to denaturalize individuals who did not respond to their calls to return to the Soviet Union for military service or any other reason. Courts had been empowered by a decree of October 31, 1924, to use denaturalization *in absentia* and exile as a criminal penalty. They used this power with greater frequency later in the 1920s.[171]

In December 1928, the NKID codified its rules on entry into and exit from the Soviet Union for both Soviet citizens and foreigners to provide guidance to its consular officials abroad. The new rules were substantially more restrictive on both types of border crossings, especially for Soviet citizens trying to leave the country. One of the larger categories of potential return migrants or emigrants was family members wishing to be reunited with their kin. The 1928 rules were hostile toward family reunification; even in the straightforward case of parents and children who wanted to return to the Soviet Union to be united with immediate family; this was allowed only if the children were thirteen or younger.

The 1928 rules also tightened restrictions on small traders in the border regions. They were allowed to bring goods across the border only in the amounts allowed for personal use (if they were allowed to cross at all by the local OGPU). Any border region small trader who entered deep into the country, left the country through a different border point than he entered, or who broke any of the other numerous rules could be banned from crossing the border for a set period or forever. Books with names and fingerprints of such banned individuals were to be kept at border points.[172]

The instructions advised consuls that when examining worker applications for visas to enter the Soviet Union they were to keep in mind that "industrial immigration to the USSR in the generally accepted concept does not exist. VSNKh SSSR [Vysshii sovet nardnogo khoziaistva (Supreme Soviet of the National Economy)] in all its activities is oriented toward employing its own personnel, both administrative-technical and laboring." At the same time, it noted that consuls should be familiar with VSNKh SSSR circulars listing the limited categories of workers and specific skills that were needed for state industry at any given moment. All offers of services and applications to immigrate should be assessed according to these priorities. As for agrarian immigration, to even be considered, peasants needed to apply with a fully formed collective. The 220,000-desiatin (240,000-hectare) land fund set aside for immigrants and return migrants was abolished because of what the NKID called the haphazard nature of the initiative and, more importantly, the need to provide land for Soviet worker-peasants in the context of ongoing strong domestic demand for land.[173] As a result, there was no longer any possibility to provide land to immigrants in the rich soil regions; land could only be provided in previously untilled regions of the north, Siberia and in the Far East. Settling these regions required investment and expenditure that was simply not possible. Therefore, immigrant collectives had to fund themselves and provide their own equipment. To this end, the NKID demanded that any potential immigrant collective deposit sums sufficient to cover all expenses for a full year. Consuls were to be sure that any such immigrants had appropriate machinery for these difficult regions. Agrarian immigration of all types to Ukraine, the Caucasus, Uzbekistan, and Turkmenistan was ruled out. There is evidence that this ban was applied not only to new immigrants. Return migrants wishing to join their families in the good soil regions of the country were given the choice of Siberia or nothing. These stringent conditions eliminated nearly all possibility of immigration. Moreover, consuls were empowered to deny any applications on the spot without asking Moscow. Even if they approved an application, several additional institutions could reject it, including, most importantly, the OGPU in Moscow.[174]

As the industrialization drive got under way, the policy dynamic switched from trying to maximize opportunities for foreign trade and interaction (which required at least some sort of market for exchangeable foreign currency) to a dynamic of outright restriction on any kind of currency export. Keeping hard currency and gold in the country rapidly became such a priority that the NKF seems to have become one of the prime movers in the overall turn toward border control and autarky. In early 1928, the NKF sent a series of memos to the foreign sections of the OGPU and NKVD complaining that the existing border controls were not sufficient to prevent large licit and illicit losses of valuta and precious metals across the border. The OGPU and NKVD both responded immediately, sending a list of possible actions to the NKF. The NKVD called an interministerial meeting to draw up measures to limit the export of valuta by Soviet citizens. The results were draconian. Among other things, the maximum personal allowance for individuals traveling abroad was reduced sharply, while visa fees to enter the country and fees for *zagranpasporta* to leave were both increased by two to three times.[175] A new set of rules required that any sums above the very low personal allowances for valuta export had to be transferred through branches of the Soviet bank abroad. The NKF concluded simply by asking the NKVD and OGPU to reduce the number of people leaving the country (because there were in its view too many ways for individuals to get around limits on valuta export).[176] The crackdown sharply reduced cross-border trade and greatly complicated travel abroad.

The restrictions on hard-currency export were applied in full force to foreigners. Word of these restrictions must have been a serious barrier to further migration of foreigners to the Soviet Union to work. The OGPU seriously entertained strict limits on the departure of foreigners and muted ideas of imposing maximum quotas on permissions to leave the country to be granted to both Soviet citizens and foreigners. The NKID overruled the idea, however, as it applied to foreigners and intervened to force the OGPU to stop delaying granting permission to foreigners to leave, saying that in international law and practice it was unacceptable to restrict the right of foreigners to leave the country. But the idea was in the air, and it would be applied to foreigners in increasing numbers in the 1930s.[177]

By the end of the 1920s, the Soviet Union had decisively embraced an autarkic path of development that reversed the 1860s attempts to link citizenship and migration policy to a globalizing model of economic development. However, the Soviet Union had launched its massive industrialization drive and still desperately needed the expertise of engineers and skilled workers from the West. In 1930, the sixteenth party congress decided to hire up to 40,000 foreign engineers, foremen, and skilled workers.[178] With the global economy mired in the Great Depression, there were plenty of applicants from abroad. By early 1931, about 10,000 foreigners had been recruited from Western countries, and by early 1932 the cap of 40,000 was slightly exceeded.[179] This wave of immigrants differed from those who came in the 1920s. Political asylum was still offered to communists from around the world, but only a small portion of those admitted came under this designation. The focus switched almost entirely to practical criteria, above all the skills and contributions the immigrant could make to industrialization. Family reunification and the return of former residents of the empire played a much smaller role (with the exception of a large group of Karelian Finns). The 1920s requirement that immigrants be of working-class origins was dropped in favor of engineers and technicians of other backgrounds with the required skill sets.

*   *   *

Foreigners were particularly prominent in the most technologically advanced projects, like Magnitogorsk, which had over 750 foreign employees. The foreign role was significant for industrialization, but it hardly signaled a new opening to the outside world. The door to immigration did not swing open. By some reports, well over a million people applied to come to the Soviet Union for work in 1930–32. The state only allowed about 42,000 (4 percent) to enter. The foreign specialists were paid in extremely scarce hard currency, usually at rates many times higher than the wages of the Russian workers at the same factories. This both strained the state budget and bred resentment among Soviet workers. When the government stopped paying wages in valuta during the 1933 famine crisis, as many as half of the foreign workers left. Even when paid in hard currency, "living and working conditions made the overwhelming majority of foreign workers quite unhappy with their situation."[180] Foreigners in the 1930s were kept under close police surveillance, making interaction with Soviet citizens difficult. Given the xenophobic tenor of the regime through most of the 1930s and the prominent role of the secret police, the position of foreigners in society was precarious throughout the decade, and especially during the purges of 1937–38, when any foreigner or Soviet citizen with foreign ties came under suspicion. Andrea Graziosi claims that more than 10,000 Western foreigners were arrested in the late 1930s (roughly half of the remaining population).[181] During arrests, it was typical for the NKVD to force former citizens of the Soviet Union or RSFSR to renounce their foreign citizenship and turn in their passports before sentencing and sending them to the camps. But this was not even necessary for many other foreigners. The most numerous were German citizens who either had no desire to return to Nazi Germany or in any case certainly would not receive diplomatic defense from that country. The stories of foreign citizens being held in the Soviet Union to work against their will brings to mind the Muscovite-era case of Patrick Gordon. Certainly nothing like it had been seen in Russian practice since Peter the Great.

The 1930s in many ways brought the citizenship story full circle, back to the era before the great reforms, but upon closer inspection, it actually went further, to a degree of closure never before seen in Russian history. Foreigners could only enter the country under extremely limited circumstances. The absolute number of foreigners on Soviet territory plummeted to less than a tenth of the level in the late imperial period. While they enjoyed better wages than Soviet citizens, they rarely had more legal protections. In fact, during the 1930s, especially during the purges, foreigners fell under greater suspicion than most. One gets the impression that the Soviet Union was working toward an ideal end point of having no foreigners in the country at all, and that the few allowed were the result of a distasteful but temporary compromise to get their expertise and send them home. Emigration was almost completely banned for Soviet citizens, and for the first time in Russian history this ban was actually enforced. The border was sealed as never before. The lively cross-border movements and trade that had been an important part of imperial Russian life for centuries came to an end. Under the old regime, residents of border regions could get special inexpensive multiexit and multientry documents and cross the border frequently to trade. By the 1930s, traders could only take tiny personal-use exemptions. Moreover, an entire regime of border zones was erected to prevent illegal crossings, contraband, smuggling of emigrants and immigrants, and normal small-scale trading.[182] An intense campaign to prevent any kind of valuta export further raised the stakes for all the branches of the government.

The great denaturalization of 1921 was strictly upheld. No former subject of the Russian Empire or citizen of the Soviet Union who had lost citizenship could enter the country until he or she acquired Soviet citizenship abroad.[183] In case after case regarding people who had the chance to opt for other citizenships but had not done so by the established deadline, the government upheld their ascribed status as Soviet citizens (even if they had no documents and had not undergone any formal ceremony, and even if another state claimed them to be eligible for their citizenship). Only after a lengthy and by no means automatic appeals process could these individuals be released from Soviet citizenship and allowed to leave the country.[184]

The closure of the citizenship boundary cannot be characterized as a return to Russian traditions. It was much more the fruit of trends that began during World War I and deepened right from the start of the Bolshevik revolution. The victory of the autarkic model was not inevitable, but once chosen, it became a defining feature of the Soviet Union.

Conclusion

The early 1930s marked the end of the era of Russia's intensive interaction with the outside world along the citizenship boundary. That era began in the 1860s when the old regime consciously embarked upon a policy to maximize the inflow of foreigners as part of its modernization strategy. It ended a half century later when Stalin embraced an autarkic model of economic modernization. The Stalinist turn marked a prevalence of security concerns over economic, legal, national, populationist, and political matters that only deepened through the 1930s and into the World War II era.

Looking inward from the citizenship boundary—from the edge of state sovereignty—provides some fresh perspectives on the perennial questions of Russian history. One is the paradox of the Russian state. Was it weak or strong? Until the 1920s, the lengthy borders of the state were hardly relevant to controlling movement. The most effective migration control was at the local level, continuing past the era of serfdom through collective responsibility and the internal passport. Roughly four of every five emigrants left illegally without documents, and did so quite openly and easily. By the turn of the century, millions of small traders, nomads, and migrant workers were entering and leaving the Russian Empire without documented checks each year.

World war and revolution brought massive increases in state aspirations to control the external borders and to scientifically and comprehensively document, register, and control both movement into and out of the country and Russian and Soviet citizenship status. From 1914 to 1930, the state exponentially increased its capacity to control the citizenship boundary, and to use it as a tool of population politics. The question of whether this indicates a stronger or weaker state is not as straightforward to answer as it might seem. By some definitions, a weak state is one that cannot get what it wants by noncoercive means. In this sense, the barbed wire, policed and cleansed border zones, enlistment of vigilantes and informants from border populations, extreme distrust of foreigners, and prophylactic operations against populations with ties abroad all point to a state with remarkably little confidence in its ability to keep its people from leaving. The mass forced denaturalizations and naturalizations of the first Soviet decades can be seen either as an impressive show of state control over the citizenship boundary or as a sign that the state had no confidence in its assimilative power or ability to "attract and hold" populations and command their loyalty.

Study of the citizenship boundary also sheds light upon the population policies of the Imperial and Soviet regimes. Citizenship and migration policies directly influenced the shape of the population and the mix of subgroups of that population by controlling or at least influencing who entered, left, stayed, naturalized, or denaturalized and left forever. Based on the assumption that wealth derives from population and that Russia desperately needed more people, technology, and trade in order to modernize, the tsars developed a long tradition of going to great lengths to "attract and hold" people in the state. This tradition ran deeper and lasted longer than in most other countries and it continued well into the age of nationalism and rural overpopulation toward the end of the imperial era.

However, the old regime also used citizenship policies like a filter to affect the ethnic balance of the population. Jews were banned from immigration or naturalization and official policies left them much more free to leave than any other population, while several Muslim populations were banned from returning if they chose to emigrate. In contrast to Austria-Hungary and Germany, which dealt with rural overpopulation by facilitating mass overseas emigration of their core populations, Russia strove to hold its Slavic populations in the country, maintaining an increasingly anachronistic set of restrictions on emigration to the very end. Conversely, it quasi-legalized emigration by Jews and other minority groups, and imposed policies on naturalization and denaturalization that made it difficult for them to return or maintain connections with their compatriots in the empire. The statistics are stunning. Ethnic Russians, comprising roughly half the population of the empire, accounted for roughly 2 percent of all emigration prior to 1914, while Jews, accounting for less than 5 percent of the imperial population, accounted for more than 40 percent of the emigrants in the same period. Germans and Poles were both over fifty times more likely to emigrate than Russians, and Jews were 184 times more likely to emigrate.

The role of ethnic population politics in citizenship and migration policy came to a sudden and dramatic end with the Provisional Government's decree of March 1917 abolishing all restrictions and discrimination on the basis of ethnicity or religion. The Soviet regime, if anything, reversed the values of the old regime's ethnic population politics by conducting a mass denaturalization that targeted hundreds of thousands of ethnic Russians, while welcoming Jewish and German return migration.

But in different ways, the Soviet regime pushed population policies via citizenship policy to new extremes—this time using criteria of class rather than ethnicity. It banned immigration and naturalization for the middle and upper classes, allowing it only for members of the working class. Early Soviet practices created a denizen category of people who were deprived of the rights of citizenship (lishentsy), while the great denaturalization of former Russian subjects abroad and other policies aimed to allow or force class enemies out of the Soviet body of citizens and residents. In principle, the primary aim of citizenship policy had shifted from ethnicity to class. In practice, because of high unemployment, general suspicion of foreigners, and the delegation of control over citizenship policies to the OGPU, the results of these policies were limited from the start. The regime never allowed a free departure of class enemies from within its borders, and quickly reasserted the principle that denaturalization abroad was not allowed. The old formula of "attract and hold" had been reduced to "hold."

The intensity of interaction along the citizenship boundary peaked on the eve of World War I, with over ten million officially recorded border crossings going each way, and millions more undocumented crossings. By 1930, this had been reduced to just thousands, and these few crossings were denuded of spontaneity, interactivity, and meaningful exchange. Small traders faced strict limits on the amounts of goods and currency they could bring both ways, and political controls made the free exchange of ideas downright dangerous. Stalin's "Great Break" sealed the country off from the outside world, and it also sealed off Russia's earlier historically evolved citizenship traditions. It brought the most decisive break in citizenship history that any major country has ever experienced.[1]

THE CITIZENSHIP BOUNDARY FROM THE 1930S
TO THE PRESENT

The citizenship boundary was crossed by millions of people during the post-1930 Soviet era. However, it was almost exclusively crossed in extraordinary ways—as a result of war or exceptional circumstances—rather than by regularized means that individuals could choose in the normal course of events. On a day-to-day basis, it proved extremely difficult for individuals to exit or enter the country or to receive permission to leave Soviet citizenship.

Emigration remained illegal, and the means to enforce this ban was formidable already in the 1930s. Stalin introduced a series of border zones from which large categories of people, including groups considered to be ethnically unreliable, were excluded from residence. The physical barriers at the border also rapidly expanded, with barbed wire, guard towers, trenches, walls, no man's land zones, and generously funded border guards (*pogranichnaia strazha*). These troops were celebrated in Soviet propaganda, and in sparsely populated areas where the borders were not so built up the local populations were drawn into the enforcement process through bounties offered to locals and vigilantes to catch illegal border crossers.

It became ever more difficult and unlikely for foreigners to exist on Soviet soil without documents and without registration with the local police. Control over Soviet citizens also took a quantum leap. Decrees of December 1932 and April 1933 launched internal passportization drives that brought greater documentation, oversight, and control over the urban and border populations and tied rural inhabitants to their localities in ways not seen since serfdom.[2] Residents of urban, industrial, strategic, and border areas, machine tractor stations, and state farms all had to register and acquire an internal passport. Rural inhabitants outside these zones did not receive an internal passport and were effectively banned from moving to these passportized regions. The system brought a bifurcation of the population into passportless rural, nomadic, and minority groups who were banned from free movement and settlement on the one hand and passportized "citizens" who were authorized to move and reside anywhere, but still restricted by strict requirements of registration with the police any time they moved from place to place on the other.[3] Not until 1976 were passports issued to rural and nomadic citizens, but even then the residence permit (*propiska*) system continued to restrict movement in similar ways.[4] Moreover, the Ministry of Internal Affairs and OGPU kept control over the system, and they continued to restrict settlement by administrative order and through their case-by-case rulings. The internal passport system had profound effects upon urban residents as well, creating a "complicated hierarchy of privileges and restrictions, of exclusions, partial exclusions, and graduated constraints on movement that affected the entire Soviet population," and differentiated the ability to move and settle based on "absurdly precise definitions of social and ethnic groups that leaders regarded as more or less loyal."[5]

The heightened stress on registration and documentation of all residents also made it much more difficult for foreigners to elude detection and registration. The 1931 Citizenship Law confirmed that when the citizenship status of an individual was in doubt, he or she would be treated as a Soviet citizen.[6] Foreigners found it increasingly difficult to exercise one of the most fundamental rights of their status, the right to depart for their own country. All foreigners had to apply for *zagranpasporta* in the 1930s, and their issuance was often expensive and fraught with red tape and delays. Former subjects of the Russian Empire who had naturalized abroad came under particular pressure to naturalize as Soviet citizens. Many foreign workers, paid in unconvertible rubles, did not have enough money to return. High and rising fees to renew residence permits and other policies put pressure on foreigners to naturalize. Finally, according to Tim Tzouliadis, Soviet officials used all kinds of subterfuge—including straightforward theft of passports—to deprive foreigners of their citizenship status and ability to leave.[7]

The 1936 constitution did away with the legal category of individual citizens deprived of the rights of citizenship *(lishentsy)*. In principle this too moved away from the variegation of rights and obligations for various categories of the citizenry toward a single uniform status. Of course, the change was introduced on the eve of the great purges to which old *lishentsy* categories and certain nationality groups fell victim more often than others, so its significance should not be overstated.[8] Moreover, differentiation of access to jobs, education, promotions, and susceptibility to being placed on police registers all continued to be linked to class background, nationality, and religion. The Citizenship Law of August 19, 1938, further sealed the citizenship border by doing away with the practice of granting foreign members of the working class voting rights.[9] This put pressure on the foreign workers remaining in the Soviet Union to naturalize because so many other rights and welfare privileges depended upon holding voting rights. The law also moved further toward a uniform singular citizenship status by eliminating nearly all reference to "republic-level" citizenship or to "union" citizenship *(soiuznoe grazhdanstvo)* and replacing it with the monolithic use of the term "Soviet citizenship" *(sovetskoe grazhdanstvo)*.

World War II raised many important citizenship issues that remain to be researched. The annexation of Eastern Poland/Western Ukraine in September 1939 was followed by a blanket act of naturalization of all individuals on the territory on November 1 and 2, 1939, with no chance to opt for any other status or citizenship.[10] These new citizens hardly enjoyed rights equal to other citizens. A series of NKVD operations ended up deporting well over a million individuals and families from the region to camps and special settlements in the Soviet interior. The pattern was similar during the occupation of the Baltic states in 1940. Collective naturalizations were again followed by brutal mass deportations of the new citizens. There are reports that refugees from German-occupied Poland who tried to refuse passports and retain their Polish or other citizenship status were most often arrested and sent to the camps.[11]

At war's end, another set of issues arose regarding the millions of Soviet prisoners of war, refugees, and forced laborers deported by the Nazi regime from Soviet territory—all of whom remained outside Soviet borders and outside areas under Red Army occupation.[12] Stalin's regime pushed the allies very hard to ensure the forcible repatriation of Soviet citizens to the Soviet Union. In a controversial set of decisions beginning at Yalta, the allies agreed to repatriate Soviet citizens held in camps in their territory. All told, roughly two million Soviet citizens were repatriated by allied officials, some voluntarily, others against their will. Many ended up in Siberian camps upon their return. Many more bore black marks in their records and faced years of discrimination in their lives and careers. Those displaced persons who were able to evade the forcible returns and find refuge were able to leave the Soviet Union in what became the largest emigration of the Soviet era since the civil war. After the war, the borders were sealed again and emigration became even more difficult than before. Those who ended up in the Soviet Union had little chance to leave. A major exception was an agreement with Poland that allowed roughly a quarter million former Polish citizens on Soviet soil to move to communist Poland. About 25,000 of them were Jews, many of whom were allowed subsequently to emigrate to Israel. However, this group had to wait until the post-Stalin 1950s before they were allowed to depart.[13]

From the 1930s to the 1950s, immigration and return migration were both extremely rare, with only episodic exceptions—like the return of two-thirds of the 300,000 former Soviet Central Asians who had fled to Xinjiang province in China to escape collectivization and famine in the 1930s. With the post-Stalin easing of repression, the Virgin Lands program increasing the demand for labor, and the rise of Chinese nationalism and social upheaval in Xinjiang, about 200,000 former citizens were naturalized by consular officials abroad and allowed to immigrate.[14] However, such cases of large-scale immigration are few, and even in these cases the immigration was limited in size and speed by a bureaucratic system and official attitudes that made immigration and naturalization very difficult. Even though conditions seemed favorable for a pro-immigration policy after the war, with a serious labor shortage, and a boom in both the standard of living and Soviet prestige as a result of the war and achievements from nuclear weapons to space exploration, immigration to the Soviet Union remained relatively infrequent and small in scale for a country of its size and level of economic development.

After World War II, the Soviet Union coerced East European regimes into communism and gained allies among many newly independent states that emerged from national, anticolonial movements in the third world. This added a whole series of complexities to the citizenship issue that require further research. Within the communist world, travel, work migration, settlement, and even naturalization and denaturalization became much easier than such interactions across borders with the capitalist world. Substantial numbers of citizens of these countries came to the Soviet Union for study, work, or leisure from the 1960s to the 1980s. Restrictions on travel and study in the Soviet Union by citizens of capitalist countries were also loosened considerably in the 1960s, and the amount of cross-border travel increased substantially. Total visitors to the Soviet Union rose from a half million in 1956 to two million in 1970, to five million in 1980, with over 60 percent of these visitors from socialist countries. Soviet travel abroad followed a nearly identical trajectory, with comparable numbers.[15] Economic and scientific cooperation also expanded between the Soviet Union and the West.[16]

Yet, the boundary between the capitalist and socialist worlds was maintained with rigor. Unauthorized emigration was treated as a form of treason, and punished with extremely harsh measures. Those who left, whether licitly or illicitly, were often denounced publicly and the families, colleagues, and acquaintances of the individuals were pressured to denounce them.[17] Tourists were shepherded by the Intourist system, which minimized uncontrolled contact with Soviet citizens, and elaborate controls were imposed upon Soviets traveling abroad.[18] Soviet citizens were barred from emigrating even after marrying foreigners.[19] High-profile individuals like Mikhail Baryshnikov, Mikhail Rostropovich, and Aleksandr Solzhenitsyn were de-naturalized *in absentia* or upon exit from the country and banned from returning.[20]

Moreover, while these changes appear substantial relative to the extreme autarky of the 1930s to the early 1950s, the changes appear meager indeed when compared to the explosion of international migration and interaction of the great wave of globalization taking place in the postwar Western world. Stalin's autarky was established in the 1930s, when the world as a whole was restricting immigration, imposing tariffs and trade barriers, and in other ways reversing the globalizing trends of the prior half century. In this comparative sense, the contrast between the Soviet Union and the rest of the world grew wider in the postwar decades. In 1970, for example, the Soviet Union recorded 2.1 million tourist arrivals—only 1 percent of global international tourism and less than 2 percent of all visitors to Europe. Twice as many people visited Yugoslavia and four times as many visited Austria during that year.[21]

The biggest exception to the generally closed border was again in Jewish emigration policy. Just as the imperial regime had quasi-legalized Jewish emigration in 1892 by allowing the Jewish colonization organizations to open emigration information bureaus throughout the country, from 1968 through the 1970s, the Soviet Union made it possible for a limited number of Jews to emigrate—albeit through a very difficult, costly, and risky procedure. In this decade, roughly a quarter million Soviet Jews were allowed to emigrate (about 10 percent of the 1970 population of 2.2 million).[22] Why the regime decided to allow this emigration is still a matter of scholarly debate.[23] It was far less a matter of population policy than the late-imperial policy had been, and more closely linked to external factors—détente, the rise of Soviet foreign trade (especially grain imports), signing of the Helsinki Accords and other international agreements that obligated the Soviet Union to respect the right to emigrate.

The 1970s Jewish emigration from the Soviet Union was an important exception to the general policy of maintaining the ban on emigration. But until the Gorbachev era, it remained an exception rather than a new rule. Even while allowing a quarter million of its citizens to emigrate, the regime went to great lengths to enforce the citizenship boundary. The regime imposed huge financial, administrative, political, and social barriers to emigration, and once an exit visa was granted, it was abundantly clear that it was a one-way ticket with no return allowed. This was important, because of all subgroups of the Soviet population, the Soviet Jews were the most highly educated (along with the Armenians) and they were a globally dispersed diaspora nationality that had the greatest potential to create a new interactive interface with the outside world. But until the late 1980s, the regime effectively prevented such interaction from occurring. The citizenship boundary remained harder than nearly any other in the world right up to the collapse of the Soviet Union in 1991.

The 1991 collapse was a watershed in the long-term history of controls over the citizenship boundary. On the eve of the dissolution of the Soviet Union, the Russian Federation adopted extremely open citizenship laws based on inclusive *jus soli* principles that automatically granted citizenship to all permanent residents of the Russian Federation and in 1992 allowed any former Soviet citizens who had not established permanent residence to apply through "simplified procedures." Along with these liberalizations of the citizenship boundary, the Russian Federation began the process of legally abolishing the *propiska* system of controls over the right to live in certain regions and guaranteed the right of all citizens to move freely within the country, rights that were finally codified in article 27 of the 1993 Russian Federation Constitution.[24] The emancipatory trend culminated in the landmark 1996 law which for the first time in all of Russian history made the right to enter and leave the country a basic legally defined right of the Russian citizen.[25] Over five million Russian citizens emigrated to countries beyond the former Soviet space from 1990 to 2010.[26] As in the Imperial era, non-Russian minorities made up a very disproportionate part of the total, with Germans and Jews together accounting for more than half of the total emigrants from 1989 to 2002. That said, ethnic Russians accounted for 36% of the emigration, making the last two decades the first period of substantial Russian emigration since the aftermaths of the two world wars.[27]

As in the wake of World War I, tens of millions of people found themselves within the boundaries of countries that did not match their origins, identities, or affinities. The sorting of nationalities and citizenships among the fifteen successor states was a drawn-out and contentious affair and one that continues to this day. It has proceeded quite differently from the process in the beginning of the 1920s. While the 1920s optation treaties and mass denaturalization were aimed against dual nationality and toward creating a loyal population of desired class backgrounds, the 1990s saw a relatively open door to naturalization without deadlines, and following global trends, proved very tolerant of dual citizenship. Former citizens of the Soviet Union residing outside the Russian Federation were allowed to receive citizenship through a "simplified procedure" that amounted to nothing more than filling out a simple form. They were not even required to enter the Russian Federation to do this. This remarkably open definition of citizenship is typical of revolutionary regimes, but in many ways went further even than the early French revolutionary laws by explicitly allowing dual citizenship.[28]

These policies have helped to avoid stateless individuals, a serious problem affecting millions in the 1920s. But they have also created large populations of Russian Federation citizens living outside the borders of the state. This has given rise to many conflicts between Russia and the host countries, especially in Latvia, Estonia, Georgia, Moldova, Transnistria, and the Crimean region of Ukraine.[29]

Since 2000, Russia has sharply pulled back on the emancipatory trends, in the process more sharply defining and more closely policing the boundary between citizen and foreigner. First, the law allowing former Soviet citizens to acquire Russian Federation citizenship by "simplified procedure" expired in 2000 and was not renewed. Then, in 2002, the law was renewed, but on a more restrictive *jus soli* basis, now only including former Soviet citizens born on Russian Federation territory. Other former Soviet citizens from that point were treated legally as no different from other foreigners.[30] Instead of a simple application, former Soviet citizens now had to provide evidence of income, demonstrate competence in Russian language, acquire a permanent residence permit, then live through five years of continuous residence in the Russian Federation before they could apply for citizenship.[31] One of the primary effects of these decisions was to finally— eleven years after the end of the Soviet Union—make clear that the open invitation to all former Soviet citizens to acquire Russian Federation citizenship had come to an end.[32] In some ways then, it amounted to a shift from the policy that the Russian Federation was the legal successor to the Soviet Union; the former Soviet space had now been divided into mutually exclusive citizenries. The 2002 law was quite openly directed toward limiting the number of non-Russians who could acquire Russian citizenship;

proponents of the law were especially concerned about preventing the naturalization of a large number of Tajiks and others from Central Asia and the Caucasus working as temporary laborers in the Russian Federation. It soon became clear that the 2002 law also made it difficult for some desired populations outside Russia to return and naturalize. A series of amendments from 2003 to 2008 addressed this perceived problem by allowing veterans of the Russian army, the Soviet army in World War II, and Soviet citizens who received higher education in Russia after 2002. In 2008, a new resettlement program for Russians in former Soviet states (the compatriots resettlement program) allowed the government to allow naturalizations of those individuals and groups it deemed worthy under expedited procedures that avoided all the barriers set by the 2002 law. The result of these changes was to accentuate the filtering function of citizenship policy—attracting and holding ethnic Russians, and preventing the influx of many non-Russian minorities.[33]

The restrictive turn did not mean an end to attempts to naturalize strategic groups in the former Soviet space—quite the contrary. In summer 2002, the Russian Federation launched a controversial drive to naturalize residents of the South Ossetian and Abkhazian regions of Georgia. Then in 2008, Russia claimed the right to protect the interests of its citizens in Abkhazia and South Ossetia during its war with Georgia.[34] Georgia has vigorously protested these naturalizations, claiming that it enacted an optation procedure in 1993 that gave all residents of the region six months to formally turn down Georgian citizenship. If they failed to exercise this option, then they were ascribed Georgian citizenship and, according to Georgian law, were not allowed to take a second citizenship without permission. The European Union independent report under Heidi Tagliavini agreed that the collective Russian naturalizations of these populations contradicted Georgian and international law. The Georgian case has been a radical departure for Russia from a long history of optation practice and adherence to territorial principles recognizing the right of states to determine the citizenship status of individuals on their territory. But in the wake of the 2008 war, Russia has pursued collective naturalization in Crimea, Transnistria, and other regions. The issue remains highly charged and unresolved.[35]

Another remarkable aspect of the shift toward a restrictive approach concerns refugees from conflicts in former Soviet states in the Russian Federation. A 1993 law created the category of "forced migrant" to cover these mostly Russian-speaking displaced people. Access to medical care, pensions, and other forms of welfare as provided to this favored immigrant category, and federal funding programs aimed to help localities provide long-term housing to accommodate people with "forced migrant" status. This amounted to one of the most aggressive and generous programs aimed at helping former Soviet citizens to migrate and integrate into the Russian Federation. However, most of these programs were allowed to expire in 2001. Moreover, the law required beneficiaries to be Russian Federation citizens. Until the 2002 law, it was easy for applicants for "forced migrant" status to quickly acquire Russian citizenship. Afterwards, it became much more difficult. The result was a sharp fall in the number of "forced migrants," from 782,000 at the beginning of 2001 to 168,000 in early 2006.[36] Symbolic of the shift of official attitude toward such migrants was the dissolution of the Federal Migration Service, created in 1992 primarily to provide social services, and transfer of its functions in 2002 to the Ministry of Internal Affairs. Observers have noted a rapid turn from a focus on welfare and integration to policing as a result. Thus, since 2002 even the most favored category of immigrant—the "forced migrants" who already had acquired Russian citizenship and most often were Russian-speakers—was less welcome and increasingly restricted in its ability to migrate and settle in the Russian Federation.[37]

All these restrictions were introduced as Russia made a nationalistic turn against foreigners, minorities, and the globalizing reforms of the 1990s. The biggest dilemma for Russian citizenship going forward will be the conflict between this trend and the intensification of a chronic shortage of labor. The opposition of these forces often plays a central role in the history of citizenship throughout the modern world, and it was important in the era analyzed in this book. But the intensity of this conflict in Russia over the past decade has rarely been matched. Russia clearly needs more workers. Even though the excess of immigration over emigration was six million between 1992 and 2008, deaths exceeded births by 12.6 million in the same period, bringing a population decline of 6.6 million. Given demographic trends and a projected sharp decline in the number of women in their twenties in the next decade, there seems to be little prospect for a sharp rise in the birthrate, and demographers predict a massive decline in the working-age population.[38] As in the late imperial era, the regime is going to great lengths to encourage ethnic Russians to stay in Russia, to have children, and to remain in the Far East to counter the perceived threat of Asian demographic dominance. But none of these policies has been very effective, and demographers are skeptical about their future prospects. Relatively high wages have pulled millions of workers into Russia for temporary or long-term work. As in the late imperial period, the regime has imposed guest worker rules that make it difficult for these laborers to naturalize, thereby preserving their temporary, marginal status. These restrictions could act as a brake on future labor immigration, especially in the very possible event that source-country economies begin to perform better relative to the Russian economy.[39] Even if guest labor flows continue at their high current rate, there will still be a massive shortage of labor. Many analysts conclude that the only realistic solution is to encourage mass immigration.[40]

But Russia has already accepted more immigrants in two decades than the entire net immigration to the Russian Empire from 1828 to 1914.[41] In the same two decades, over five million people have emigrated, including an unprecedented number of ethnic Russians. All this has happened at a time of intense political and social search for a Russian national idea and for the creation of a Russian national identity. Public attitudes are not adjusting to this unparalleled era of mass emigration and immigration nearly as quickly as the demand for labor is increasing, and there has been a backlash that may make future immigration difficult.[42] Exacerbating the problem is the fact that those most willing to come have been Muslims from the Caucasus and Central Asia or Asians in the Far East—both the targets of Russian nationalists and popular prejudice. In both cases, immigrants have been portrayed as security risks—whether because of purported sympathies with Muslim extremism or because of fears of Chinese aims in the Far East and China's massive demographic advantage on the other side of the border.[43] Political and national tensions over immigration show no signs of abating, and questions about naturalization and the treatment of a large population of immigrant and guest worker foreigners are likely to remain central to debates about Russian citizenship for a long time to come.

The dilemma is perhaps even more acute if we turn from unskilled low-wage labor to the questions of attracting skilled labor and investors and increasing the intensity of interactions between the domestic and global economies. In the aftermath of the 1998 economic crisis, many foreign investors, employees, students, and others in the foreign community left the country. Vladimir Putin then turned away from the 1990s attempts to draw foreign investment and asserted control over key industries in the gas and oil sector through renationalization or acquisition by loyal oligarchs. This model has been servicable as natural-resource prices climbed, but most economists agree that even continuation of an undiversified, fossil-fuel export economy will be difficult without a return to a more open economy. Citizenship policies are a small part of this larger set of choices, but just as the 1860s and 1920s changes in citizenship policy were direct results of larger economic policy choices, so too will the future of citizenship and migration policies in the Russian Federation be closely linked to the general economic line. In the broader picture, then, Russia continues to face a fundamental dilemma about globalization. Whether it leans toward the strategy launched in the 1860s and continued right up to 1914, or follows an updated variant of the autarkic path is one of the most important questions the country faces. As has been true throughout Russian history, its citizenship and migration policies will be determined by the choices it makes on this larger agenda.

Tables

TABLE I. Aggregate Immigration to the Russian Empire by Decade

1851–60	195,000
1861–70	533,000
1871–80	776,000
1881–90	864,000
1891–1900	465,000
1901–10	708,000
1911–15	543,000

Source: Walter F. Willcox, *International Migrations,* vol. II, National Bureau of Economic Research Demographic Monographs, vol. 8 (New York: Gordon and Breach Science Publishers, 1969), 566.

TABLE 2. Seasonal Chinese Laborers in the Far East

	Primorskaia oblast'	Amurskaia oblast'
1884	8000	
1886	13,000	14,500°
1890	6215	
1891	7648	14891°
1892	8508	
1893	8275	20272°
1894	9371	
1895	10,663	
1896	13781	8828
1897	29284	8597
1898	33809	12199
1899	38655	7891
1900	31448	9048
1901	25000	7709
1902	31039	7561
1905		11436
1906	47390	17303
1909	65409	22368
1910	60587	31809
1911	57447	29619
1912	53698	36441
1913	52239	32201
1914	38779	40740
1916		42015

°Includes Manchurian Chinese subjects resident in the Zeia River basin.

Source: O. A. Timofeev, *Rossiisko-kitaiskie otnosheniia v Priamur'e (ser. XIX–nach. XX vv.)* (Blagoveshchensk: Blagoveshchenskii gos. pedagogicheskii universitet, 2003), 263, 265.

TABLE 3. Emigration from the Russian Empire to North and South America (in Thousands)

1821–30	—
1831–40	0.5
1841–50	0.6
1851–60	1.6
1861–70	4.9
1871–80	68.0
1881–90	300.7
1891–1900	692.8
1901–10	1778.4
1911–20	1134.1
1821–1920	3981.6

Source: Vladimir M. Kabuzan, *Emigratsiia i reemigratsiia v Rossii v XVIII-nachale XX vek* (Moscow: Nauka, 1998),, 88–89; Imre Ferenczi and Walter F. Willcox, *International Migrations,* vol. I, National Bureau of Economic Research Demographic Monographs vol. 7, (New York: Gordon and Breach Science Publishers, 1969), 377–383; *Statistical Abstract of the United States* (Washington, D.C.: U.S. G.P.O., 1929), 95.

TABLE 4. Net Migration to the Russian Empire (Immigrants and Returning Emigrants Minus Emigrants, in Thousands)

Year	Total	Russian subjects	Foreign subjects	Germany	Austria-Hungary	Persia	Ottoman Empire	China
1828–30	4.1	0.4	3.7	2.8	0.6	-1.3	-0.3	—
1831–40	57.9	35	22.9	8.4	11.1	4.8	-2.4	—
1841–50	43.3	5	38.3	13.5	2.4	11.6	4.8	—
1851–60	-67.7	-262.8	195	64.4	42.9	40.7	26.8	—
1861–70	336.7	-196.3	533	271.1	145.7	15.9	69.7	—
1871–80	399.5	-378.8	778.3	292.3	267.9	90.7	52.8	0.1
1881–90	449.7	-414	863.7	439.3	308	73.1	33	-0.4
1891–1900	-256.6	-722.2	465.6	118.4	37.8	200.4	51.9	6.8
1901–10	-851.1	-1559.1	708.0	193.4	-29.1	194.4	107.6	-15.8
1911–15	-471.6	-1014.9	-543	58.6	40	214.5	58.5	132.4
TOTAL	-355.8	-4507.7	4151.9	1462.5	827.3	844.8	402.4	123.1

Source: Kabuzan, *Emigratsiia i reemigratsiia*, 62–63; Ferenczi and Willcox, *International Migrations*, vol. 1, 261–272, 794–797. The emigration data are gathered from records of the primary countries of destination.

TABLE 5. The Movement of Foreigners across the International Borders of the Russian Empire (according to Statistics Gathered by the Third Section of the Imperial Chancellery)

Year	Entered	Left	Net entry of foreigners	Naturalized	Naturalized as a % of net entry of foreigners	Deported	Russian subjects going abroad
1839	12229	3404	8825	502	6	25	
1845	17912	6706	11206	496	4	18	
1846	21373	7959	13414	550	4	9	
1847	29162	10452	18710	682	4	19	
1848	13093	2487	10606	957	9	31	2204
1857	21349	11385	9964	3419	34	38	
1860	31233	16257	14976	1318	9	51	
1861	39740[a]	15070	24670	1144	5	27	
1862	24928						27303[b]
1863	30524	16909	13615	1106	8	212	28048
1864	28173	17245	10928	1648	15	259	
1865	39556	9392	30164	783	3	153	12418
1866	36867	6312	30555	546	2	107	
1867	43134	7645	35489	355	1	108	
1868	102775	29705	73070	112	0.2	184	21702
1869[c]	99687	29705	69982	179	0.3	81	18380

a. The Third Section attributes this increase to the new passport rules for foreigners, which were temporary until the final review of the passport statute, but in the meantime, "significantly eased the passport formalities faced by foreigners coming into the country, and along with that have significantly eased bureaucratic burdens." GARF, f. 109, op. 223, (1861), l. 151.

b. The Third Section report for the year attributes this sharp increase to the "easing of passport rules for Russian subjects going abroad."

c. The 1869 report notes that the new rule allowing double entry within six months may be resulting in underreporting of numbers entering in that year.

All the above statistics are from the yearly reports of the Third Section of the Imperial Chancellery, 1839–1869. GARF, f. 109, op. 223, dd. 4–34. To compare with Germany, see charts in Eli Nathans, *The Politics of Citizenship in Germany: Ethnicity, Utility, and Nationalism* (Oxford and New York: Berg, 2004), 93, 95, 99. I was unable to find an explanation for the anomalously large naturalization rate in 1857.

This table should not be used as anything but a crude indicator of general changes over time. As much as 90 percent of all emigration was illegal, unregistered, and thus would not be reflected in these official statistics (see chapter 4). The immigration figures are probably much closer to reality, since most immigrants (other than temporary workers from the Far East, Caucasus, and Central Asia) had incentive to register legally in order to acquire the privileges that accrued. This is not to say that Russian statistics are less reliable than those of other states in this era.

TABLE 6. Movement of Populations across the External Boundaries of the Russian Empire, 1897–1907: Leaving the Empire

	1897	1900	1903	1906	1907	1908	1909
By *zagranpasport*	399,000	451,000	531,000	596,000	581,000	530,000	571,000
By multiexit visa or border crossing card[a]	3,480,000	3,507,000	5,374,000	8,199,000	8,151,000	8,232,000	9,826,000
Russian subjects	1,606,000	2,210,000	3,003,000	5,890,000	6,262,000	6,032,000	6,982,000
Foreign subjects	2,273,000	1,749,000	2,884,000	2,905,000	2,834,000	2,732,000	3,415,000
Through European borders	3,796,000	3,859,000	5,725,000	8,623,000	8,908,000	8,575,000	18,201,000
Through Asian borders[***]	83,000	100,000	161,000	163,000	188,000	189,000	197,000
	—	—	274,000	493,000	524,000	569,000	513,000
Total	3,879,000	3,958,000	5,887,000	8,795,000	9,097,000	8,764,000	10,398,000

TABLE 7. Movement of Populations across the External Boundaries of the Russian Empire, 1897–1907: Arriving in the Empire

	1897	1900	1903	1906	1907	1908	1909
By *zagranpasport*	420,000	443,000	494,000	537,000	566,000	548,000	584,000
By multiexit visa or border crossing card*	3,452,000	3,449,000	5,318,000	8,140,000	8,423,000	8,186,000	9,815,000
Russian subjects	1,519,000	2,081,000	2,845,000	5,571,000	6,051,000	5,920,000	6,877,000
Foreign subjects	2,353,000	1,811,000	2,966,000	1,926,000	2,938,000	2,814,000	3,523,000
Through European borders	3,758,000	3,775,000	5,614,000	8,459,000	8,736,000	8,503,000	10,148,000
Through Asian borders**	114,000	117,000	198,000	218,000	253,000	231,000	252,000
	—	—	262,000	464,000	511,000	553,000	499,000
Total	3,872,000	3,892,000	5,812,000	8,677,000	8,989,000	8,734,000	10,400,000

*legitimizatsionnyi billet

**Including the Caucasus borders.

Note: On average, both for numbers departing and arriving, the number of men exceeded women by about a quarter through the entire era.

Source: RGIA, f. 565, op. 12, d. 134, l. 1ob.

TABLE 8. Population of the United States Born in the Russian Empire (Excluding Finland) according to the 1910 Census (by Mother Tongue)

Mother Tongue	Number	%
Yiddish and Hebrew	838,193	52.3
Polish	418,370	26.1
Lithuanian and Lettish (Latvian)	137,046	8.6
German	121,638	7.6
Russian	40,542	2.5
Finnish	5,865	0.4
Ruthenian	3,402#	0.2
All other	37,696	2.4
Total	1,602,752	100

#Includes 728 reporting "Little Russian."

Source: U.S. Bureau of the Census, *Thirteenth Census of the United States Taken in the Year 1910: Abstract of the Census* (Washington, DC: GPO, 1913), 193.

TABLE 9. Share of Emigration by Ethnic Group

	1901–10 estimate	1904–9 estimate	Emigrants per 100,000
Jews	41%	47%	1662
Poles	29%	26%	514
Lithuanians	9%	9%	456
Finns	7%	7%	182
Slavs (Russians, Ukrainians, Belarus)	7%	5%	9
Germans	6%	5%	491

Source: For 1901–9: Robin Cohen, *Cambridge Survey of World Migration* (Cambridge: Cambridge University Press, 1995), 90. For 1904–9: RGIA, f. 565, op. 12, d. 134, l. 149; RGIA, P. Z. 2531 (*Ocherk istorii i sovremennogo sostoianiia otkhoda na zarabotki za granitsu v Zapadnoi Evrope i v Rossii*), 13. Emigrants per 100,000 is based on figures for 1904–9 taken from RGIA, P. Z. 2531, l. 13.

The Statute on Soviet Citizenship

1. For the citizens of the Soviet Socialist republics, a union* citizenship is created (Constitution of the USSR, art. 7). The citizen of one of the union republics within the composition of the USSR is at the same time a citizen of the USSR and possesses all the rights and carries all the obligations established by the constitution and laws of the USSR as well as by the constitution and laws of the Soviet republic in which he resides.
2. Foreign citizens living on the territory of the USSR for work and belonging to the working class or to that part of the peasantry that does not employ hired labor are granted all the political rights of citizens of the USSR.
3. Every individual on the territory of the USSR is considered to be a citizen of the USSR insofar as it is not proven that he is a foreign citizen.
4. A child whose parents are both citizens of the USSR is considered a citizen of a Soviet republic and at the same of the USSR, no matter where he was born.

    A child is considered a citizen of a Soviet republic and at the same time of the USSR if one of his parents at the time of birth was a citizen of the USSR, on the condition that one of his parents lived at that moment on the territory of the USSR.

    The citizenship of a child, one of whose parents was a Soviet citizen at the moment of his birth, but both of whose parents lived outside the territory of the USSR at that moment, is determined by agreement of the parents. At adulthood this individual, may acquire citizenship in a simplified procedure.
5. In a marriage between an individual with Soviet citizenship and an individual with foreign citizenship, each individual preserves his or her citizenship. A change in the citizenship of these individuals can follow in a simplified procedure established by Soviet Union law.

6. A change in the citizenship of one spouse who is a citizen of the USSR and is living on the territory of the USSR has no effect on the citizenship of his or her children.

The citizenship of children in cases when one of the parents has been a citizen of the USSR, but has been living outside the territory of the union and leaves the citizenship of the USSR, is decided by agreement of the parents.

    Note 1. In cases where both parents leave the citizenship of the USSR or when both parents become citizens of the USSR, the citizenship of children under fourteen years old changes accordingly.

    Note 2. Individuals who have ceased to be citizens of the USSR because of their parents' denaturalization are given the right to acquire citizenship of the USSR through a simple declaration to the *guberniia, oblast,'* or corresponding *guberniia* executive committee—or in autonomous republics in which the *guberniia* administration is absent—to the TsIK of the republic.

7. The TsIK of each Soviet republic conducts the naturalization of foreign citizens living on the territory of that Soviet republic.

Note. Naturalization of foreign citizens with residence for work and belonging to the working class or to the peasantry not employing labor, and also those seeking political asylum as a result of repression for social activity, is conducted by the *guberniia, oblast,'* and other corresponding executive committee, and—in autonomous republics in which the *guberniia* administration is absent—the TsIK of the republic.

8. The order of naturalization in the USSR of individuals wishing to settle on the territory of the USSR as agricultural or industrial immigrants—and equally the order of naturalization into the citizenship of the USSR of repatriates, return migrants, and individuals returning to the USSR on the basis of treaties with foreign states—is established by special legislation of the USSR, which should in these questions respect the sovereignty of the Soviet republics.

9. The naturalization of foreigners living abroad—but not falling under article 8 of this Statute—is conducted by diplomatic, consular, or organs of the USSR fulfilling their functions abroad, by the decisions of the TsIKs of the Soviet republics according to the declaration of the representative of the NKID at the SNK of the given Soviet republic and of the TsIK USSR by declaration of the NKID.

10. Restoration of the citizenship of individuals who have lost it may be granted by decree of the TsIK USSR or of TsIKs of the Soviet republics in the order described in article 9.

11. Foreign citizens who have been accepted into the citizenship of the USSR do not carry the rights and do not carry the obligations linked with membership in the citizenship of another state.

12. The following are recognized as having lost citizenship in the USSR:
    a) individuals who have been deprived of citizenship according to the legal acts of the union republics published up to July 6, 1923, or who were deprived of it on the basis of the laws of the USSR;
    b) individuals who left the territory of the USSR with or without the permission of the organs of the USSR or the Soviet republics but did not return or are not returning in response to the demands of corresponding organs of the authorities;
    c) individuals who have left citizenship of the USSR according to the established legal order;
    d) individuals who have been deprived of citizenship by order of the courts;
    e) individuals who have opted for foreign citizenship on the basis of treaties with foreign states;

13. Exit from Soviet citizenship is allowed with the permission of the TsIK of the Soviet republics or TsIK USSR.

Chairman of the TsIK of the USSR M. Kalinin
Secretary of the TsIK of the USSR A. Enukidze
October 29, 1924

Translated by the author from Sergei Kishkin, *Sovetskoe grazhdanstvo* (Moscow: NKIu RSFSR, 1925), 93–96.
*The term is "sovetskoe grazhdanstvo." I translate it here as "union" rather than "Soviet" to reflect the dance in the text between "republic" and "union" citizenships.

Archival Sources

ARKHIV VNESHNEI POLITIKI ROSSIISKOI IMPERII (AVPRI)

f. 133 Kantseliariia Ministerstva inostrannykh del, 1797–1917, op. 468–470

f. 137 Otchety MID Rossii, 1830–1916, op. 475 (1830–1916)

f. 148 Tikhookeanskii stol, op. 487

f. 150 Iaponskii stol, op. 493

f. 256 Gen-konsul'stvo v Londone, op. 555 a, b

f. 161 St. Peterburg Glavnyi arkhiv, op. 44, 45, 61, 64, 93

f. 170 Rossiiskoe posol'stvo v Vashingtone, op. 512/1–5

f. 249 Genkonsul'stvo v Konstantinople, op. 1

f. 149 Turetskii stol, op. 502 a.

f. 167 Posol'stvo v Berline, op. 509/1

f. 340 Nol'de, B. E., op. 610

f. 340 Martens, F. F., op. 787

f. 156 Iuriskonsul'skaia chast', op. 457

GOSUDARSTVENNYI ARKHIV ROSSIISKOI FEDERATSII (GARF)

f. 102 Departament politsii
    I deloproizvodstvo
    II deloproizvodstvo
    Op. 260
    Op. 269
    Op. 76a

f. 109 Tret'e otdelenie sobstvennoi Ego Imperatorskogo Velichestva kantseliarii
    (1826–1880)

f. r-130 RSFSR Sovnarkom 1917–1923

f. 215 Kantseliariia Varshavskogo general-gubernatora

f. r-364 USSR STO Permanent Commission for Immigration and Emigration, 1922–1930

f. r-393 Narodnyi komissariat vnutrennikh del RSFSR

f. r-1235. VTsIK RSFSR

f. r-1318 Narkomat po delam natsional'nostei RSFSR (1917–1924)

f. 3316 VTsIK SSSR

f. r-5209, 1 op. (1124 d.) Mezhduvedomstvennaia komissiia po provedeniiu amnistii soglasno mezhdunarodnym dogovoram zakliuchennym RSFSR, 1921–1923

f. r-5404, 11 op. (12,822 d.) 1925–1938 Mezvedomstvennaia komissiia pri prezidiume vserossiiskogo tsentral'nogo ispolnitel'nogo komiteta po predvaritel'nomu rasssmotreniiu zhalob i khodataistv o vosstanovlenii v pravakh grazhdanstva, 1925–1938

f. 6001, op. 1 Konsul'skaia chast' rossiiskoi diplomaticheskoi missii v Konstantinople

NATIONAL ARCHIVE RECORDS ADMINISTRATION (NARA), WASHINGTON, DC

NARA, U.S. State Department: Records Relating to Relations with the Soviet Union, 861.602/210

ROSSIISKII GOSUDARSTVENNYI VOENNO-ISTORICHESKII ARKHIV (RGVIA)

f. 1 Kantseliariia voennogo ministerstva

f. 401 Voenno-uchenyi komitet glavnogo shtaba

f. 2000 Glavnoe upravlenie glavnogo shtaba (GUGSh)

ROSSIISKII GOSUDARSTVENNII ISTORICHESKII ARKHIV (RGIA)

f. 821 MVD Departament dukhovnikh del, inostrannykh ispovedanii

f. 1276 Sovet ministrov

f. 1284 MVD Departament obshchikh del

f. 1286 MVD Departament politsii ispol'nitel'noi

Pechatnye zapiski (P. Z.)

317 Sovet ministrov, 3 noiabria 1910. Kratkii obzor uzakonenii, kasaiushchikhsia prav russkikh urozhentsev v Finliandii (po proektu zakona ob uravnenii v pravakh s finliandskimi grazhdanami drugikh russkikh poddannykh v gosudarstvennuiu dumu).

450 Traktaty, deklaratsii i konventsii 1825–1882.

460 Materialy o korpuse pogranichnoi strazhei (1896–1916).

462 Zhurnaly komissii o merakh k preduprezhdeniiu naplyva inostrantsev v zapadnye okrainy (1891).

463 Spravka po voprosu o pereselenii vykhodtsev iz Severnoi Ameriki v primor-skuiu oblast' i predstavleniia Dept. obshchikh del MVD ob usloviiakh posele-niia inostrannykh poddannykh v priamurskom gen-gub i o merakh po sele-niiu preobladavshaia na murmanskom poberezhe russkikh, 1897–1914.

464 Materialy po voprosu o naime i perevozke rabochikh kitaitsev i koreitsev dlia raboty na gornykh promyslakh, 1913–1917.

465 Zhurnaly komiteta po zaseleniiu Dal'nego Vostoka i drugie materialy po voprosu o merakh bor'by protiv naplyva v Priamurskii krai kitaitsev i koreit-sev, 1908–1911.

466 Materialy po proektu pravilo priem v russkoe poddanstvo i uvol'nenii iz nego, 1891–1898.

467 Proekt pravil o rasstorzhenii braka inostrantsev v Rossii i russkikh poddan-nykh za granitsei, 1916.

471 Spisok inostrannykh poddannykh bezvozvratno vyslannykh zagranitsu o po-semu nepodlezhashchikh dopushcheniiu v predely imperii.

477 Tsirkuliary DP MVD kasaiushchiesia inostrannykh poddannykh, 1891–1907.

511 Ogranichitel'nye uzak. i osobye zakonopolozhenie izd. po soobrazheniiam natsional'nogo ili veroispovednogo svoistva libo obuslovlivaemym razlichicm polov. Ch. 1–3 (St. Petersburg: tip. MVD, 1906–1907).

516 Zhurnal pasportnoi komissii, 1886–1888.

2530 Ministerstvo torgovli i promyshlennosti: otdel torgovogo moreplavaniia, July 8, 1909. Po voprosu ob obrazovanii mezhduvedomstvennogo soveshcha-niia dlia vyrabotki zakona ob emigratsii.

2531 Ocherk istorii i sovremennogo sostoianiia otkhoda na zarabotki za granitsu v Zapadnoi Evrope i v Rossii.

97697 MVD. Zhurnaly vysochaishe uchrezhdennoi komissii o merakh k predu-prezhdeniiu naplyva inostrantsev v zapadnye okrainy. Otdel III. Vopros o priniatii i ostavlenii russkogo poddanstva (St. Petersburg, 1891).

102751 Spravka k delu o vysylke iz imperii porochnykh inostrantsev i merakh na sluchai neispolneniia poslednimi trebovanii ob ostavlenii predelov imperii ili samovol'nogo ikh vozvrashcheniia posle vysylki (1902).

Notes

INTRODUCTION

1. There are many reasons for this, several of which are discussed in Eric Lohr, "The Ideal Citizen and Real Subject in Late Imperial Russia," *Kritika: Explorations in Russian and Eurasian History* 7, no. 2 (2006): 173–194. Existing works tend to focus relatively narrowly on citizenship law: Oleg Emel'ianovich Kutafin, *Rossiiskoe grazhdanstvo* (Moscow: Iurist, 2004); Vladimir Gessen, *Poddanstvo: ego ustanovlenie i prekrashchenie* (St. Petersburg: Pravda, 1909); George Ginsburgs, *The Citizenship Law of the USSR* (The Hague, Boston: M. Nijhoff Publishers, 1983); N. Ia. Korzh, *Grazhdanstvo Rossiiskoi Federatsii: istoriko-pravovoi aspekt* (St. Petersburg: "Neva," 2004); Sergei Kishkin, *Sovetskoe grazhdanstvo* (Moscow, 1925); Sergei Pavlovich Orlenko, *Vykhodtsy iz zapadnoi Evropy v Rossii: pravovoi status i real'noe polozhenie* (Moscow: Drevlekhranilishche, 2004).

2. See: Andreas Fahrmeir, *Citizenship: The Rise and Fall of a Modern Concept* (New Haven and London: Yale University Press, 2007); Rogers Brubaker, *Citizenship and Nationhood in France and Germany* (Cambridge: Harvard University Press, 1992); Andreas Fahrmeir, *Citizens and Aliens: Foreigners and the Law in Britain and the German States, 1789–1870* (New York, Oxford: Berghahn Books, 2000); Patrick Weil, *How to Be French: Nationality in the Making Since 1789* (Durham: Duke University Press, 2008); Eli Nathans, *The Politics of Citizenship in Germany: Ethnicity, Utility and Nationalism* (Oxford: Berg, 2004); Ricko Karatani, *Defining British Citizenship: Empire, Commonwealth, and Modern Britain* (London: Frank Cass, 2003); Waltraud Heindl and Edith Saurer, *Grenze und Staat: Passwesen, Staatsbürgerschaft, Heimatrecht und Fremdengesetzgebung in der österreichischen Monarchie*

1750–1867 (Vienna: Böhlau, 2000); Peter Sahlins, *Unnaturally French: Foreign Citizens in the Old Regime and After* (Ithaca: Cornell University Press, 2004); Mary Dewhurst Lewis, *The Boundaries of the Republic: Migrant Rights and the Limits of Universalism in France, 1918–1940* (Stanford: Stanford University Press, 2007); Saskia Sassen, *Guests and Aliens* (New York: The New Press, 1999); Andreas Fahrmeir, Olivier Faron, and Patrick Weil, *Migration Control in the North Atlantic World: The Evolution of State Practices in Europe and the United States from the French Revolution to the Inter-War Period* (New York, Oxford: Berghahn Books, 2003); James H. Kettner, *The Development of American Citizenship, 1608–1870* (Chapel Hill: University of North Carolina Press, 1978); John Torpey, *The Invention of the Passport: Surveillance, Citizenship, and the State* (Cambridge: Cambridge University Press, 2000); Ulrich Herbert, *A History of Foreign Labor in Germany, 1880–1980: Seasonal Workers/Forced Laborers/Guest Workers* (Ann Arbor: University of Michigan Press, 1990); Patrick Weil, "Nationalities and Citizenships: The Lessons of the French Experience for Germany and Europe," in David Cesarani and Mary Fulbrook, eds., *Citizenship, Nationality and Migration in Europe* (London and New York: Routledge, 1996): 74–87.

3. Margaret R. Somers, "Citizenship and the Place of the Public Sphere: Law, Community, and Political Culture in the Transition to Democracy," *American Sociological Review* 58 (1993): 588.

4. For different reasons having to do with the lack of linkage between subjecthood status and membership in the English or British nations, scholars of Britain have said similarly that "there is no such thing [as British citizenship]—not, at least, as citizenship is understood in other countries." Ann Dummett, "The Acquisition of British Citizenship: From Imperial Traditions to National Definitions," in Rainer Bauböck, ed., *From Aliens to Citizens: Redefining the Status of Immigrants in Europe* (Aldershot, UK: Avebury, European Centre Vienna, 1994), 75–84; Rieko Karatani, *Defining British Citizenship: Empire, Commonwealth, and Modern Britain* (London: Frank Cass, 2003), 3.

5. Gessen, *Poddanstvo.*

6. For a more extensive treatment of the history of the concept of citizenship, see: Eric Lohr, "Grazhdanstvo i poddanstvo: istoriia kontseptsii," in A. Miller, D. Sdvizhkov, and I. Shirle, eds., *Poniatiia o Rossii: K istoricheskoi semantike imperskogo perioda*, vol. 1 (Moscow: Novoe literaturnoe obozrenie, 2012), 197–222 and "The Ideal Citizen."

7. Numerous studies address the question of the history of rights and obligations of various groups before the law in imperial Russia. For the classic nineteenth-century treatment, see Vasilii Kliuchevskii, *Istoriia soslovii*

Rossii (Hattiesburg: Academic International, 1969). Some important recent overviews include: Elise Wirtschafter, *Social Identity in Imperial Russia* (DeKalb: Northern Illinois University Press, 1997); Gregory L. Freeze, "The Soslovie (Estate) Paradigm and Russian Social History," *The American Historical Review* 91, no. 1 (1986), 11–36; Alfred Rieber, "The Sedimentary Society," *Russian History* 16, nos. 2–4 (1989): 353–376; W. Bruce Lincoln, *The Great Reforms: Autocracy, Bureaucracy, and the Politics of Change in Imperial Russia* (DeKalb: Northern Illinois University Press, 1990). For a few examples of studies of individual social groups in a rich and deep literature, see: Alfred Rieber, *Merchants and Entrepreneurs in Imperial Russia* (Chapel Hill: University of North Carolina Press, 1982); Thomas C. Owen, *Capitalism and Politics in Russia: A Social History of the Moscow Merchants, 1855–1905* (New York: Cambridge University Press, 1981); Daniel Field, *The End of Serfdom: Nobility and Bureaucracy in Russia, 1855–1861* (Cambridge: Harvard University Press, 1976); Jeffrey Burds, *Peasant Dreams and Market Politics: Labor Migration and the Russian Village, 1861–1905* (Pittsburgh: University of Pittsburgh Press, 1998); Gregory L. Freeze, *The Parish Clergy in Nineteenth-Century Russia: Crisis, Reform, Counter-Reform* (Princeton: Princeton University Press, 1983); Laurie Manchester, *Holy Fathers, Secular Sons: Clergy, Intelligentsia, and the Modern Self in Revolutionary Russia* (DeKalb: Northern Illinois University Press, 2008); Elise Kimerling Wirtschafter, *Structures Of Society: Imperial Russia's "People of Various Ranks"* (DeKalb : Northern Illinois University Press, 1994); Jane Burbank, *Russian Peasants Go to Court: Legal Culture in the Countryside, 1905–1917* (Bloomington: Indiana University Press, 2004).

8. In practice, many exemptions were granted. John Torpey, "Revolutions and Freedom of Movement: An Analysis of Passport Controls in the French, Russian, and Chinese Revolutions," *Theory and Society* 26, no. 6 (1997): 837–868.

9. On the methodological agenda of writing "entangled histories" of empires, see Alexei Miller, *The Romanov Empire and Nationalism: Essays in the Methodology of Historical Research* (Budapest, New York: Central European University Press, 2008), 10–43 and Eric Lohr, "Germanskoe zaimstvovanie?": poddanstvo i politika v oblasti immigratsii i naturalizatsii v Rossiiskoi imperii kontsa XIX–nachala XX veka," in *Imperium inter pares: rol' transferov v istorii Rossiiskoi imperii (1700–1917)*, edited by Martin Aust, Ricarda Vilpius, Aleksei Miller (Moscow: Novoe literaturnoe obozrenie, 2010), 330–353.

10. Rogers Brubaker, *Citizenship and Nationhood in France and Germany* (Cambridge: Harvard University Press, 1992); Hans Kohn, *A History of*

Nationalism in the East (New York: Harcourt, Brace and Co., 1929) and *The Idea of Nationalism: A Study in its Origins and Background* (New York: Macmillan, 1945). For a more recent variant, see Liah Greenfeld, *Nationalism: Five Roads to Modernity* (Cambridge: Harvard University Press, 1992). For a critique of the notion, see Catherine Evtuhov and Stephen Kotkin, eds., *The Cultural Gradient: The Transmission of Ideas in Europe, 1789–1991* (Lanham: Rowman & Littlefield Publishers, 2003).

11. Andreas Fahrmeir, *Citizenship: The Rise and Fall of a Modern Concept* (New Haven and London: Yale University Press, 2007) and *Citizens and Aliens: Foreigners and the Law in Britain and the German States, 1789–1870* (New York, Oxford: Berghahn Books, 2000); Patrick Weil, *How to Be French: Nationality in the Making Since 1789* (Durham: Duke University Press, 2008).

12. See Torpey, *The Invention of the Passport;* Paul Werth, "In the State's Embrace? Civil Acts in an Imperial Order," *Kritika: Explorations in Russian and Eurasian History* 7, no. 3 (2006): 433–458.

13. Jane Caplan and John Torpey, eds., *Documenting Individual Identity: The Development of State Practices in the Modern World* (Princeton and Oxford: Princeton University Press, 2001), 67–82; Yanni Kotsonis, "'No Place to Go': Taxation and State Transformation in Late-Imperial and Early-Soviet Russia," *Journal of Modern History* 76, no. 3 (2004): 531–577 and "'Face to Face': The State, the Individual, and the Citizen in Russian Taxation, 1863–1917," *Slavic Review* 63, no. 2 (2004): 221–246; Peter Holquist, "'Information is the Alpha and Omega of Our Work': Bolshevik Surveillance in Its Pan-European Context," *The Journal of Modern History* 69 (1997): 415–450.

I. BOUNDARIES AND MIGRATION BEFORE 1860

1. For a classic statement of the central role of long-distance trade in the founding of Kievan Rus', see Omelian Pritsak, *The Origins of Rus'* (Cambridge: Harvard University Press, 1981). On the centrality of the long-distance fur trade throughout the first half millennium of the Kievan and Muscovite eras, see Janet Martin, *Treasure of the Land of Darkness: The Fur Trade and its Significance for Medieval Russia* (Cambridge and New York: Cambridge University Press, 1986). On the benefits of long-distance trade in the Mongol era, see Nicola Di Cosmo, "Black Sea Emporia and the Mongol Empire: A Reassessment of the Pax Mongolica," *Journal of the Economic and Social History of the Orient* 53, no. 1 (2010): 83–108; Peter Jackson, *The Mongols of the West 1221–1410* (Harlow: Pearson, 2005).

2. A. S. Muliukin, *Priezd inostrantsev v Moskovskoe gosudarstvo: iz istorii russkogo prava XVI i XVII vekov* (St. Petersburg: Tip. "Trud," 1909), 2, 27.

See also Ivan Efimovich Andreevskii, *O pravakh inostrantsev v Rossii* (St. Petersburg: Ia. Treia, 1854).

3. Valentina Grigor'evna Chernukha, *Pasport v Rossii, 1719–1917* (St. Petersburg: Liki Rossii, 2007); P. M. Vvedenskii, "Pasportnaia politika Russkogo tsarizma i ee vliianie na krest'ianskii otkhod," in Vladimir Terent'evich Pashuto et al., *Sotsial'no-politicheskoe i pravovoe polozhenie krest'ianstva v dorevoliutsionnoi Rossii* (Voronezh: Izd. Voronezhskogo universiteta, 1983).

4. Richard Hellie, *Enserfment and Military Change in Muscovy* (Chicago: University of Chicago Press, 1971).

5. See for example, M. I. Mysh, *Ob inostrantsakh v Rossii* (St. Petersburg: A. Bekt, 1911), vii.

6. In the era of Peter the Great, passports were required for anyone leaving his district *(uezd)* or traveling more than fifty versts from his place of residence (a verst equated to 1.07 kilometers or 0.66 miles). In the early twentieth century, the radius was set at thirty versts. GARF, f. 102, 7oe deloproizvodstvo (1910 g.), d. k8, ch. 150b, l. 168.

7. Chernukha, *Pasport v Rossii*; Vvedenskii, "Pasportnaia politika."

8. The law was first promulgated in 1834, but it recognized administrative practices going back much earlier. RGVIA f. 405, op. 6, d. 3933, l. 2.

9. Oswald P. Backus, *Motives of West Russian Nobles in Deserting Lithuania for Moscow, 1377–1514* (Lawrence: University of Kansas Press, 1957); Brian Boeck, *Imperial Boundaries: Cossack Communities and Empire-Building in the Age of Peter the Great* (Cambridge: Cambridge University Press, 2009); Barbara Pendzich, "The Burghers of The Grand Duchy of Lithuania during the War of 1654–1667: Resiliency and Cohesion in the Face of Muscovite Annexation" (Ph.D. diss., Georgetown University, 1998).

10. Hellie, *Enserfment and Military Change.*

11. Horace W. Dewey and Ann M. Kleimola, "Suretyship and Collective Responsibility in Pre-Petrine Russia," *Jahrbücher für Geschichte Osteuropas* 18 (1970): 337–354.

12. Gustav Alef, "Das Erlöschen des Abzugsrechts der moskauer Bojaren," in *Forschungen zur osteuropäischen Geschichte* 10 (1965): 39–41. See the famous case of Patrick Gordon, who was denied permission to leave several times. When he was finally allowed to go, his wife had to remain behind as insurance that he would return. *Passages from the Diary of General Patrick Gordon in the Years 1635–1699* (New York: De Capo Press, 1968), 110.

13. PSZ, t. 1, no. 408, pp. 85–86, cited in Mysh, *Ob inostrantsakh*, vii; Alexei Miller, "The Romanov Empire and the Jews," in Alexei Miller, *The Romanov*

Empire and Nationalism: Essays in the Methodology of Historical Research (Budapest: Central European University Press, 2008).

14. A. S. Muliukin, *Ocherki po istorii iuridicheskogo polozheniia inostrannykh kuptsov v Moskovskom gosudarstve* (Odessa: Tip. "Tekhnik," 1912), 308–327; Sergei Pavlovich Orlenko, *Vykhodtsy iz zapadnoi Evropy v Rossii: pravovoi status i real'noe polozhenie* (Moscow: Drevlekhranilishche, 2004).

15. Orlenko, *Vykhodtsy*, 265.

16. William M. Reger IV, "Baptizing Mars: The Conversion to Russian Orthodoxy of European Mercenaries during the Mid-Seventeenth Century," in Eric Lohr and Marshall Poe, eds., *The Military and Society in Russia, 1450–1917* (Leiden: Brill, 2002), 391; Hellie, *Enserfment and Military Change.*

17. For an important recent reevaluation of the significance of seventeenth-century foreign trade, see Jarmo Kotilaine, *Russia's Foreign Trade and Economic Expansion in the Seventeenth Century* (Leiden: Brill, 2005).

18. Joseph T. Fuhrmann, *The Origins of Capitalism in Russia: Industry and Progress in the Sixteenth and Seventeenth Centuries* (Chicago: Quadrangle Books, 1972); Kotilaine, *Russia's Foreign Trade.*

19. Orlenko, *Vykhodtsy*, 266–268.

20. Marc Szeftel, "The Legal Condition of the Foreign Merchants in Muscovy," *Recueils de la Société Jean Bodin* 33 (1972): 335–358.

21. Orlenko, *Vykhodtsy*, 213–223, 268.

22. Evgenii Zviagintsev, "Slobody inostrantsev v Moskve XVII veka," *Istoricheskii zhurnal* 126, no. 2 (1944): 81. On the power of the church vis-à-vis the tsar on policy toward foreigners, see Orlenko, *Vykhodtsy*, 102–168.

23. Reger, "Baptizing Mars"; Muliukin, *Priezd inozemtsev*, 152–153.

24. Dmitrii Vladimirovich Tsvetaev, *Protestanstvo i protestanty v Rossii* (1890), 340–343. The focus on conversion was far less apparent in the cases of Muslims and Jews, neither of whom was typically pressured to convert. Perhaps, counterintuitively, this deeper sense of recognition of religious difference was combined with greater familiarity. This was reflected in the linguistic bifurcation of foreigners into *nemtsy* (dumb, Germans), a term used to describe West Europeans, and *inozemtsy* (foreigners), a more general term often used to refer to non-European foreigners. See Martha Luby Lahana, "Novaia nemetskaia sloboda: Seventeenth Century Moscow's Foreign Suburb" (Ph.D. diss., University of North Carolina at Chapel Hill, 1983), 342, 350.

25. Tsvetaev, *Protestanstvo*, 329.

26. D. V. Tsvetaev, *Obrusenie zapadnoevropeitsev v moskovskom gosudarstve* (Warsaw: Tip. Varshavskogo uchebnogo okruga, 1903), 12; Vladimir Matveevich Gessen, *Poddanstvo: ego ustanovlenie i prekrashchenie*

(St. Petersburg: Pravda, 1909), 203; A. S. Muliukina, "Priezd inostrantsev
v drevniuiu Rus'," *Zhurnal Ministerstva narodnogo prosveshcheniia*
(November 1907), 144.

27. Vladimir Borisovich Nikolaev, "Poddanstvo Rossiiskoi Imperiii: ego ustanovlenie i prekrashchenie (istoriko-pravovoi analiz)" (Kand. diss., Nizhegorods-
kaia akademiia MVD Rossii, Nizhnii Novgorod, 2008), 21; N. I. Nazarenko,
"Pravovoe polozhenie inostrantsev v otechestvennom zakonodatel'stve XI–
pervoi poloviny XVII vv., Avtoref" (Kand. diss., Moscow, 2004), 23. See also
the analogous problem for the Muslims: Janet Martin, "Multiethnicity in
Muscovy: A Consideration of Christian and Muslim Tatars in the 1550s–
1580s," *Journal of Early Modern History* 5, no. 1 (2001): 1–23.

28. Only 12 percent of Reger's database of foreign mercenaries in the mid-
seventeenth century converted. Reger, "Baptizing Mars," 393.

29. Tsvetaev, *Protestanstvo*, 385, citing a decree of Tsar Mikhail Feodorovich
in 1629.

30. Aleksandr Nikolaevich Pypin, "Inozemtsy v Moskovskoi Rossii," *Vestnik
Evropy* 23, no. 1 (1888): 255–296 (review of Tsvetaev on p. 295); Dmitrii
Tsvetaev, "Obrusenie inozemtsev-protestantov v Moskovskom gosudarstve,"
Russkii vestnik 8, 10 (1886).

31. Gessen, *Poddanstvo*.

32. Margarete Woltner, "Zur Frage der Untertanenschaft von Westeuropäern
in Russland bis zur Zeit Peters des Grossen Einschliesslich," *Jahrbücher
für Geschichte Osteureopas* 3, no. 1 (1938): 47–60.

33. Muliukin, *Priezd inostrantsev*, 31–38, 60–62.

34. Muliukin, *Ocherki*, 341.

35. Ibid., 347–348.

36. Woltner, "Zur Frage," 54.

37. *The Muscovite Law Code (Ulozhenie) of 1649*, trans. and ed. Richard
Hellie (Irvine, California: Charles Schlacks, Jr., 1988), 23.

38. *The Muscovite Law Code*, 34. See also Nancy Kollmann, *By Honor Bound:
State and Society in Early Modern Russia* (Ithaca: Cornell University Press,
1999).

39. One of the most important legal disabilities faced by foreigners in the seventeenth century was the ban on non-Orthodox foreigners owning Orthodox serfs or slaves. Concerned that such Orthodox slaves in the households
of non-Orthodox foreigners were being served meat during fasts and were
dying without confession, Tsar Mikhail Fedorovich issued a decree of 1627
that both banned Orthodox from being enserfed to non-Orthodox foreigners and granted emancipation to any foreigners who were baptized into the
Orthodox faith. Interestingly, the clause of this decree says nothing about
whether such foreigners were required to take the oath of subjecthood. *The*

Muscovite Law Code, 182; Tatiana Oparina, "Ukazy 1627 i 1652 godov protiv 'nekreshchennykh inozemtsev'," *Otechestvennaia istoriia* 1 (2005): 22–39.

40. *The Muscovite Law Code*, 105. Likewise, if a foreigner was killed in service to the tsar, his widow received the exact same benefits as Russian nobles and servitors. *The Muscovite Law Code*, 109.

41. Samuel H. Baron, "The Origins of Seventeenth-Century Moscow's *Nemetskaia sloboda*," *California Slavic Studies* 5 (1970): 5; *The Muscovite Law Code*, 228–231.

42. *The Muscovite Law Code*, 80. For an excellent analysis of the complex origins of this provision, see Orlenko, *Vykhodtsy*, 90–94.

43. Andrei Vladimirovich Demkin, *Zapadnoevropeiskoe kupechestvo v Rossii XVII v.*, vol. 1 (Moscow 1994), 57, 129. Orlenko, *Vykhodtsy*, 95.

44. Lindsay Hughes, *Russia in the Age of Peter the Great* (New Haven: Yale University Press, 1998), 13.

45. Baron, "The Origins," 6; Konstantin Vasilevich Bazilevich, "Kollektivnye chelobitiia kupechestva i bor'ba za russkii rynok v pervoi polovine XVII veka," *Izvestiia Akademii nauk SSSR, Otdelenie obshchestvennykh nauk*, no. 2 (1932), 109–118.

46. Baron, "The Origins," 10; Vladimir Vasilevich Leshkov, "Vzgliad na sostoianie prava inostrantsev, po nachalam evropeiskogo narodnogo prava voobshche, i v osobennosti po zakonam otechestvennym" (1841), held in the general collection of the Russian National Library in St. Petersburg.

47. Vladimir Leontevich Snegirev, *Moskovskie slobody: ocherki po istorii Moskovskogo posada XIV–XVIII vv* (Moscow: Moskovskii rabochii, 1956); Baron, "The Origins," 11–12; Sergei K. Bogoiavlenskii, "Moskovskaia nemtskaia sloboda," *Izvestiia Akademii nauk SSSR. Seriia istorii i filosofii* (1947), no. 3, 20-32.

48. Mysh, *Ob inostrantsakh*, vi–viii.

49. Gordon, *Passages from the Diary;* Woltner, "Zur Frage," 56.

50. Hughes, *Russia in the Age*, 154.

51. Roger P. Bartlett, *Human Capital: The Settlement of Foreigners in Russia, 1762–1804* (Cambridge and New York: Cambridge University Press, 1979), 17.

52. PSZt., 26, no. 1910, 593–5; Erik Amburger, *Die Anwerbung ausländerischer Fachkräfte für die Wirtschaft Russlands vom 15ten bis ins 19te Jahrhundert* (Wiesbaden: O. Harrassowitz, 1968), 75–76.

53. PSZt., 7, no. 4378, 167–74.

54. Petr Guliaev, *Prava i obiazannosti gradskoi i zemskoi politsii i vsekh voobshche zhitelei rossiiskogo gosudarstva po ikh sostoianiiam* (Moscow: Universitetskoi tip., 1824).

55. Alison K. Smith, "'The Freedom to Choose a Way of Life': Fugitives, Borders, and Imperial Amnesties in Russia," *Journal of Modern History* 83, no. 2 (June 2011): 243–271.

56. Bartlett, *The Settlement*, 17–18; Vanik Akopovich Khachaturian, "Naselenie armianskoi kolonii v Astrakhani vo 2-oi polovine XVIII v.," *Izvestiia A.N. Armianskoi S.S.R. (obshchestvennye nauki)*, no. 7 (1965): 77–87.

57. Woltner, "Zur Frage," 57; Gessen, *Poddanstvo*, 204.

58. Hughes, *Russia in the Age*, 66; Georg Grund, *Bericht über Russland in den Jahren 1705–1710. Doklad o Rossii v 1705–1710 godakh* (Moscow: RAN, 1992), 22–26.

59. Woltner, "Zur Frage," 59; D. Polenov, "O prisiage inozemtsev, priniatykh v russkuiu sluzhbu pri Petre Velikom," *Russkii arkhiv* (1869): 1729–1766; C. Peterson, *Peter the Great's Administrative and Judicial Reforms* (Stockholm, 1979), 136–137.

60. Woltner, "Zur Frage," 53.

61. There were also many cases of servitors on the temporary oath being denied permission to leave the empire. For one of the most famous cases, see Gordon, *Passages from the Diary*, 110.

62. RGVIA, f. 405, op. 2, d. 2816, ll. 1–1ob.

63. Ibid., l. 2.

64. Peter Sahlins, *Boundaries: The Making of France and Spain in the Pyrenees* (Berkeley: University of California Press, 1989).

65. Polkovnik Chernushevich, *Sluzhba v mirnoe vremia: stychki s kontrabandirami i prochiia proisshestviia na granitse*. vols. 1–3 (St. Petersburg, 1900), 43; RGVIA, f. 4888 Otdel'nyi korpus pogranichnoi strazhi, op. 1 (Shtab otdel'nogo korpusa pogranichnoi strazhi, predislovie).

66. Chernushevich, *Sluzhba v mirnoe*, 46.

67. Grigorii Vol'tke, *Zakony o pogranichnykh zhiteliakh i pogranichnykh snosheniiakh* (St. Petersburg: Tip. G. A. Bernshteina, 1903), 15.

68. RGVIA, f. 1, op. 1, t. 1, d. 2097 (Delo o massovom pobege krest'ianshliakhtichei iz Kamenets-Podol'skoi gubernii v Avstriiu i Pol'shu, 1809–10).

69. Chernushevich, *Sluzhba v mirnoe vremia*, 46, 51.

70. *O pasportakh russkikh poddannykh v Rossii* (b.m.[St. Petersburg], 1860); Chernukha, *Pasport v Rossii*.

71. Mikhail Mikhailovich Bogoslovskii and Vladimir Ivanovich Lebedev, *Petr Pervyi: materialy dlia biografii*, vol. II: *pervoe zagranichnoe puteshestvie* (The Hague: Mouton, 1941).

72. GARF, f. 109, op. 223, d. 4, papka 4 (1839), l. 49.

73. Ibid.

2. ANNEXATION AND NATURALIZATION

1. Vladimir M. Gessen, *Poddanstvo: ego ustanovlenie i prekrashchenie* (St. Petersburg: Pravda, 1909).

2. Boris E. Nolde, "Essays in Russian State Law," *The Annals of the Ukrainian Academy of Arts and Sciences in the U.S.* 4, no. 3 (13) (1955), 873.

3. "The Diplomatic Report of Vasilii Buturlin," in John Basarab, *Pereiaslav 1654: A Historiographical Study* (Edmonton: The University of Alberta, 1982), 256; also in Panteleimon P. Gudzenko, ed., *Vossoedinenie Ukrainy s Rossiei: dokumenty i materialy v trekh tomakh,* vol. 3 (Moscow: Izd-vo Akademii nauk SSSR, 1953), 459–466.

4. Orest Subtelny, *Ukraine: A History,* 2nd ed. (Toronto: University of Toronto Press, 1994), 134. For analysis stressing the clash between two fundamentally different concepts of subjecthood in the Polish-Lithuanian Commonwealth, see Andrzej Kaminski, *Republic vs. Autocracy: Poland-Lithuania and Russia, 1686–1697* (Cambridge: Harvard University Press, 1993).

5. Oleksander Ohoblyn, "Pereiaslav Treaty of 1654," in *Encyclopedia of Ukraine,* Danylo H. Struk, ed., vol. 3 (Toronto: University of Toronto Press, 1993), 838. "Svodnye dannye iz zapisnykh knig o privedennykh k prisiage zhiteliakh ukrainskikh sel i gorodov posle vossoedineniia Ukrainy s Rossiei," in Gadzen to, ed., *Vossoedinenie Ukrainy* vol. 3 (Moscow: AN SSSR, 1953), 534–543.

6. Basarab, *Pereiaslav 1654.*

7. Most important was the tsar's pledge to accept 60,000 registered Cossack soldiers (Poland only offered to allow 20,000).

8. Nolde, "Essays in Russian State Law," 877; Boris E. Nolde, "Edinstvo i nerazdelnost'" in *Ocherki russkago gosudarstvennago prava* (St. Petersburg: Pravda, 1911).

9. Viacheslav Prokopovych, "The Problem of the Juridical Nature of the Ukraine's Union with Muscovy," *The Annals of the Ukrainian Academy of Arts and Sciences in the U.S.* 4, no. 3 (13): 935.

10. Ibid., 931. PSZ, I, nos. 10218, 10258, 10486.

11. Prokopovych, "The Problem," 918–919; *Akty, otnosiashchiesia k istorii iuzhnoi i zapadnoi Rossii,* X, 502–503.

12. Bohdan Kohut, *Russian Centralism and Ukrainian Autonomy: Imperial Absorption of the Hetmanate, 1760s–1830s* (Cambridge: Harvard University Press, 1988). According to Nolde, full absorption was completed with the abolition of local courts (1781) and local control over taxation (1783). Nolde, "Essays in Russian State Law," 890.

13. Nolde, "Essays in Russian State Law," 873.

14. Barbara Pendzich, "The Burghers of the Grand Duchy of Lithuania during The War of 1654–1667: Resiliency and Cohesion in the Face of Muscovite Annexation" (Ph.D. diss., Georgetown University, 1998); Evdokina D. Rukhmanova, "K istorii peregovorov o priniatii Kurliandii v poddanstvo Rossii v 1658 godu," *Istoriia SSSR* 1 (1975), 158–163.

15. RGIA, P. Z. 317 (Sovet ministrov, 3 Noiabria 1910. Kratkii obzor uzakonenii, kasaiushchikhsia prav russkikh urozhentsev v Finliandii [po proektu zakona ob uravnenii v pravakh s finliandskimi grazhdanami drugikh russkikh poddannykh v gosudarstvennuiu dumu]).

16. Oleg Emilianovich Kutafin, *Rossiiskoe grazhdanstvo* (Moscow: Iurist, 2004), 141.

17. RGIA, P. Z. 317.

18. Liubomir Grigorevich Beskrovny, *The Russian Army and Fleet in the Nineteenth Century: Handbook of Armaments, Personnel, and Policy* (Gulf Breeze: Academic International Press, 1996), 44–52.

19. George F. Jewsbury, *The Russian Annexation of Bessarabia, 1774–1828: A Study of Imperial Expansion* (Boulder and New York: Columbia University Press, 1976), 66–69.

20. Ibid., Charles King, *The Moldovans: Romania, Russia, and the Politics of Culture* (Stanford: Hoover Institution Press, 2000), 20–24.

21. Albert Kaganovich, "The Legal and Political Situation of the Chalah: The Muslim Jews in Russian Turkestan, 1865–1917," *Shvut* 6 (1997): 65. A. M. Matveev, *Zarubezhnye vykhodtsy v Turkestane na putiakh k velikomu oktiabriu (1914—oktiabr' 1917 g.)* (Tashkent: FAN, 1977).

22. Mikhail Ignatevich Mysh, *Rukovodstvo k russkim zakonam o evreiakh* (St. Petersburg, 1914), 19; Kaganovich, "The Legal and Political," 57–78.

23. RGVIA, f. 400, op. 1, d. 904, l. 30; RGVIA, f. 400, op. 1, d. 888 (Perepiska aziatskoi chasti glavnogo shtaba o priniatii russkogo poddanstva Mervskimi turkmenami).

24. Gerhard von Glahn, *The Occupation of Enemy Territory: A Commentary on the Law and Practice of Belligerent Occupation* (Minneapolis: University of Minnesota Press, 1957), 56–57.

25. Lawrence Farley, *Plebiscites and Sovereignty: The Crisis of Political Illegitimacy* (Boulder: Westview Press, 1986), 33; Edwin Borchard, "Collective Naturalization after Conquest—Its Inapplicability to Non-Residents," *The American Journal of International Law* 37, no. 4 (1943), 637.

26. Farley, *Plebiscites and Sovereignty*, 33.

27. Regulations of 1899 respecting the laws and customs of war on land (annex to the convention), article 45, in James B. Scott, *The Proceedings of the Hague Peace* (New York: Oxford University Press, 1920–1921), vol. 3, p. 72. James Molony Spaight claims that by the late nineteenth century "belligerents

generally adhered to the principle that no oath of allegiance should be asked of people in occupied regions." J. M. Spaight, *War Rights on Land* (London: Macmillan, 1911), 372. See also Doris Appel Graber, *The Development of the Law of Belligerent Occupation, 1863–1914: A Historical Survey* (New York: AMS Press, 1968), 266.

28. S. C. M. Paine, *Imperial Rivals: China, Russia, and Their Disputed Frontier* (Armonk: M. E. Sharpe, 1996).

29. John J. Stephan, *The Russian Far East: A History* (Stanford: Stanford University Press, 1994), 45.

30. Oleg A. Timofeev, *Rossiisko-kitaiskie otnosheniia v Priamur'e (seredina XIX–nachalo XX vv.)* (Blagoveshchensk: RAN DVO, 2003), 71. V. M. Kabuzan estimates only 3,000 settled Chinese in the region in 1859. V. M. Kabuzan, *Dal'nevostochnyi krai v XVII–Nachale XX vv. (1640–1917): Istoriko-demographicheskii ocherk* (Moscow: Nauka, 1985), 51, 61.

31. See David Habecker, "Ruling the East: Russian Urban Administration and the Chinese, Koreans, and Japanese in Vladivostok, 1884-1922" (Ph.D. diss., University of Maryland, 2003), 208–215. For the most detailed account of the Russian side of the negotiations, see Vladimir Viktorovich Sinichenko, *Vostochnaia Sibir' v rossiisko-kitaiskih otnosheniiakh, 50–80-x gg. XIX veka* (Irkutsk: Irkutskoi gosudarstvennyi pedagogicheskii universitet, 1999), 12–40. A contemporary expert estimated roughly 14,000 under the Aigun provisions, occupying 108,000 desiatin (118,000 hectares) of land according to the census, a figure that grew to about 23,000 by 1894. I. G. Matiunina, "Zapiska o kitaitsakh i manchzhurakh, prozhivaiushchikh na levom beregu Amura," in *Sbornik geograficheskikh, topograficheskikh i statisticheskikh materialov po Azii*, vol. 58 (St. Petersburg: Voennaia tip., 1894), 37–38.

32. "Dogovor, zakliuchennyi v Aigune," May 16, 1858, in T. Iuzefovich, ed., *Dogovory Rossii s Vostokom politicheskie i torgovye* (St. Petersburg: Tip. O.I. Baksta, 1869), 252.

33. "Dopolnitel'nyi dogovor, zakliuchennyi v Pekine," November 2, 1860, in Iuzefovich, ed., *Dogovory Rossii*, 260.

34. *Svod mezhdunarodnykh postanovlenii opredeliaiushchikh vzaimnye otnosheniia mezhdu Rossieiu i Kitaem, 1689–1897* (St. Petersburg: Tip. V. O. Kirshbaum, 1900), 26.

35. Tatiana Nikolaevna Sorokina, *Khoziaistvennaia deiatel'nost' kitaiskikh poddannykh na Dal'nem Vostoke Rossii i politika administratsii Priamurskogo kraia (Kontets XIX–nachalo XX)* (Omsk: OmGU, 1999), 27–45.

36. Paine, *Imperial Rivals*; Sorokina, *Khoziaistvennaia deiatel'nost'*.

37. David Wolff, "Crossing Borders," in David Wolff and Stephen Kotkin, eds., *Rediscovering Russia in Asia: Siberia and the Russian Far East* (Armonk: M.E. Sharpe, 1995), 43.

38. Iulia Nikolaevna Popovicheva, "'Zheltyi vopros' v deiatel'nosti vysshei dal'nevostochnoi administratsii (1883–1900)," in D. P. Bolotin, ed., *Rossiia i Kitai na dal'nevostochnykh rubezhakh* (Blagoveshchensk: AmGU, 2001), 15.

39. I. G. Matiunina, "Zapiska o kitaitsakh i manchzhurakh, prozhivaiushchikh na levom beregu Amura," in *Sbornik geograficheskikh, topograficheskikh i statisticheskikh materialov po Azii,* vol. 58 (St. Petersburg: Voennaia tip., 1894), 38.

40. This was not simply a wartime emergency measure, but was preceded by open discussion among Russian officials in the Far East in the 1890s of proposals to expel the entire Aigun Chinese population. See, for example, Matiunina, "Zapiska o kitaitsakh," 38–39.

41. Sorokina, *Khoziaistvennaia deiatel'nost',* 116–120.

42. Lewis Siegelbaum, "Another 'Yellow Peril': Chinese Migrants in the Russian Far East and the Russian Reaction before 1917," *Modern Asian Studies* 12, no. 2 (1978): 318–319; "Blagoveshchenskaia 'Utopia'," *Vestnik Evropy* 7 (1910), 231–241; "Khronika," *Russkoe Bogatstvo* 9 (1900), 218–224.

43. Sorokina, *Khoziaistvennaia deiatel'nost',* 124.

44. However, especially in more remote mountainous areas, this Muslim faith differed substantially from most forms of Islam and had interesting admixtures of Orthodox ritual and practice. The *Brokhaus-Efron Encyclopedia* claims that Laz are members of the Megrelo-Chan (Mingrelian) and Adzhars members of the Kartelian branches of the Georgian ethnolinguistic family. Others claim that Laz and Adzhar are primarily geographic designations for the same people. See "Lazy," *Entsiklopedicheskii slovar'* vol. 33 (St. Petersburg: I. A. Efron, 1896), 252–253.

45. Aslan Khuseinovich Abashidze, *Adzhariia: istoriia, diplomatiia, mezhdunaronoe pravo* (Moscow: RAU universitet, 1998); Oliver Reisner, "Integrationsversuche der muslimishcen Adscharer in die georgische Nationalbewegung," in Raoul Motika and Michael Ursinus, eds., *Caucasia between the Ottoman Empire and Iran, 1555–1914* (Wiesbaden: Reichert, 2000), 217–219; Merab Vachnadze and Vakhtang Guruli, *Istoriia Gruzii (XIX–XX veka): uchebnik dlia IX klassa* (Tbilisi: Artanudzhi, 2001), 62–65.

46. *Adjara and the Russian Empire, 1878–1917: British Archives on the Caucasus: Georgia* (London: Archival Publications, 2003) 3; McCarthy, Justin, *Death and Exile: The Ethnic Cleansing of Ottoman Muslims, 1821–1922* (Princeton: Darwin Press, 1995), 114–115. The British vice-consul in Batum claimed 80,000 Laz emigrated between 1878 and 1882, leaving only 40,000 Laz in the region. "Report by Vice-Consul Peacock on Batoum and its Future Prospects, April 8, 1882" in *Adjara and the Russian Empire,* 91–95.

47. Abashidze, *Adzhariia,* 111–113.

48. Andor Frenkel, *Ocherki Churuk-su i Batuma* (Tbilisi: A.A. Mikhel'son, 1879); A. Chkheidze, "Batumskii vopros na Berlinskom kongresse," *Trudy Tbilisskogo gosudarstvennogo pedagogicheskogo instituta im. A. S. Pushkina,* v. 19 (1966), 278.; Aleksandr Aleksandrovich Bashmakov, *Posle San-Stefano: zapiski grafa I. P. Ignat'eva* (Petrograd: Novoe vremia, 1916), 75–76. Article 9 of Treaty of San Stefano (superseded by the Treaty of Constantinople) gave a longer three-year window to sell property and opt for Ottoman subjecthood.

49. Vladimir E. Grabar, *The History of International Law in Russia: A Bio-bibliographical Study* (New York: Oxford University Press, 1990), 499.

50. Sharon Korman, *The Right of Conquest: The Acquisition of Territory by Force in International Law and Practice* (Oxford: Clarendon Press, 1996), 85.

51. Korman, *The Right of Conquest,* 91.

52. "O poriadke priema v Russkoe poddanstvo ostavshikhsia v Rossii turetskikh voenno-plennykh," Tsirkuliar departamenta politsei ispolnitel'noi, November 4, 1878, no. 162, in *Sbornik tsirkuliarov i instruktsii MVD za 1878 god* (St. Petersburg, 1880), 275–276.

53. "Optation" later became the standard international law term to refer to this period when individuals could opt for one citizenship or the other. The heyday of optation treaties came after World War I. The topic is addressed in Chapter 6.

54. The first mass action was the local iteration of empire-wide policies that had analogs among all the belligerents, namely, the internment of enemy subjects. Russia rounded up more than a quarter million enemy subjects during the war and sent them to internment camps in the interior. About 10,000 Ottoman-subject Laz were interned near Riazan and Tambov for the duration of the war. Many of them were migrant tobacco-farm workers. The conditions of their internment were very poor and many died of typhus. The internment of civilian enemy aliens was a novel feature of the war, but one that was widely practiced.

55. RGVIA, f. 1218, op. 1, d. 155, l. 93; Gosudarstvennaia duma, *Stenograficheskie otchety* 4, session 4, meeting 1, col. 129; meeting 2, cols. 153–154; meeting 10, col. 829.

56. Malkhaz Makarovich Sioradze, "Batumskaia oblast' v imperialisticheskikh planakh zapadnykh derzhav (1914–1921 gg.)," (Kand. diss., Tblisi, 1986), 79; RGIA, f. 1276, op. 19, d. 1061, ll. 1–4 (Pederson to A. P. Nikol'skii, January 17, 1915).

57. Robert Conrood, "The Duma's Attitude toward War-time Problems of Minority Groups," *American Slavic and East European Review* 13 (1954): 44; Sioradze, "Batumskaia oblast'," 60–79.

58. RGIA, f. 1276, op. 19, d. 1061, ll. 61–62.

59. The decade-long standoff over Armenian refugees in the 1890s was not explicitly mentioned but those making this decision must have been conscious of it.

3. IMMIGRATION AND NATURALIZATION

1. Richard Hellie, *Enserfment and Military Change in Muscovy* (Chicago: University of Chicago Press, 1971).

2. Willard Sunderland, *Taming the Wild Field: Colonization and Empire on the Russian Steppe* (Ithaca: Cornell University Press, 2004); Roger P. Bartlett, *Human Capital: The Settlement of Foreigners in Russia, 1762–1804* (Cambridge, New York: Cambridge University Press, 1979).

3. Note the important exclusion of Jews from this otherwise enlightened invitation to foreigners. *Manifest Imperatritsy Ekateriny Vtoroi*, "O vykhode k poseleniiu v Rossiiu vsem inostrannym," cited in Rossiiskaia gosudarstvennaia biblioteka (RGB), Otdel rukopisei, f. 261, kor. 20, d. 6, l. 84.

4. RGVIA, f. 401, op. 4/928, d. 60, l. 14; Vladimir M. Kabuzan, *Emigratsiia i reemigratsiia v Rossii v XVIII-nachale XX vek* (Moscow: Nauka, 1998), 59.

5. Most Jesuits in the Russian Empire lived in the lands Russia acquired during the partitions of Poland. Jesuit orders came under serious pressure in the early nineteenth century, culminating in the 1815 expulsion from St. Petersburg and 1820 expulsion from the empire as a whole. James T. Flynn, "The Role of the Jesuits in the Politics of Russian Education, 1801–1820," *The Catholic Historical Review* 56, no. 2 (July 1970): 249–251; Mikhail Moroshkin, *Iezuity v Rossii s tsarstvovaniia Ekateriny II-oi do nashego vremeni* (St. Petersburg, 1870), 520–530.

6. PSZ, Zakony o sostoainiiakh, t. 9 (1899), art. 821.

7. *Obozrenie deistvuiushchikh v Rossii uzakonenii o inostrantsakh* (St. Petersburg, 1859), 6–8.

8. GARF, f. 102, II deloproizvodstvo (1884), d. 515; PSZ, vol. 14, no. 487 (O pasportakh).

9. Mikhail Ignatevich Mysh, *Rukovodstvo k Russkim zakonam o evreiakh* (St. Petersburg: M. P. Frolovoi, 1904), 15–16.

10. Mysh, *Rukovodstvo*, 16.

11. PSZ, Zakony o sostoainiiakh, t. 9 (1899), art. 819, primechanie 3, cited in RGIA, P. Z. 102751 (Spravka k delu o vysylke iz imperii porochnykh inostrantsev i merakh na sluchai neispolneniia poslednimi trebovanii ob ostavlenii predelov imperii ili samovol'nogo ikh vozvrashcheniia posle vysylki, 1902). On the formation of the Pale, see John D. Klier, *Russia Gathers Her Jews: The Origins of the "Jewish Question" in Russia, 1772–1825* (DeKalb: Northern Illinois University Press, 1986).

12. The relevant clause was article 819, t. IX, *Svod Zakonov* (1899), "Inostrantsy iz evreev ne dopuskaiutsia k pereseleniiu v Rossiiu ili vstupleniiu v Rossiiskoe poddanstvo." Published in *Prava evreev i inostrantsev* (St. Petersburg, 1908).

13. GARF, f. 102, op. 76a, d. 1732, l. 7 (Po voprosu o prave pereseleniia v Rossiiu inostrannykh evreev); GARF, f. 102, II deloproizvodstvo (1885), op. 42, d. 435, l. 4 (governor-general of Kiev, Podolia, and Volynia to Ministry of Internal Affairs, July 9, 1885).

14. M. A. Lozina-Lozinskogo, "Priniatie v russkoe poddanstvo," *Pravo*, no. 4 (1898): 10–15; no. 1 (1899): 22–29; no. 2 (1899): 79–84; *Svod Zakonov*, t. 14, (1890), *Ustav o pasportakh*, st. 290.

15. For a collection of such cases, see GARF, f. 102, op. 76a, d. 1732 (Po voprosu o prave pereseleniia v Rossiiu inostrannykh evreev).

16. GARF, f. 102, op. 76a, d. 2103, l. 5ob. The Ministry of Internal Affairs seems to have been primarily concerned with the possibility that Jews could evade the ban on their immigration by claiming "no faith." Its circulars ordered Russian consuls to deny former Jews visas and, in the event that they were discovered in Russia, ordered governors to deport them from the country. More generally, the Russian "confessional state" simply could not handle atheists. Traditionally, all acts of registering births, marriages, and deaths went through religious institutions. Foreigners needed a religion to be slotted into the system. Paul Werth, "In the State's Embrace? Civil Acts in an Imperial Order," *Kritika: Explorations in Russian and Eurasian History* 7, no. 3 (2006): 433–458; Robert Crews, "Empire and the Confessional State: Islam and Religious Politics in Nineteenth-Century Russia," *American Historical Review* vol. 108, no. 1 (2003): 50–83.

17. Vladimir Matveevich Gessen, *Poddanstvo: ego ustanovlenie i prekrashchenie* (St. Petersburg: Pravda, 1909), 227.

18. AVPRI, f. 137, Otchety Ministerstvo inostrannykh del, d. 24 (1849), ll. 257–262. GARF, IIIoe otdelenie, op. 223, d. 4, papka 4 (1839), ll. 1–80, 151–167.

19. AVPRI, f. 137, Otchety Ministerstvo inostrannykh del, d. 44, ll. 30–32.

20. AVPRI, f. 137, Otchety Ministerstvo inostrannykh del, op. 475, d. 43, ll. 266–271ob.

21. AVPRI, f. 137, Otchety Ministerstvo inostrannykh del, (1858 g.), d. 42, ll. 215–216; AVPRI, f. 137, op. 475, d. 86, l. 304ob.

22. AVPRI, f. 137, Otchety Ministerstvo inostrannykh del, op. 475, d. 43, ll. 266–271ob.

23. Peter Sahlins, *Unnaturally French: Foreign Citizens in the Old Regime and After* (Ithaca: Cornell University Press, 2004); Hannelore Bürger, "Passwesen und Staatsbürgerschaft," in Waltraud Heindl and Edith Saurer, eds., *Grenze und Staat: Passwesen, Staatsbürgerschaft, Heimatrecht und Fremdengesetzgebung in der österreichischen Monarchie 1750–1867* (Wien: Bohlau, 2000), 98.

24. John Torpey, "Revolutions and Freedom of Movement: An Analysis of Passport Controls in the French, Russian, and Chinese Revolutions," *Theory and Society* 26, no. 6 (1997): 848.

25. Eric Hobsbawm, *The Age of Capital, 1848–1875* (London: Weidenfeld and Nicolson, 1975), 35, cited in Torpey, "Revolutions and Freedom," 848.

26. M. I. Mysh, *Pravo nasledovaniia posle inostrantsev v Rossii* (St. Petersburg, 1887), 9.

27. Ibid., 8. For greater detail on the abolition of the "repatriation tax" (*vyvoznaia poshlina*) see Johann Caspar Bluntschli, *Sovremennoe mezhdunarodnoe pravo tsivilizovannykh gosudarstv, izlozhennoe v vide kodeksa* (Moscow: Indrikh, 1876), 245.

28. "O novykh pravilakh vydachi pasportov inostrantsam," Tsirkuliar Departamenta politsii ispolnitel'noi, August 18, 1860, in *Sbornik tsirkuliarov i instruktsii MVD za 1858, 1859, 1860 i 1861 gody,* ed. Dmitrii Nikolaevich Chudovskii (St. Petersburg: Tip. Ministerstvo vnutrennikh del, 1873), 105, 152. For the new rules, see Prodolzhenie 1863 goda k XIV t. Svod Zakonov, izd. 1857, v prilozhenii k st. 436 Ustav o pasportakh.

29. M. I. Mysh, *Ob inostrantsakh v Rossii* (St. Petersburg: A. Bekt, 1911), x.

30. PSZ, vol. 29, no. 22418, cited in Mysh, *Ob inostrantsakh,* xi.

31. RGIA, P. Z. 97697 (*Zhurnaly vysochaishe uchrezhdennoi komissii o merakh k preduprezhdeniiu naplyva inostrantsev v zapadnye okrainy. Otdel III: vopros o priniatii i ostavlenii russkogo poddanstva,* 1891), 6.

32. Mysh, *Ob inostrantsakh,* xii. See also Ministerstvo Finansov, *Vysochaishchee povelenie o priniatii mer dlia privlecheniia inostrannykh kapitalov,* September 13, 1859.

33. GARF, f. 109, op. 223 (Otchety III otdeleniia Tsarskoi kantseliarii i korpusa zhandarmov), d. 26 papka XXIV (1861), ll. 228–237.

34. Ibid., ll. 152ob–153.

35. Ibid., ll. 151, 159.

36. "O nedopushchenii medlennosti po delam inostrantsev," Tsirkuliar Dept. Politsii Isp., March 8, 1861, no. 33, in *Sbornik tsirkuliarov i instruktsii MVD za 1858, 1859, 1860 i 1861 gody,* ed. D. Chudovskii (St. Petersburg: Tip. Ministerstvo vnutrennikh del, 1873), 303.

37. GARF, f. 109, op. 223 (1862), d. 27, l. 336.

38. RGIA, P. Z. 97697, 10.

39. GARF, f. 109, op. 223 (1862), d. 27, l. 335.

40. RGIA, P. Z. 97697, 4.

41. Ibid.

42. AVPRI, f. 137, Otchety Ministerstvo inostrannykh del, d. 54 (1865), l. 234.

43. I. V. Potkina, "Zakonodatel'noe regulirovanie predprinimatel'skoi deiatel'nosti inostrantsev v Rossii, 1861–1916," in V. I. Bovykin, ed., *Inostrannoe*

predprinimatel'stvo i zagranichnye investitsii v Rossii: Ocherki (Moscow: Rosspen, 1997), 20.

44. Ivan N. Beliaev, *Dva veka pochetnogo grazhdanstva: XIX–XX vv.: istoriia, pravo, sovremmenost'* (Smolensk: Smolenskaia oblast' tip., 2001); *Obozrenie deistvuiushchego*, 37.

45. *Proekt polozheniia o sostoianii inostrantsev* (St. Petersburg, 1861), 19, 22. On the direct link between this reform and the aim of drawing foreign capital, see *Vysochaishchee povelenie o priniatii mer dlia privlecheniia inostrannykh kapitalov*, September 13, 1859.

46. See for example, the case of Alfred Dattan, who used his position as a German diplomat to great advantage in building his commercial career. Lothar Deeg, *Kunst & Albers Wladiwostok: Die Geschichte eines deutschen Handelshauses im russischen Fernen Osten 1864–1924* (Tubingen: Klartext, 1996).

47. S. A. Pros'bin, *Torgovo-promyshlennyi sbornik: svod deistvuiushchikh uzakonenii po chasti promyshlennosti i torgovli* (St. Petersburg, 1907), 373–374; Potkina, "Zakonodatel'nye," 26.

48. *Zakony o sostoianiiakh* (Svod zak, vol. IX (1899), article 850). Moreover, the children of naturalized foreigners were not automatically naturalized (unless born after naturalization of the parents). But children could enter the civil service by taking the oath of service without taking the oath of subjecthood (there were two separate oaths).

49. *O Prisiage: o prisiage voobshche: prisiaga na poddanstvo: prisiaga na vernost' sluzhby: prisiaga po delam grazhdanskim: prisiaga po delam torgovym* (St. Petersburg: "Mirskii vestnik," 1864); *Prisiaga na vernost' sluzhby imperatoru Nikoalaiu II* (Kazan': Tip. Gran., 1910).

50. RGVIA, f. 400, op. 14, d. 16108.

51. Andreas Fahrmeir, *Citizens and Aliens: Foreigners and the Law in Britain and the German States, 1789–1870* (New York, Oxford: Berghahn Books, 2000), 30.

52. *Obozrenie deistvuiushchikh*, 35–38.

53. RGIA, f. 1343, op. 58, d. 653; A. A. Shumkov, "Iuridicheskie polozheniia o priznanii inostrantsev v pravakh rossiiskogo dvorianstva," 45–46, in *Problemy priznaniia i utverzhdeniia v pravakh rossiiskogo dvorianstva vysshikh soslovii narodov Rossiisikoi Imperii i inostrannykh dvorian: materialy k tret'emu nauchnomu seminaru 5–6 aprelia 1997* (St. Petersburg: Sankt-Peterburgskoe Dvorianskoe Sobranie, 1997).

54. All the above statistics are from the yearly reports of the Third Section of the Imperial Chancellery, 1839–1869, in GARF, f. 109, op. 223, dd. 4–34.

55. Gessen, *Poddanstvo*, 220. See James Kettner, *The Development of American Citizenship, 1608–1870* (Chapel Hill: University of North Carolina Press, 1978), 3–130.

56. For example, naturalized prisoners of war received passports with a notation that they were banned from living in Poland, Kurland, Finland, Bessarabia, St. Petersburg, or Moscow. *Proekt polozheniia,* 49.

57. Gessen, *Poddanstvo,* 226–231.

58. RGIA, P. Z. 97697, 4.

59. M. A. Lozina-Lozinskogo, "Priniatie v russkoe poddanstvo," *Pravo: ezhenedel'naia iuridicheskaia gazeta* no. 4 (1898): 10–15; no. 1 (1899): 22–29; no. 2 (1899): 79–84. Governors and local officials were also given substantial authority to waive the onerous regular procedures for naturalization (especially the requirement of five years of continuous residence). A late-nineteenth-century jurist claimed that the expedited form of naturalization was a fairly popular and common path to naturalization.

60. For analyses of this transition that frame it in Foucauldian terms of the emergence of governmentality and individuals' integration in the state and disciplinary webs of power (rather than in Gessen's terms of the emergence of the autonomous liberal subject), see Charles Steinwedel, "Making Social Groups, One Person at a Time: The Identification of Individuals by Estate, Religious Confession, and Ethnicity in Late Imperial Russia," in Jane Caplan and John Torpey, eds., *Documenting Individual Identity: The Development of State Practices in the Modern World* (Princeton and Oxford: Princeton University Press, 2001), 67–82; Yanni Kotsonis, "'Face to Face': The State, the Individual, and the Citizen in Russian Taxation, 1863–1917," *Slavic Review* 63, no. 2 (2004): 221–246. On Gessen's philosophy, see Eric Lohr, "The Ideal Citizen and Real Subject in Late Imperial Russia," *Kritika: Explorations in Russian and Eurasian History* 7, no. 2 (Spring 2006): 173–194.

61. Gessen, *Poddanstvo,* 283

62. Ibid., 285.

63. See Nikolai Reinke, *Ocherk russko-pol'skogo mezhduoblastnogo chastnogo prava* (St. Petersburg: Senatskaia tip., 1909). This was also true for the Bukhara and Khiva emirates, but they were legally "protectorates" in a category of their own with their own subjecthoods. See Aleksandra Iur'evna Balchturina *Okrainy Rossiiskoi Imparii: gosudarstrennal uparlance i natsienal'naia politikav gody Pervoi miroroi voiny (1914–1917gg.)* (Moscow: Rosspen, 2004), 316–334.

64. GARF, f. 109, op. 223, d. 26 papka XXIV (1861). Governors often complained that Finland provided a loophole through which foreigners could enter and Russian subjects depart the empire, evading all the checks and restrictions imposed in other parts of it. The Finnish route is well known as the preferred path for political revolutionaries to enter and leave the country, but many others used the route as well. See, for example: GARF, f. 102, II deloproizvodstvo (1889g.), d. 46, l. 105.

65. "Pasportnye pravila na vremia voennogo polozheniia v Tsarstve Pol'skom (1865)," article 28 in RGIA, P. Z. 520.

66. RGIA, f. 1284, op. 190, d. 85, l. 29.

67. The relevant clause was article 819, t. IX, *Svod Zakonov* (1899), "Inostrantsy iz evreev ne dopuskaiutsia k pereseleniiu v Rossiiu ili vstupleniiu v rossiiskoe poddanstvo," also in *Prava evreev i inostrantsev* (St. Petersburg, 1908).

68. Norman Saul, *Distant Friends: The United States and Russia, 1763–1867* (Lawrence: University Press of Kansas, 1991) contains a great deal about this dispute. See also V. V. Engel', *Evreiskii vopros v russko-amerikanskikh otnosheniiakh: na primere 'pasportnogo voprosa' 1864–1913* (Moscow: Nauka, 1998); Viktoriia I. Zhuravleva, "Evreiskii vopros v Rossii glazami Amerikantsev," *Vestnik evreiskogo universiteta* 3, no. 13 (1996): 64–87.

69. GARF, f. 215, op. 1, d. 411, l. 35. (Circular of the governor–general of Warsaw on the order of granting visas to the passports of foreign Jews upon their entry into Russia, July 9, 1891).

70. RGIA, f. 1289, op. 1, d. 2281, l. 1 (Ministry of Internal Affairs, Department of General Affairs, confidential circular, December 21, 1864).

71. Ibid., ll. 1–6.

72. *Proekt polozheniia o sostoianii inostrantsev* (1863), in the general collection of the Russian National Library, St. Petersburg, p. 41; Vladimir M. Gessen, "O pripiske naturalizovannykh inostrantsev k meshchanskim obshchestvam," *Zhurnal Ministerstva iustitsii* (April 1896).

73. Gessen, *Poddanstvo*, 87; Zapiska kommisii pri II'm otdelenii sobstvennoi Ego Imperatorskogo Velichestva kantseliarii dlia razsmotreniia voprosa ob ostavlenii russkogo poddanstva, December 15, 1870. Unpublished manuscript in the general collection of the Russian National Library, St. Petersburg.

74. Victor Dönninghaus, *Die Deutschen in der Moskauer Gesellschaft: Symbiose und Konflikte (1494–1941)* (Munich: R. Oldenbourg Verlag, 1992), 306–328.

75. The first public organization of the Moscow merchants was the Moscow Merchants' Club, founded by a foreigner in 1786. See Alfred Rieber, *Merchants and Entrepreneurs in Imperial Russia* (Chapel Hill: University of North Carolina Press, 1982), 22.

76. Ibid., 67.

77. Ibid., 73.

78. Ibid., 71–73.

79. Thomas C. Owen, *Dilemmas of Russian Capitalism: Fedor Chizhov and Corporate Enterprise in the Railroad Age* (Cambridge: Harvard University Press, 2005), 55.

80. For example, a series of articles in *Den'* in March–April 1864 seems to have helped defeat a proposal to loosen the strict ban on Jesuits entering the empire. *Den',* March 14 and 21, and April 4, 1864.

81. AVPRI, f. 137, op. 475, d. 59.

82. Dietmar Neutatz, *Die "deutsche Frage" im Schwarzmeergebiet und in Wolhynien: Politik, Wirtschaft, Mentalitäten und Alltag im Spannungsfeld von Nationalismus und Modernisierung (1856–1914)* (Stuttgart: Franz Steiner Verlag, 1993); Christoph Schmidt, *Russische Presse und Deutsches Reich, 1905–1914* (Köln: Böhlau, 1988), 100–108.

83. After 1871, the legal term was changed from "kolonist" to "sobstvennik-poseliane" ("colonist" to "landholding settler").

84. RGIA, f. 381, op. 13, d. 7813 (Delo o podchinenii kolonii iuzhnogo kraia saratovskoi i samarskoi gubernii gubernskim uchrezhdeniia); RGIA, f. 385, op. 1, d. 555, ll. 19–24ob (F. Minkov, Zapiska kasatel'no voinskoi povinnosti bolgarskikh kolonistov, January 14, 1872). The pacifist Mennonites were able to negotiate a civil form of service (mostly in forestry) in place of active military duty.

85. Mysh, *Ob inostrantsakh,* 19–25; Mysh, *Rukovodstvo.*

86. AVPRI, f. 149, op. 502a, d. 932, ll. 206–207ob.

87. Fahrmeir, *Citizens and Aliens,* 139.

88. P. Bazarov, *Gosudarstvennaia granitsa* (St. Petersburg: Tip. Shtaba verkhovnogo glavnokomanduiushego, 1917).

89. GARF, f. 215, op. 1, d. 463, l. 2 (Ministry of Internal Affairs circular to governors, June 9, 1873); AVPRI, f. 137, op. 475 Otchety Ministerstvo inostrannykh del Rossii, 1830–1916.

90. Eli Nathans, *The Politics of Citizenship in Germany: Ethnicity, Utility and Nationalism* (Oxford and New York: Berg, 2004); Richard Blanke, *Prussian Poland in the German Empire (1871–1900)* (Boulder and New York: Columbia University Press, 1981); Pamela Susan Nadell, "The Journey to America by Steam: the Jews of Eastern Europe in Transition" (Ph.D. diss., The Ohio State University, 1982), 95.

91. William W. Hagen, *Germans, Poles, and Jews: The Nationality Conflict in the Prussian East, 1772–1914* (Chicago and London: University of Chicago Press, 1980), 124–158; Eric Lohr, *Nationalizing the Russian Empire: The Campaign Against Enemy Aliens during World War I* (Cambridge: Harvard University Press, 2003), 92–94.

92. Of course, these foreigners did not have the right to vote, and German naturalization law was notoriously restrictive, leading to some of the smallest rates of naturalization in Europe in the late nineteenth century—with much higher rates of denial of applications for naturalization than Russia and most other countries. So there is not a direct or fully logical relationship here.

93. Gessen, *Poddanstvo*, 103.
94. GARF, f. 102, II deloproizvodstvo (1885), op. 38, d. 277 ch. 1, l. 2 (Minister of Foreign Affairs Giers to Minister of Internal Affairs Durnovo, May 10, 1885).
95. GARF, f. 102, op. 76a, d. 41, l. 1.
96. GARF, f. 102, II deloproizvodstvo (1881), d. 38, l. 527.
97. GARF, f. 102, II deloproizvodstvo (1884), op. 41, d. 236, l. 4 (Russian Embassy in Vienna to Giers, February 1, 1884).
98. Durnovo was a long-time proponent of maintaining a strong alliance with the conservative European monarchies. He is best known for his memo three decades later on the eve of World War I which called for, among other things, a renewal of that alliance. David McDonald, "The Durnovo Memorandum in Context: Official Conservatism and the Crisis of Autocracy," *Jahrbücher für Geschichte Osteuropas* 44, no. 4 (1996): 481–502.
99. GARF, f. 102, II deloproizvodstvo (1881), d. 277 ch.1, ll. 62–65.
100. GARF, f. 102, op. 269, d. 52, ll. 10–11ob.
101. AVPRI, f. 137, op. 475, d. 96 (1885), ll. 87ob–88.
102. GARF, f. 102, II deloproizvodstvo (1881), d. 38, l. 527.
103. GARF, f. 102, II deloproizvodstvo (1885), d. 277 ch. 1, ll. 119–124 (Mouravieff to Bismarck, September 12, 1885).
104. AVPRI, f. 137, op. 475, d. 97 (1886), ll. 99–100.
105. GARF, f. 102, II deloproizvodstvo (1885), d. 277 ch. 1, l. 209 (governor-general of Vilna, Kovno, and Grodno to Ministry of Internal Affairs, November 19, 1885).
106. AVPRI, f. 137, op. 475, d. 100 (1887), l. 93ob.
107. GARF, f. 102, II deloproizvodstvo (1885), op. 38, d. 277 ch. 2, ll. 196–197 (Ministry of Foreign Affairs to Ministry of Internal Affairs, October 2, 1886).
108. AVPRI, f. 137, op. 475, d. 97 (1886), ll. 103ob.
109. Nathans, *The Politics of Citizenship*, 122–123.
110. GARF, f. 102, II deloproizvodstvo (1885), 277 ch. 1, ll. 119–124 (Mouravieff to Bismarck, September 12, 1885).
111. AVPRI, f. 137, op. 475, d. 97 (1886), l. 105.
112. *Svod vysochaishikh otmetok po vsepoddannieishim otchetam za 1881–1890* (St. Petersburg: Gos. tip., 1893), 199.
113. Ibid., 199–200.
114. Ibid., 200–201.
115. Nathans, *The Politics of Citizenship*, 124.
116. GARF, f. 102, II deloproizvodstvo (1890), op. 47, d. 104 ch. 12, ll. 15–16. In 1891–92, officials on the border with the Ottoman Empire and Austria both reported similar refusals to admit Russian-subject Jews. Austria likewise imposed an inflated 250-ruble per Jewish person cash requirement. GARF, f. 102, II deloproizvodstvo (1891), d. 48, l. 202.
117. Nathans, *The Politics of Citizenship*, 125.

118. Ulrich Herbert, *A History of Foreign Labor in Germany, 1880–1980* (Ann Arbor: University of Michigan Press, 1990), 13–23.

119. Herbert, *A History of Foreign Labor,* 22–23; K. S. Leites, *Russkie rabochie v germanskom sel'skom khoziaistve* (Petrograd: Tip. Ministerstva finansov, 1914).

120. The significance of demographics was present in Russian debates, though not so central as in Prussia. Bismarck's demagogic use of the issue was not necessary in a land with few electoral institutions. Moreover, the elected *zemstva* (local government bodies introduced in Russian provinces in 1864) were not introduced into most of the non-Russian provinces where the issue would have been most intense). However, the Pleve committee did note that the threat that naturalized immigrant communities could become a majority of the population in select districts raised the question either of limiting their electoral rights or sharply restricting their ability to naturalize. RGIA, P. Z. 97697, 13.

121. The 1865 decree applied only to "gentry estates," but a ruling of 1866 expanded its scope to include all nonurban land. See Witold Rodkiewicz, *Russian Nationality Policy in the Western Provinces of the Empire: 1863–1905* (Lublin: Scientific Society of Lublin, 1998), 58–59; PSZ, 2nd ed., vol. 40, no. 42759.

122. Rodkiewicz, *Russian Nationality Policy,* 65.

123. Ibid., 74. One reason why the measures were applied to all foreigners without distinguishing exemptions for such favored nationalities as the Czechs was the objections of the ministers of justice and foreign affairs. Both argued that it would not be within the practices of international law to distinguish between various nationalities and subjecthoods in policies of this type. RGVIA, f. 401, op. 4/928, d. 60, l. 19ob (Zhurnaly zasedanii komissii dlia razrabotki voprosa o merakh k prekrashcheniiu naplyva inostrantsev v nashi zapadnye okrainy, 1885–1886).

124. RGVIA, f. 401, op. 4/928, d. 60, 19ob.

125. The exception for inheritance is quite a contrast to the 1865 decree restricting Russian subjects of Polish origins. The explanation probably lies in the long and strong tradition in the Russian Empire of granting rights of inheritance to foreigners who had acquired property in the empire. Mysh, *Pravo nasledovaniia,* 12.

126. Rodkiewicz, *Russian Nationality Policy,* 75.

127. GARF, f. 102, II deloproizvodstvo, op. 49 (1892), d. 287, l. 1 (governor-general of Vilna, Kovno, and Grodno correspondence with the Ministry of Internal Affairs, September 1892).

128. GARF, f. 102, II deloproizvodstvo (1888), d. 178, ll. 1–11 (Ministry of Finance, Department of Trade and Manufacturing report, April 19, 1888). This case dealt with a complaint from the Ministry of Internal Affairs that

foreign workers in the mining and steelmaking industry were abusing the legitimation ticket system. The Ministry of Finance responded by arguing strongly that it had its own approach to "nationalizing" the economy that involved new tariffs on iron imports. It noted that skilled foreign labor comprised about 20 percent of the labor force and 50 percent of the management of the factories in these industries. Because there was no higher school for the training of mining and steelmaking experts, it would undermine Russian companies' ability to compete if they were deprived of trained foreigners.

129. RGIA, P. Z. 97697, 13; Rodkiewicz, *Russian Nationality Policy*, 88.

130. GARF, f. 215, op. 1, d. 429 (O narushenii inostrantsami zakona 14 Marta 1887).

131. Rodkiewicz, *Russian Nationality Policy*, 88–89.

132. GARF, f. 215, op. 1, d. 411, ll. 24–26 (governor-general of Warsaw to governors of the Privislenskii Krai, February 25, 1889).

133. GARF, f. 102, II deloproizvodstvo (1885 g.), op. 42, d. 435, ll. 13, 33–35 (governor-general of Kiev, Podolia, and Volynia to Ministry of Internal Affairs, February 13, 1886 and August 20, 1887).

134. One interesting result of the breakdown of cooperation with Germany and Austria was a switch from close collaboration in arresting and returning draft evaders and deserters to a system whereby such foreigners were arrested and then often were allowed to naturalize (on the condition that they serve in the Russian army). GARF, f. 102, II deloproizvodstvo (1889 g.), d. 46, l. 254.

135. RGVIA, f. 401, op. 4/928, d. 60, l. 19ob.

136. RGIA, P. Z. 466 (Proekt rezoliutsii po delu ob ogranichenii inostrannogo zemlevladeniia na Kavkaze. Vypiska iz zhurnalov Komiteta ministrov, May 19 and June 2, 1898).

137. AVPRI, Tikhookeanskii stol, op. 487, d. 762, l. 170. The law expired on April 27, 1901, spurring a renewed debate about limits upon further immigration from China and Korea.

138. T. N. Sorokina, *Khoziaistvennaia deiatel'nost' kitaiskikh poddannykh na Dal'nem Vostoke Rossii i politika administratsii Priamurskogo kraia (konets XIX–nachalo XX)* (Omsk: OmGU, 1999), 29–31.

139. V. V. Sinichenko, *Vostochnaia Sibir' v Rossiisko-kitaiskih otnosheniiakh, 50–80-x gg. XIX veka* (Irkutsk: Irkutskoi gosudarstvennyi pedagogicheskii universitet, 1999), 50–51.

140. See AVPRI, Tikhookeanskii stol, op. 487, d. 762, l. 382 for a map of settlements as of 1901. The striking features of this map include the large amount of land given to Cossack settlements along the border, the relatively small amount of land distributed to settlers from European Russia, and the fact that settlement did not generally occur outside a narrow band along the border.

141. The 1860 Treaty of Peking included many clauses opening and protecting trade of Russians in China and Chinese in Russia on a mutual basis, presumably with the assumption that Russian traders in China would be more successful than Chinese traders in Russia. Two decades later, the results of the open trade regime were quite the opposite of these expectations. "Dopolnitel'nyi dogovor, zakliuchennyi v Pekine," November 2, 1860, in T. Iuzefovich, ed., *Dogovory Rossii s Vostokom politicheskie i torgovye* (St. Petersburg: Tip. O.I. Baksta, 1869), 259–269.

142. On the concept of the foreign, Jewish, and German *zasil'e*, see Eric Lohr, "Russian Economic Nationalism during World War I: Moscow Merchants and Commercial Diasporas," *Nationalities Papers* 31, no. 4 (2003): 471–484.

143. Sorokina *Khoziaistvennaia deiatel'nost'*, 79.

144. Chia Yin Hsu, "The Chinese Eastern Railroad and the Making of Imperial Orders in the Far East" (Ph.D. diss., New York University, 2006).

145. AVPRI, Tikhookeanskii stol, op. 487, d. 471, ll. 184–186 (Ministry of Internal Affairs to Ministry of Foreign Affairs, July 26, 1902).

146. Sorokina, *Khoziaistvennaia deiatel'nost'*, 86–89; AVPRI, Tikhookeanskii stol, op. 487, d. 770, l. 73 (Gondotti to Chair of the Council of Ministers, November 2, 1912).

147. Erika Lee, *At America's Gates: Chinese Immigration during the Exclusion Era, 1882–1943* (Chapel Hill and London: University of North Carolina Press, 2003); Sucheng Chan, ed., *Entry Denied: Exclusion and the Chinese Community in America, 1882–1943* (Philadelphia: Temple University Press, 1991).

148. AVPRI, Tikhookeanskii stol, op. 487, d. 471, ll. 194–209 (governor-general of the Priamur region to the Ministry of Internal Affairs, September 23, 1902).

149. The governor-general of the Priamur region's annual report for 1885, in *Svod vysochaishikh otmetok po vsepoddanneishim otchetam za 1881–1890* (St. Petersburg: Gos. Tip., 1893), 500; AVPRI, Tikhookeanskii stol, op. 487, d. 471, l. 195 (governor-general of the Priamur region to the Ministry of Internal Affairs, September 23, 1902); Prim. 1 k st. 818 Zakony o sostoianiiakh, Svod zakonov, vol. 9 (1899); PSZ (1886), no. 4035.

150. George Ginsburgs, "The Citizenship Status of Koreans in Pre-Revolutionary Russia and the Early Years of the Soviet Regime," *Journal of Korean Affairs* 5, no. 2 (1975): 1–19.

151. AVPRI, Tikhookeanskii stol, op. 487, d. 471, l. 195 (governor-general of the Priamur region to the Ministry of Internal Affairs, September 23, 1902).

152. *Sbornik deistvuiushikh traktatov, konventsii i soglashenii, zakliuchennykh Rossiei s drugimi gosudarstvami*, vol. 3 (St. Petersburg: Tip. Trenke i Fiusno, 1891), 292; *Zakony o sostoianiiakh* (Svod zak, t. IX, izd. 1899), art. 818, primechanie 1.

153. AVPRI, op. 487, d. 471, ll. 184–186.
154. Sorokina, *Khoziaistvennaia deiastel'nost'*, 144–148. The committee drew on discussions of similar policies in the western provinces.
155. AVPRI, Iaponskii stol, op. 493, d. 1904, ll. 2–167, 352.
156. AVPRI, Iaponskii stol, op. 493, d. 212, ll. 1–15; Ginsburgs, "The Citizenship Status," 6.
157. Lewis Siegelbaum, "Another 'Yellow Peril': Chinese Migrants in the Russian Far East and the Russian Reaction before 1917," *Modern Asian Studies* 12, no. 2 (1978): 318–319.
158. AVPRI, Tikhookeanskii stol, op. 487, d. 751, ll. 3–196.
159. AVPRI, Tikhookeanskii stol, op. 487, d. 770, l. 45 (Kollektivnaia zapiska kitaiskikh komersantov, zhivushchikh v g. Vladivostoke, 1908).
160. AVPRI, Tikhookeanskii stol, op. 487, d. 762, l. 9ob (Ministry of Internal Affairs report on a review of the laws on settlement in the Priamur region, March 17, 1901).
161. AVPRI, Tikhookeanskii stol, op. 487, d. 770, ll. 4–33 (*Zhurnal soveshchaniia po voprosu o dostavke russkikh rabochikh na Dal'nyi Vostok*, December 15/16, 1911). The policy of providing inducements for Russian émigrés to return has a fascinating pre-history in the nineteenth century. See Alison K. Smith, " 'The Freedom to Choose a Way of Life': Fugitives, Borders, and Imperial Amnesties in Russia," *Journal of Modern History* 83, no. 2 (June 2011): 243–271.
162. AVPRI, Tikhookeanskii stol, op. 487, d. 770, l. 3 (*Zhurnal soveshchaniia po voprosu o dostavke Russkikh rabochikh na Dal'nyi Vostok*, December 15/16, 1911).
163. RGVIA, f. 1759, op. 3 dop., 1405s, l. 3 (governor-general of Kiev, Podolia, and Volynia to the chief of staff of the regional military administration, secret, July 25, 1914); GARF, f. 102, II deloproizvodstvo, op. 71, d. 105, ll. 1–7. The Petrograd deportations of Chinese were completed by August 4, 1914. A circular of the general staff on September 7, 1914, ordered the deportation of all Chinese subjects from all areas under military rule. GARF, f. 102, II deloproizvodstvo, op. 75 (1916), d. 29, l. 9 (copy of secret circular of the main administration of the general staff headquarters, September 7, 1914).
164. GARF, f. 102, II deloproizvodstvo, op. 71 (1914), d. 105, l. 98 (Department of Police secret circular to governors and city heads, July 28, 1914).
165. Full statistics on the number of Chinese deported from the country are not available. Several thousand were deported from areas under military rule, and 963 from Moscow. Numbers from provinces outside the area under military rule were usually in the tens or low hundreds. GARF, f. 102, II deloproizvodstvo, op. 71 (1914), d. 105.

166. Ibid., l. 9 (Dzhunkovskii circular to governors and city heads, August 17, 1914).

167. GARF, f. 102, II deloproizvodstvo, op. 75, d. 29, l. 75.; GARF, f. 102, II deloproizvodstvo, op. 75, d. 10 ch. 7, l. 6. GARF, f. 102, II deloproizvodstvo, op. 75, d. 29, l. 76; Reinhard Nachtigal, *Die Murmanbahn: Die Verkehrsanbindung eines kriegswichtigen Hafens und das Arbeitspotiential der Kriegsgefangenen (1915 bis 1918)* (Grunbach: Greiner, 2001).

168. Ibid., ll. 136–137ob (Deputy Minister of Internal Affairs A. Stepanov to Ministry of Transport, August 2, 1916).

169. GARF, f. 1791, op. 2, d. 4, l. 6.

170. GARF, f. 1791, op. 2, d. 398, l. 2 (Provisional Government Chancery to Minister of Finance, September 21, 1917).

171. Sorokina, *Khoziaistvennaia deiatel'nost'*, 42; F. V. Solov'ev, *Kitaiskoe otkhodnichestvo na Dal'nem Vostoke Rossii v epokhu kapitalizma (1861–1917)* (Moscow: Nauka, 1989); George Ginsburgs, "The Citizenship Status"; RGIA, P. Z. 464 (Materialy po voprosu o naime i perevozke rabochikh-Kitaitsev i Koreitsev dlia raboty na gornykh promyslakh); RGIA, P. Z. 465 (Zhurnaly Komiteta po zaseleniiu Dal'nego Vostoka i drugie materialy po voprosu o merakh bor'by protiv naplyva v Priamurskii krai Kitaitsev i Koreitsev).

4. EMIGRATION AND DENATURALIZATION

1. *Zakony o sostoianiiakh*, vol. 9 (1876) in RGIA, P. Z. 466 (Materialy po proektu pravilo priem v Russkoe poddanstvo i uvol'nenii iz nego, 1891–1898), 8.

2. Nikolai Lavrent'evich Tudorianu, *Ocherki rossiiskoi trudovoi emigratsii perioda imperializma* (Kishinev: Shtiintsa, 1986), 11.

3. *Ustav o pasportakh i beglykh, Svod zakonov*, t. XIV (1890) in RGIA, P. Z. 466, l. 240.

4. Valentina G. Chernukha, *Pasport v Rossii, 1719–1917* (St. Petersburg: Liki Rossii, 2007).

5. Many efforts were undertaken to reform both passport systems, beginning with a committee in the 1860s. During the Duma era, a very serious and comprehensive set of proposals focused explicitly on switching the primary function of the passport from a document regulating movement to a document verifying identity were worked out, but not passed. See RGIA, P. Z. 516 (Zhurnal pasportnoi komissii, 1886–1888); GARF, f. 102, 7oe deloproizvodstvo (1910), d. 207 k. 8, ch. 150a, ll. 155–167, 198–207; GARF, f. 102, 7oe deloproizvodstvo (1910), d. k. 8, ch. 150b, l. 156 *Spravka po proektu novogo ustava o pasportakh* (St. Petersburg, 1913), in the general collection of the Russian National Library in St. Petersburg.

6. "Pasport," *Entsiklopedicheskii slovar'*. 44 (St. Petersburg: I. A. Efron, 1897), 923–925; Chernukha, *Pasport v Rossii*, 177; Mervyn Matthews, *The Passport Society: Controlling Movement in Russia and the USSR* (Boulder: Westview Press, 1993), 9–11; GARF, f. 102, op. 269, d. 25, l. 4; Zhurnal zasedanii vedomstvennogo soveshchaniia obrazovannogo dlia razsmotreniia sostavlennom dept. politsii proekta "Polozheniia ob uchete naseleniia i o pasportakh," December 30, 1914.

7. GARF, f. 102, VII deloproizvodstvo (1910), d. 207 k. 8, ch. 150b, l. 168.

8. For an excellent recent contribution to the literature on overpopulation, see Fiona Hill and Clifford Gaddy, *Siberian Curse: How Communist Planners Left Russia out in the Cold* (Washington, DC: Brookings Institution Press, 2003). On the internal migration that resulted, see Barbara A. Anderson, *Internal Migration during Modernization in Late Nineteenth Century Russia* (Princeton: Princeton University Press, 1980); Bohdan Krawchenko, *Social Change and National Consciousness in Twentieth-Century Ukraine* (New York: St. Martin's Press, 1985). On the link between land shortage and emigration, see: Tudorianu, *Ocherki rossiiskoi*, 23–24. See also: NARA, RG 59, M316, roll 128 (decimal files 861.55–861.56, 1910–1929, 242–243 ("Russian Emigration," report of John Grout, consul in Odessa, April 2, 1910).

9. John Klier, "Emigration Mania in Late Imperial Russia: Legend and Reality," in Aubrey Newman and Stephen Massil, eds., *Patterns of Migration, 1850–1914* (London: The Jewish Historical Society of England, 1996), 21–30.

10. Vladimir Alekseevich Iontsev, *Emigratsiia i repatriatsiia v Rossii* (Moscow: Popechitel'stvo o nuzhdakh rossiiskikh repatriantov, 2001), 29. Canada saw a more substantial Slavic immigration, though most were Ukrainian rather than ethnic Russian (approximately 92,000 Slavs from the Russian Empire migrated to Canada between 1900 and 1913). Vadim Kukushkin, "Protectors and Watchdogs: Tsarist Consular Supervision of Russian-Subject Immigrants in Canada, 1900–1922," *Canadian Slavonic Papers* 44, no. 3/4 (2002). For a good discussion of the ethnic mix of emigrants to North America, see Vadim Kukushkin, *From Peasants to Labourers: Ukrainian and Belarusan Immigration from the Russian Empire to Canada* (Montreal: McGill-Queen's University Press, 2007), 5–6.

11. A border guard official claimed in 1906 that one of the biggest causes of emigration was primogeniture, with the younger sons going abroad permanently or temporarily for work. GARF, f. 102, II deloproizvodstvo (1890), op. 47, d. 104 ch. 6, ll. 242–245 (secret report of the head of the 2nd region of the separate corps of the border guards, July 3, 1906).

12. Vladimir M. Kabuzan, *Emigratsiia i reemigratsiia v Rossii v XVIII-nachale XX vek* (Moscow: Nauka, 1998), 131; Kukushkin, *From Peasants*, 12–29.

13. Dietmar Neutatz, *Die "deutsche Frage" im Schwarzmeergebiet und in Wolhynien: Politik, Wirtschaft, Mentalitäten und Alltag im Spannungsfeld von Nationalismus und Modernisierung (1856–1914)* (Stuttgart: Franz Steiner Verlag, 1993); Detlef Brandes, *Von den Zaren Adoptiert: Die Deutschen Kolonisten und die Balkansiedler in Neurussland und Bessarabien 1751– 1914* (München: R. Oldenbourg Verlag, 1993); Victor Dönninghaus, *Revolution, Reform und Krieg: Die Deutschen an der Wolga im ausgehenden Zarenreich.* Veröffentlichungen zur Kultur und Geschichte der Deutschen im östlichen Europa, vol. 23 (Essen: Klartext, 2002).

14. Robert F. Baumann, "The Debates over Universal Military Service in Russia, 1870–1874" (Ph.D. diss., Yale University, 1982).

15. RGIA, f. 385, op. 1, d. 555 (T. Fedor Minkov, "Zapiska kasatel'no voinskoi povinnosti bolgarskikh kolonistov," January 14, 1872).

16. In the end, the government conceded to Mennonites an alternative form of civilian service (mostly in forest work). See Norman Saul, *Concord and Conflict: The United States and Russia, 1867–1914* (Lawrence: University Press of Kansas, 1996), 78–85; John F. Schmidt, "When a People Migrate. Footnote to the Mennonite Migration of the 1870's," *Mennonite Quarterly Review* 33(2) (1959): 152–155; Gerhard Wiebe, *The Causes and History of the Emigration of the Mennonites from Russia to America* (Manitoba: Manitoba Historical Society, 1981).

17. GARF, f. 102, II deloproizvodstvo (1881), op. 38, d. 527, ll. 91ob–92 (governor of Lomzha's report to Ministry of Internal Affairs, 1875–1877).

18. GARF, f. 102, II deloproizvodstvo (1881), op. 38, d. 527, ll. 30–82.

19. Amirkhan Magomedovich Magomeddadaev, "Dagestanskaia diaspora v Turtsii i Sirii genezis i problemy assimiliatsii" (Kand. diss., RAN Dagestanskii nauchnyi tsentr institut istorii, Makhachkala, 1996), 75.

20. Andreas Fahrmeir, "From Economics to Ethnicity and Back: Reflections on Emigration Control in Germany, 1800–2000," in Nancy L. Green and François Weil, eds., *Citizenship and Those Who Leave: The Politics of Emigration and Expatriation* (Urbana: University of Illinois Press, 2007), 176–177.

21. Nikolai L. Tudorianu, *Emigratsionnaia politika i zakonodatel'stvo Rossii v nachale XX veka* (Kishinev: Ministerstvo obrazovaniia i nauki Respubliki Moldova, 2000), 4.

22. Hannelore Burger, "Passwesen und Staatsbürgerschaft," in Waltraud Heindl and Edith Saurer, eds., *Grenze und Staat: Passwesen, Staatsbürgerschaft, Heimatrecht und Fremdengesetzgebung in der österreichischen Monarchie 1750–1867* (Wien: Bohlau, 2000), 139.

23. The Russian legalization debate included extensive commentary on the Austrian laws. See "Proekt avstriiskogo zakona ob emigratsii," *Pravo; ezhenedel'ny: ivridicheskii zhurnal* (1914), 528–532.

24. Carine Pina Guerassimoff and Eric Guerassimoff, "The 'Overseas Chinese': The State and Emigration from the 1890s through the 1990s," in Green and Weil, eds., *Citizenship and Those Who Leave*, 249.

25. Green and Weil, eds., *Citizenship and Those Who Leave*, 1–62.

26. AVPRI, f. 159, op. 502a, d. 932, l. 2ob; GARF, f. 102, op. 269, l. 52. The ban on returning was stamped on their *zagranpasporta*. According to David Cuthel, this policy was reinforced on the other side of the border by an Ottoman policy in the 1860s to confiscate the passports of immigrants as part of an attempt to limit their ability to return to the Russian Empire and to force them to become solely subjects of the Ottoman Empire. See David Cuthel, "The Circassian Sürgün," *Ab Imperio* 2 (2003): 148–149.

27. GARF, f. 102, II deloproizvodstvo (1899), op. 56, d. 22, ch. 8, ll. 7–13.

28. Since return migration is normally a frequent (and much underestimated) phenomenon, this policy could have massive implications for turning one-time decisions into permanent demographic transformation.

29. GARF, f. 102, II deloproizvodstvo (1885 g.), op. 38, d. 277 ch. 2.

30. RGIA, f. 1286, op. 53, d. 270, ll. 15–41.

31. RGIA, P. Z. 477 (Ministry of Internal Affairs circular to governors and city heads, February 19, 1892).

32. James Meyer, "Immigration, Return, and the Politics of Citizenship: Russian Muslims in the Ottoman Empire, 1860–1914," *International Journal of Middle East Studies* 39, no. 1 (2007): 15–32.

33. AVPRI, f. 137, op. 475 (1891), d. 108, l. 195.

34. Meyer, "Immigration, Return," 24.

35. While there is a substantial literature on return migration for most countries, there is a gaping hole in the Russian historiography. However, the sources I have seen strongly suggest that return migration was relatively rare, especially among Jews and Germans, two of the largest groups of emigrants.

36. AVPRI, f. 137, op. 475, d. 141 (1909); GARF, f. 102, VII deloproizvodstvo (1910), d. 207, k. 8, ch. 150a, l. 126.

37. AVPRI, f. 137, op. 475, d. 100, ll. 137–152.

38. Ibid., AVPRI, f. 137, op. 475 (1891), d. 108.

39. On the accession of a new tsar, the Russian diplomatic corps went to great lengths to administer an oath to all subjects abroad. The progress in registering and keeping track of Russian subjects abroad was apparent in the much greater efficiency of the 1894 operation than the 1881 attempt to locate Russian subjects outside the country. AVPRI, Posol'stvo v Vashingtone, op. 521.1, d. 63, ll. 2–15; AVPRI, Posol'stvo v Konstantinople, op. 616, d. 220 (1881–1882), ll. 2–59; *O prisiage* (St. Petersburg: "Mirskii vestnik," 1864), 6.

40. AVPRI, f. 137, op. 475, d. 108, ll. 191–192ob; GARF, f. 102, op. 76a, d. 29, ll. 39–46ob.

41. Tudorianu, *Emigratsionnaia politika*, 11; Chernukha, *Pasport v Rossii*, 253.

42. GARF, f. 102, VII deloproizvodstvo (1910), d. 207, k. 8, ch. 150a, ll. 124–126; A. Ia[novskii], "Pasport zagranichnyi," *Entsiklopedicheskii slovar'* 44 (St. Petersburg: I. A. Efron, 1897), 925–927.

43. Kukushkin, *From Peasants*, 58.

44. RGIA, P. Z. 2530 (Ministerstvo torgovli i promyshlennosti otdel torgovogo moreplavania, July 8, 1909. Po voprosu ob obrazovanii mezhduvedomstvennogo soveshchaniia dlia vyrabotki zakona ob emigratsii), 5; RGIA, P. Z. 2531 (Ocherk istorii i sovremennogo sostoianiia otkhoda na zarabotki za granitsu v Zapadnoi Evrope i v Rossii).

45. GARF, f. 102, II deloproizvodstvo, (1890), d. 104 ch. 3, l. 18 (governor-general of Warsaw to Ministry of Internal Affairs, February 28, 1894).

46. Tudorianu, *Emigratsionnaia politika*, 13.

47. GARF, f. 102, II deloproizvodstvo, (1882), op. 39, d. 555, ll. 9–10.

48. GARF, f. 102, II deloproizvodstvo, (1890), d. 104, ch. 1, ll. 50–62 (governor-general of Warsaw to Ministry of Internal Affairs, October 18, 1890).

49. GARF, f. 215, op. 1, d. 46, ll. 1–15. Promoting emigration was not legal in most European countries at the time, but the Russian penalties and efforts to enforce this principle were uniquely aggressive. Pamela Susan Nadell, "The Journey to America by Steam: the Jews of Eastern Europe in Transition" (Ph.D. diss., The Ohio State University, 1982), 56.

50. GARF, f. 102, II deloproizvodstvo (1890), d. 104 ch. 2, l. 32. A report from Brazil claimed only one in five emigrants from Russia had a foreign passport. An interdepartmental committee examining proposals for a new emigration law claimed as few as 10 percent of emigrants had proper documents. GARF, f. 102, VII deloproizvodstvo (1910), d. 207 k. 8 ch. 150n, ll. 170–171ob. A *Vestnik Finansov* report for 1909 claims only 25 percent of emigrants had *zagranpasporta*.

51. GARF, f. 102, OO (1906), d. 250, l. 21 (letter intercepted by the Okhrana of Zakhar to Shlim Itskovits in Odessa, November 6, 1906).

52. GARF 102, OO (1906), d. 250, l. 6 (Volynia Gendarme Administration to the Department of Police, April 24, 1906).

53. GARF, f. 102, II deloproizvodstvo, (1890), d. 104, ch. 4, l. 261 (assistant to the head of the Kurland Gendarme Administration to the Department of Police, March 18, 1903).

54. Boris Bogen, *Born a Jew* (New York: Macmillan, 1930), 30; Nadell, "The Journey," 62.

55. RGIA, P. Z. 367, 2530, and 2531.

56. GARF, f. 102, II deloproizvodstvo (1890 g.), op. 47, d. 104, ch. 6, l. 3.

57. GARF, f. 102, 7oe deloproizvodstvo (1910), d. 207k. 8, ch. 150a, ll. 124–126.

58. GARF, f. 265, op. 1, d. 1362, l. 14 (assistant governor-general of Warsaw to the Department of Police, January 5, 1904).

59. Ibid., l. 75.

60. GARF, f. 102, II deloproizvodstvo, (1890), d. 104, ch. 4, ll. 507–08 (report of the governors-general of Kiev, Podolia, and Volynia, May 27, 1911).

61. GARF, 102, OO, (1907g), d. 212, 94 (report of the Suvalki Provincial Gendarme Administration, November 13, 1908).

62. See, for example, the exchange between Minister of Finance Bunge and Minister of Internal Affairs Tolstoi in 1881 in GARF, f. 102, II deloproizvodstvo (1881), op. 38, d. 534, ll. 68–69.

63. Kukushkin, *From Peasants,* 59; P. Tizenko, *Emigratsionnyi vopros v Rossii, 1820–1910* (Libava: Libavskii vestnik, 1909), 38–41.

64. GARF, f. 102, VII deloproizvodstvo (1910), d. 207 k. 8 ch. 150a, ll. 135–168.

65. GARF, f. 102, II deloproizvodstvo (1890), d. 104 ch. 4, ll. 512–533 (Ministerstvo torgovli i promyshlennosti Otdel torgovogo moreplavaniia, Mezhduvedomstvennoe soveshchanie dlia vyrabotki proekta zakona ob emigratsii. Zhurnal zasedanii, January 1910).

66. RGIA, P. Z. 2531, l. 27.

67. GARF, f. 102, II deloproizvodstvo, (1890), d. 104, ch. 4, ll. 512–533.

68. Kukushkin, *From Peasants*; Andrzej Brozek and James Barrett, "Polish Immigrant Workers in Europe and the Labor Movement," *Polish American Studies* 46, no. 1 (1989), 61–73; RGIA, P. Z. 2531, ll. 10–35.

69. RGIA, P. Z. 2531, ll. 23–24. The workers ended up striking and in 1917 many were arrested by a spooked governor who thought they were trying to foment a revolution. AVPRI, Tikhookeanskii stol, op. 487, d. 1440, l. 1–345; R. M. Brodski, "Russian Immigrants in Hawaii," *Novaia i noveishaia istoriia* 3 (1981): 172–177.

70. RGIA, P. Z. 2531, l. 22.

71. AVPRI, Posol'stvo v Berline, op. 509a, d. 4347, ll. 135–167.

72. RGIA, P. Z. 97697 (Ministry of Internal Affairs, *Zhurnaly vysochaishe*), 223; Tudorianu, *Emigratsionnaia politika,* 10.

73. Nikolai Mikhailovich Korkunov, "Ukorenenie inostrantsev i prekrashchenie poddanstva," *Zhurnal Ministerstva iustitsii* 10 (1895), 120.

74. James H. Kettner, *The Development of American Citizenship, 1608–1870* (Chapel Hill: University of North Carolina Press, 1978). At the same time, a Ministry of Internal Affairs committee on passports was puzzling over the treatment of communities of foreign subjects that had lived for generations in Russia as foreigners long after their own countries had denaturalized them because of their extended absence from their homelands.

75. AVPRI, f. 512, op. 1, d. 27, ll. 7–9; Kettner, *The Development of American Citizenship*, 344; Rieko Karatani, *Defining British Citizenship: Empire, Commonwealth, and Modern Britain* (London: Frank Cass, 2003), 39–69.

76. RGIA, P. Z. 97697 (Ministry of Internal Affairs, *Zhurnaly vysochaishe*), 228.

77. *Ustav o pasportakh i beglykh, Svod zakonov*, vol. 9 (1890), art. 304, in M. I. Mysh, *Ob inostrantsakh v Rossii* (St. Petersburg: A. Bekt, 1911), 36.

78. Galina Ia. Tarle, "Emigratsionnoe zakonodatel'stvo Rossii do i posle 1917 goda (analiz istochnikov)," in *Istochniki po istorii adaptatsii rossiiskikh emigrantov v XIX–XX vv.* (Moscow: RAN, 1997).

79. Korkunov, "Ukorenenie inostrantsev," 113.

80. AVPRI, f. 137, op. 475 (1890), d. 104, l. 91.

81. Korkunov, "Ukorenie inostrantsev." On the remarkably strict general policies toward divorce in late imperial Russia, see: Barbara Alpern Engel, *Breaking the Ties that Bound: the Politics of Marital Strife in Late Imperial Russia* (Ithaca: Cornell University Press, 2011); Gregory Freeze, "Bringing Order to the Russian Family: Marriage and Divorce in Imperial Russia, 1760–1860," *The Journal of Modern History* 62, no. 4 (1990): 709–746.

82. RGIA, P. Z. 466 (Prilozhenie k predstavleniiu po proektu pravil o priniatii i ostavlenii russkogo poddanstva: otzyvy vedomstv), 11.

83. Vladimir Matveevich Gessen, *Poddanstvo: ego ustanovlenie i prekrashchenie* (St. Petersburg: Pravda, 1909).

84. Green and Weil, eds., *Citizenship and Those Who Leave*, 181; Korkunov, "Ukorenenie inostrantsev," 113.

85. RGIA, P. Z. 97697 (Ministry of Internal Affairs, *Zhurnaly vysochaishe*), 145–195; GARF, f. 102, VII deloproizvodstvo (1910), d. 2007, k. 8, ch. 150a (Ministry of Foreign Affairs to Department of Police, July 19, 1913).

86. Vladimir Matveevich Gessen, "O prekrashchenii poddanstva," *Zhurnal iuridicheskogo obshchestva pri Imperatorskom St. Peterburgskom universitete* 26, no. 8 (1896): 1–40; no. 9 (1896): 1–40.

87. This is the central argument of his doctoral thesis: Gessen, *Poddanstvo.*

88. RGIA, P. Z. 466 (Prilozhenie k predstavleniiu po proektu pravil o priniatii i ostavlenii russkogo poddanstva: otzyvy vedomstv, zapiska Ministerstvo inostrannykh del, June 11, 1892), ll. 36–43.

89. Korkunov, "Ukorenenie inostrantsev," 120.

90. S. Tukholka, *Russkie poddannye v Turtsii* (St. Petersburg: V. F. Kirshbaum, 1900), 1–3.

91. Ibid., 4–5.

92. Ibid., 25.

93. For example, in 1894 several young men were caught using the cheap and expedited legal route out of the country to do a pilgrimage to Jerusalem, but then stayed in the Ottoman Empire. The Russian consulates detained them as draft-dodgers when they tried to renew their passports.

The result was a new set of restrictions on the issuance of special pilgrimage passports. RGVIA, St. Peterburg Glavnyi Arkhiv, II-8, op. 44, d. 3, l. 1894.

94. Mysh, *Ob inostrantsakh*, 37.

95. GARF, f. 102, op. 76a, d. 29, l. 35 (Ministerstvo vnutrennikh del, izlozhenie dela po II deloproizvodstvo, December 1881).

96. *Novoe vremia*, May 14, 1910.

97. John D. Klier, "Kievlianin and the Jews: A Decade of Disillusionment, 1864–1873," *Harvard Ukrainian Studies* 5, no. 1 (March 1981): 83–101.

98. Kukushkin, *From Peasants,* 68–71; NARA, RG 59 (State Department Central Files), M316 (Soviet Union), roll 128 (decimal files 861.55–861.56, 1910–1929).

99. GARF, f. 102, op. 76a, d. 29, l. 35.

100. On this point, see Dietmar Neutatz, *Die "deutsche Frage" im Schwarzmeergebiet und in Wolhynien: Politik, Wirtschaft, Mentalitäten und Alltag im Spannungsfeld von Nationalismus und Modernisierung (1856–1914)* (Stuttgart: Franz Steiner Verlag, 1993).

101. Valerii Viktorovich Engel', *"Evreiskii vopros" v russko-amerikanskikh otnosheniiakh: Na primere 'pasportnogo' voprosa 1864–1913* (Moscow: Nauka, 1998), 42–43; A. Ginzburg, "Emigratsiia evreev iz Rossii," *Evreiskaia entsiklopediia* (Moscow: Terra, 1991), 264–267.

102. Ambassador Rockwill to Secretary of State Adee, April 16, 1910, National Archives, RG 59, M316, roll 128, pp. 261–262.

103. Kukushkin, *From Peasants,* 57.

104. GARF, f. 102, op. 76a, d. 1569, l. 25 (Zhurnal evreiskogo kolonizatsionogo obshchestva, August 10, 1893).

105. RGIA, P. Z. 2531, l. 20.

106. Engel', *"Evreiskii vopros."*

107. Ibid., 9.

108. Vasilii Nikiforovich V. N. Aleksandrenko, *O poddanstve i naturalizatsii* (Warsaw: Tip. Varshavskogo uchebnogo okruga, 1904), 38. Among others, France, Italy, the Ottoman Empire, and Switzerland explicitly banned denaturalization of men owing active military service, and many countries retained more extensive limits on the ability to denaturalize.

109. Alan J. Ward, "Immigrant Minority 'Diplomacy': American Jews and Russia, 1901–1912," *Bulletin: British Association for American Studies* 9 (December 1964), 16.

110. The relevant clause was article 819, t. IX, *Svod zakonov* (1899), "Inostrantsy iz evreev ne dopuskaiutsia k pereseleniiu v Rossiiu ili vstupleniiu v rossiiskoe poddanstvo," published in *Prava evreev i inostrantsev* (St. Petersburg, 1908). GARF, f. 102, op. 76a, d. 1732, l. 7 (po voprosu o prave pereseleniia

v Rossiiu inostrannykh evreev); GARF, f. 102, II deloproizvodstvo, (1885 g.), op. 42, d. 435, l. 4 (governors-general of Kiev, Podolia, and Volynia to Ministry of Internal Affairs, July 9, 1885); Mysh, *Ob inostrantsakh*, 19–21.

111. Clifford L. Egan, "Pressure Groups, the Department of State, and the Abrogation of the Russian-American Treaty of 1832," *Proceedings of the American Philosophical Society* 115, no. 4 (1971), 328–334.

112. Ward, "Immigrant Minority 'Diplomacy'," 14–16.

113. Saul, *Concord and Conflict*, 577; Engel', *"Evreiskii vopros."*

114. Engel', "Evreiskii vopros," 17.

115. On the expansion of the consular system abroad, see the yearly reports of the Ministry of Foreign Affairs to the tsar, 1885–90 in AVPRI, f. 137, Otchety Ministerstvo inostrannykh del, op. 475, dd. 95–100, and Kukushkin, "Protectors and Watchdogs."

116. Leland J. Gordon, "The Turkish-American Controversy over Nationality," *American Journal of International Law* 25 (October 1931); Kemal Karpat, "Ottoman Emigration to America, 1860–1914," *International Journal of Middle Eastern Studies* 17 (1985), 189–192; Robert R. Trask, *The United States Response to Turkish Nationalism and Reform, 1914–1939* (Minneapolis: University of Minnesota Press, 1971), 189.

117. Richard W. Flournoy, Jr., "Observations on the New German Law on Nationality," *The American Journal of International Law* 8, no. 3 (1914), 477–486; Vsevolod N. Durdenevskii, "Germanskoe dvupoddanstvo," *Problemy velikoi Rossii* (1916), 11: 10–12; 13: 11–13; 15: 9–10.

118. AVPRI, Tikhookeanskii stol, op. 487, d. 760, l. 13 (*Osobyi zhurnal Soveta ministrov*, March 13, 1908).

119. Ibid., ll. 17–60.

120. Ibid., ll. 13, 56; *Osobyi zhurnal Soveta ministrov*, September 30, 1908; AVPRI, Tikhookeanskii stol, op. 487, d. 762, ll. 1760–382 has a good set of materials, maps, and memos on the demographic concerns for the region and the kind of immigration policies that could best address the problem. NARA, RG 59, M316, roll 128 (decimal files 861.55–861.56, 1910–1929), ll. 1–3 (report of the U.S. ambassador on Stolypin's 1910 trip to the Amur region).

121. AVPRI, Tikhookeanskii stol, op. 487, d. 760, l. 15 (*Osobyi zhurnal Soveta ministrov*, March 13, 1908).

5. CITIZENSHIP IN WAR AND REVOLUTION

1. Valentina G. Chernukha, *Pasport v Rossii, 1719–1917* (St. Petersburg: Liki Rossii, 2007), 179.

2. GARF, f. 102, VII deloproizvodstvo (1910) d. k. 8, ch. 150b, l. 166ob (*Spravka po proektu novogo ustava o pasportakh*, St. Petersburg, 1913).

3. Chernukha, *Pasport v Rossii*, 180–81.

4. GARF, f. 102, VII deloproizvodstvo (1910 g.), d. k8 ch. 150b, l. 168.

5. Yanni Kotsonis, "'Face to Face': The State, the Individual, and the Citizen in Russian Taxation, 1863–1917," *Slavic Review* 63, no. 2 (2004): 221–246. Kotsonis, "'Face to Face.'"

6. GARF, f. 102, op. 269, d. 39 (Zhurnaly mezhduvedomstvennogo soveshchaniia, obrazovannogo dlia razsmotreniia proekta 'polozheniia ob udostoverenii lichnosti, ob uchete naseleniia i o pasportakh', 1914–1915); GARF, f. 102, VII deloproizvodstvo (1910 g.) d. k. 8, ch. 150b, l. 166ob (*Spravka po proektu novogo ustava o pasportakh,* St. Petersburg, 1913).

7. See, for example, Aleksei K. Dzhivelegov, *Prava i obiazannosti grazhdan' v pravovom gosudarstve* (Moscow, 1906); Georg Ellinek, *Pravo men'shinstva* (Moscow: Sytin, 1906); Liudvig L. Gervagen, *Obiazannosti, kak osnovanie prava* (St. Petersburg: Shtoltsenburg, 1908); Pavel Briunelli, *Prava russkogo grazhdanina: kak ikh opredeliat', kak ikh osushchestvliat', kak ikh otstaivat'* (St. Petersburg: Izd. Vestnika znaniia (V. V. Bitnera), 1913); Vasilii P. Alekseev, *Svobodnyi grazhdanin i ego prava* (Moscow: "Universal'naia biblioteka," 1917); Nikolai Arsen'ev, *O svobode i obiazannostiakh grazhdanina* (Moscow, 1917); Vsevolod N. Durdenevskii, *Prava i obiazannosti grazhdanina* (Moscow, 1917). On the means by which consciousness of the rule of law was spread, see Michel Tissier, "L'éducation aux libertés: culture juridique et changements socio-politiques en Russie des années 1890 à 1917" (Ph.D. diss., Université Paris I—Panthéon-Sorbonne, 2009).

8. GARF, f. 102, II deloproizvodstvo, op. 73, ch. 1, d. 10, ch. 36, ll. 1–117 (materials on the project to create a new citizenship law, with extensive materials and memos on the prewar history of the project from the late nineteenth century). Similar materials can be found in: RGIA, P. Z., 2534. Shortly after the revolution, the Ministry of Internal Affairs published a massive collection of the laws that limited the rights of various parts of the population as if to concretely refute the notion of universal equal rights and obligations in the new order: *Ogranichitel'nie uzakoneniia i osobiea zakonopolozheniia: izdanniia po soobrazheniiam natsional'nogo ili veroispovednogo svoistva libo obuslovlivaemym razlichiem polov,* 3 vols. (St. Petersburg: Tip. Ministerstva vnutrennikh del, 1906–1907).

9. Isaak I. Levin, *Germanskie kapitaly v Rossii*, 2nd ed. (Petrograd, 1918), 60.

10. Edwin Borchard, "Enemy Private Property," *American Journal of International Law* 18, no. 2 (1924), 523.

11. Several hundred Japanese subjects were expelled from the country and delivered to Japan through the intermediation of the neutral United States. Roughly 700 Japanese subjects were gathered from the Far East in September 1904 and interned in Perm until the end of the war. When the war ended, they were immediately released and allowed to return to their previous place of residence, and the Japanese subjects expelled to Japan were allowed to return. Though this was an important precedent, it was conducted with extensive third-party involvement by the United States and with close attention to the norms of international law. AVPRI, Iaponskii stol, op. 493, d. 352, ll. 2–167; Amos Hershey, *The International Law and Diplomacy of the Russo-Japanese War* (New York: Macmillan, 1906), 298.

12. Boris Nolde, *Russia in the Economic War* (New Haven: Yale University Press, 1928), 6–8; S. Dobrin, "Voprosy Ministra iustitsii Prav. senatu o prave nepriiatel'skikh poddannykh na sudebnuiu zashchitu," *Pravo: ezhenedel'naia iuridicheskaia gazeta* 6 (February 8, 1915): 348–349.

13. GARF, f. 215, op. 1, d. 174, l. 180.

14. "Russkie poddannye v Germanii i Avstro-vengrii vo vremia voiny," *Russkie vedomosti* (July 22, 1914), 2.

15. GARF, f. 102, II deloproizvodstvo, op. 71, d. 80, ll. 1, 55 (correspondence between Stavka and the Ministry of Internal Affairs, July 26-October 7, 1914); Panikos Panayi, *The Enemy in Our Midst: Germans in Britain during the First World War* (New York: Berg, 1991), 134–137; Adolf von Vogel, *Der Wirtschaftskrieg: Die Massnahmen und Bestrebungen des feindlichen Auslandes zur Bekämpfung des deutschen Handels und zur Förderung des eigenen Wirtschaftslebens*, Part 2, Russland (Jena: Kommissionsverlag von Gustav Fischer, 1918).

16. On February 9, 1915, the Senate confirmed the September decision to deny enemy subjects access to the courts, while not denying Russian subjects the right to bring suits against them. Such trials were held without the presence of the accused. RGIA, f. 1483, op. 1, d. 14, l. 151; L. M. Zaitsev, *Poddannye vrazhdebnogo gosudarstva i russkie sudy* (Kiev: "Petr Barskii v Kieve", 1915); Dobrin, "Voprosy Ministra," 345–356.

17. GARF, f. 215, op. 1, d. 432, l. 29 (Dzhunkovskii circular to governors, September 21, 1914).

18. The governors of Warsaw and Lvov both reported that large numbers of enemy subjects left their regions in the days surrounding the declaration of war, but neither they nor others provided any figures. It seems that few of those departing were permanent residents; most were temporary visitors. GARF, f. 102, II deloproizvodstvo, op. 73, d. 351, l. 40 (Assistant Governor–General of Warsaw to the Department of Police, December 22, 1914). The

one exception to the rule appears to have been the Finnish border with Sweden, through which those with the means and determination were able to leave in small numbers.

19. Sergei Nelipovich, "Repressii protiv poddannykh 'tsentral'nykh derzhav'," *Voenno-istoricheskii zhurnal* 6 (1996): 35.

20. AVPRI, f. 138, op. 474, d. 370, ll. 2–5.

21. AVPRI, f. 323, op. 617, d. 83, l. 70 (Chief of Quartering and Military Service at the General Staff to Chief of the Headquarters of the Supreme Commander M. V. Alekseev, December 31, 1915).

22. RGVIA, f. 2005, op. 1, d. 24, l. 261 (General Oranovskii to Iu. N. Danilov, January 10, 1915).

23. RGVIA, f. 2005, op. 1, d. 24, l. 395 (obligatory decree, signed by General Trotskii, n.d.).

24. Nelipovich, "Repressii protiv," 40.

25. The German organization for the settlement of Germans from abroad processed 30,000 Germans arriving in Germany from 1915 through early 1918. The bulk of the arrivals were German citizens who left the country either shortly before the war or during the chaos of late 1917–18. See: Alfred Borchardt, "Deutschrussische Rückwanderung," *Preussische Jahrbücher* 162 (1915): 133–150; NARA, Washington DC, Listen und Fragebogen aus Russland ausgewanderter Reichsdeutscher, angelegt durch das Deutsche Auslandsinstitut Stuttgart: German Records, T-81, R. 630–632; H. S. Weder, "Deutsch-russische Rücksiedlung," *Bibliothek für Volks- und Weltwirtschaft* 32 (Dresden and Leipzig, 1917): 1–66.

26. The records of these exchanges are in AVPRI, f. 160, op 708 (II Department: otdel o voennoplennykh, 1914–1918); f. 157 Pravovoi departament, 1914–1918, op. 455a.

27. RGVIA, f. 2003, op. 1, d. 1452, l. 53 (Glavnoe upravlenie glavnogo shtaba [GUGSh], quartermaster to general quartermaster at Stavka, January 9, 1916).

28. RGIA, f. 1276, op. 10, d. 106, ll. 1–26.

29. AVPRI, Posol'stvo v Vashingtone, op. 512/1, d. 338, ll. 145–149, 180–220.

30. GARF, f. 215, op. 1, d. 174 (Ministry of Internal Affairs circular to all city and provincial governors, July 26, 1914). Those arrested in European Russia and the Caucasus were sent to Viatka, Vologda, and Orenburg provinces for internment in camps under the supervision of the Ministry of War; those arrested in Siberia were sent to Iakutia.

31. GARF, f. 215, op. 1, d. 174.

32. RGVIA, f. 2005, op. 1, d. 24, l. 1, (Ministry of Internal Affairs Maklakov circular to provincial and city governors, August 11, 1914); GARF, f. 215, op. 1, d. 174, l. 159.

33. GARF, f. 102, II deloproizvodstvo, op. 71, d. 102 (1914), ll. 1–10; 15–127; *Deutsche und das Orenburger Gebiet (Sammelung der Materialien der Wissenschaftlichen Gebietskonferenz zum 250 Jahrestag des Orenburger Gouvernements und zum 60 Jahretag des Orenburger Gebiets)* (Orenburg, 1994), 25–26.

34. GARF, f. 270, op 1, d. 91, l. 46 (Chief of the Lifliand Gendarme Administration to Assistant Minister of Internal Affairs and Commander of the Corps of Gendarmes V. F. Dzhunkovskii, September 4, 1914).

35. GARF, f. 215, 1, 432, l. 61 (chief of the chancery of the supreme commander of military supplies of the Northwest Front to General Tumanov, December 13, 1914).

36. For detailed records of major orders to clear Poland of enemy subjects (and Russian-subject Germans) see GARF, f. 215 Kantseliariia varshavskogo general-gubernatora, op. 1, d. 524.

37. RGVIA, f. 2005, op. 1, d. 24, ll. 38–50 (*Osobyi zhurnal Soveta ministrov. Proekt sovershenno doveritel'no.* "O nekotorykh merakh v otnoshenii poddannykh voiuiushchikh s Rossiiu derzhav," October 17 and 21, 1914).

38. RGVIA, f. 2005, op. 1, d. 24, l. 133 (Chief of Army Headquarters N. N. Ianushkevich to Commander of the Sixth Army K. P. Fan der Flit, December 20 1914); RGVIA, f. 2005, op. 1, d. 14, l. 214; RGVIA, f. 2000s, op. 1, d. 4430, ll. 52, 61 (Main Administration of the General Staff, secret report, April 24, 1916).

39. For a discussion of the statistical issues, see Eric Lohr, *Nationalizing the Russian Empire: The Campaign against Enemy Aliens during World War I* (Cambridge: Harvard University Press, 2003), 127; Nelipovich, "Repressii protiv," 41; RGVIA, f. 400, op. 8, d. 697, l. 242; f. 400, op. 8, d. 704, ll. 1–63.

40. J. Spiropulos, *Ausweisung und Internierung feindlicher Staatsangehöriger* (Leipzig: Rossbergische Verlagsbuchhandlung, 1922), 67; Jean-Claude Farcy, *Les camps de concentration français de la premiere guerre mondiale (1914–1920)* (Paris: Anthropos, 1995), 129.

41. Spiropulos, *Ausweisung,* 67, 78; Richard B. Speed, III, *Prisoners, Diplomats, and the Great War: A Study in the Diplomacy of Captivity* (London: Greenwood Press, 1990), 146.

42. Annemarie Sammartino, *The Impossible Border: Germany and the East, 1914–1922* (Ithaca: Cornell University Press, 2010); James Wilford Garner, "Treatment of Enemy Aliens: Measures in Respect to Personal Liberty," *American Journal of International Law* 12, no. 1 (1918): 27–55. As late as March 1915, Germany had not interned any civilian enemy aliens. However, internment began in the spring of 1915, and by June that year there were

48,513 civilian enemy alien internees. See Wilhelm Doegen, *Kriegsgefangene Volker: Der Kriegsgefangenen Haltung und Schicksal in Deutschland* (Berlin: Dietrich Reimer, 1919), table G. Italy interned several thousand enemy aliens during the war. See Spiropulos, *Ausweisung,* 90–92. The number of enemy aliens interned in countries outside Europe is not available. In the United States 2,300 enemy aliens were interned and in Australia 4,500. For a survey of other countries' internment policies, see Spiropulos, *Ausweisung,* 92–102. Unfortunately, figures for the important cases of Austria-Hungary and the Ottoman Empire are not available.

43. Lohr, *Nationalizing the Russian Empire.*

44. Michael Cherniavsky, *Prologue to Revolution: Notes of A. N. Iakhonotov on the Secret Meetings of the Council of Ministers, 1915* (Upper Saddle River, N.J.: Prentice Hall, 1967), 56–72.

45. Bachschi Ischchanian, *Die ausländischen Elemente in der russischen Volkswirtschaft* (Berlin: Franz Siemenroth, 1913). Ischchanian's figures were based on surveys in the 1890s. The absolute numbers of foreigners in these positions had risen by 1914, but the relative share of foreigners had fallen substantially; Eric Lohr, "Russian Economic Nationalism during the First World War: Moscow Merchants and Commercial Diasporas," *Nationalities Papers* 31, no. 4 (2003): 471–484.

46. John McKay, *Pioneers for Profit: Foreign Entrepreneurship and Russian Industrialization, 1885–1913* (Chicago and London: University of Chicago Press, 1970); Vol'fgang Sartor, "Torgovyi dom 'Shpis': Dokumental'noe nasledie dinastii nemetskikh predprinimatelei v Rossii (1846–1915 gg.)," *Otechestvennaia istoriia* 2 (1997): 174–183; Fred V. Carstensen, "Foreign Participation in Russian Economic Life: Notes on British Enterprise, 1865–1914," in Gregory Guroff and Fred V. Carstensen, eds., *Entrepreneurship in Imperial Russia and the Soviet Union* (Princeton: Princeton University Press, 1983), 140–158; Erik Amburger, *Deutsche in Staat, Wirtschaft und Gesellschaft Russlands: Die Familie Amburger in St. Petersburg 1770–1920* (Wiesbaden: Otto Harrassowitz, 1986), 178–185; Aleksandr Aleksandrovich Fursenko, "Mozhno li schitat' kompaniiu Nobelia russkim kontsernom?" in *Issledovaniia po sotsial'no-politicheskoi istorii Rossii,* Akademiia nauk SSSR Institut istorii SSSR Leningradskoe otdelenie, Trudy, vol. 12 (Leningrad: Nauka, 1971), 352–361.

47. Thomas C. Owen, *Russian Corporate Capitalism from Peter the Great to Perestroika* (New York and Oxford: Oxford University Press, 1995), 188. These figures cover managers in the ten leading cities of the empire.

48. Anders Henriksson, "Nationalism, Assimilation and Identity in Late Imperial Russia: The St. Petersburg Germans, 1906–1914," *The Russia Review*

52 (1993), 341–353. The leading demographer Vladimir Maksimovich Kabuzan comes to a similar conclusion for the empire as a whole: that the process of assimilation accelerated in the early twentieth century. Vladimir M. Kabuzan, "Nemetskoe naselenie v Rossii v XVIII-nachale XX veka (chislennost' i razmeshchenie): 28.

49. For an overview of its views on the issue, see its official journal: *Promyshlennost' i torgovlia*. On the organization, see Ruth Amende Roosa, "Russian Industrialists during World War I: The Interaction of Economics and Politics," in Guroff and Carstensen, eds., *Entrepreneurship in Imperial Russia*, 159–187.

50. For background on the prewar history of these kind of programs and the regional, class, ethnic, and state barriers to their successful mobilization, see Alfred Rieber, *Merchants and Entrepreneurs in Imperial Russia* (Chapel Hill: University of North Carolina Press, 1982); Thomas C. Owen, *Capitalism and Politics in Russia: A Social History of the Moscow Merchants, 1855–1905* (New York: Cambridge University Press, 1981); Muriel Joffe, "Regional Rivalry and Economic Nationalism: The Central Industrial Region Industrialists' Strategy for the Development of the Russian Economy, 1880s–1914," *Russian History/Histoire Russe* 11, no. 4 (1984), 389–421.

51. See *Promyshlennaia Rossiia*, a journal that included articles by many leading liberal and moderate economists with essays on ways to promote an economically independent Russia during the war years. See also Ivan Khristoforovich Ozerov, *Na novyi put'! K ekonomicheskomu osvobozhdeniiu Rossii* (Moscow: Tip. A. I. Mamontova, 1915; *Zadachi, programma i deiatel'nosti torgovo-promyshlennogo otdela Obshchestva 1914 goda v 1915 godu* (Petrograd: Rassvet, 1916); Otchet soveta o deiatel'nosti 'Obshchestva 1914 goda' za 1915 god (Petrograd: Rassvet, 1916); *Zhurnal "1914 god": bor'ba s nemetskim zasil'em i vozrozhdenie Rossii, Russkaia budushchnost'*, and the collection of articles on the theme from *Novoe vremia* published as A. Rennikov, *Zoloto Reina: o nemtsakh v Rossii* (Petrograd: A. S. Suvorin, 1915).

52. Eric Lohr, "Patriotic Violence and the State: The Moscow Riots of 1915," *Kritika: Explorations in Russian and Eurasian History* 4, no. 3 (2003): 607–626; Iurii Il'ich Kir'ianov, "'Maiskie besporiadki' 1915 g. v Moskve," *Voprosy istorii* 12 (1994): 137–150.

53. Eric Lohr, "Enemy Alien Politics within the Russian Empire during World War I" (Ph.D. diss., Harvard University, 1999), 305–344; Russian State Library (RGB), Otdel rukopisei, f. 261, kor. 20, d. 6; RGIA, f. 1405, op. 533, d. 2536 (memoir of Nikolai Kharlamov), ll. 1–15ob (report of Senator Krasheninnikov to the Ruling Senate, September 10, 1915. The government

interpreted the riot as a sign that it needed to scale up its own measures against enemy subjects.

54. GARF, f. 58, op. 5, d. 399, ll. 6, 28, 38, 83–84; GARF, f. 102, Osobyi otdel, op. 245, d. 247, ll. 1–3, 12, 13, 61, 132; GARF, f. 102, op. 245, d. 247; RGVIA, f. 1759, op. 3, d. 1420; GARF, f. 102, II, op. 73, d. 162, l. 132.

55. Nolde, *Russia in the Economic War*, 8.

56. Borchard, "Enemy Private Property," 523. James A. Gathings, *International Law and American Treatment of Alien Enemy Property* (Washington, DC: American Council on Public Affairs, 1940), vi.

57. *Sbornik uzakonenii, rasporiazhenii, raziasnenii i tsirkuliarov ob ogranichenii prav nepriiatel'skikh poddannykh i o pravitel'stvennom nadzore za torgovo-promyshlennymi predpriiatiiami* (Petrograd: Izd. Ministerstva finansov, 1915), 5–6. GARF, f. r-546, op. 1, d. 9, l. 19 (memo compiled for the Brest-Litovsk negotiations, n.d.).

58. The original interpretation defining the "nationality" of a firm was issued on October 7, 1914, by the Minister of Justice: "The nationality [natsional'nost'] of a firm is defined not by the composition of its participants and members of its administration, but by the order of foundation of the firm or partnership. If the charter and statutes regulating its activity was confirmed under Russian laws, then the organization is considered a Russian organization." *Osobyi zhurnal Soveta ministrov*, October 7, 1914.

59. RGIA, f. 23, op. 28, d. 3178, ll. 1–2ob [memo of the liquidation division of the People's Commissariat of Trade and Industry on the situation of firms liquidated according to official decrees, n.d. (late 1917)]. On the Provisional Government's policies, see Leonid Efimovich Shepelev, "Aktsionernoe zakonodatel'stvo Vremennogo pravitel'stva," *Issledovaniia po sotsial'no-politicheskoi istorii Rossii Akademiia nauk SSSR Institut istorii SSSR leningradskoe otdelenie*, Trudy, vol. 12 (Leningrad: Nauka, 1971), 369–381.

60. *Sbornik uzakonenii, rasporiazhenii, raziasnenii i tsirkuliarov*, 25; David Rempel, "The Expropriation of the German Colonists in South Russia during the Great War," *Journal of Modern History* 4, no.1 (1932): 49–67; Karl Lindeman, *Prekrashchenie zemlevladeniia i zemlepol'zovaniia poselian sobstvennikov: ukazy 2 fevralia i 13 dekabria 1915 goda i 10, 15 Iiulia i 19 avgusta 1916 goda i ikh vliianie na ekonomicheskoe sostoianie iuzhnoi Rossii* (Moscow: K. L. Men'shova, 1917).

61. *Sbornik uzakonenii, rasporiazhenii, raziasnenii i tsirkuliarov*, 25.

62. Mark von Hagen, "The Great War and the Mobilization of Ethnicity," in Barnett R. Rubin and Jack Snyder, eds., *Post-Soviet Political Order: Conflict and State-Building* (London and New York: Routledge, 1998), 34–57; Arkadii L. Sidorov et al., *Pervaia mirovaia voina 1914–1918* (Moscow: Nauka, 1968).

63. AVPRI, f. 157, op. 455a, d. 21b, ll. 3–22 (Ministry of Foreign Affairs correspondence with the Ministry of Internal Affairs regarding a new law on rules concerning entry and exit from the empire). The law is published as: "Ob ustanovlenii vremennykh pravil o vydache zagranichnykh pasportov," *Osobyi zhurnal Soveta ministrov,* July 7, 1915 (signed by the tsar, July 14, 1915). Among other changes, this law introduced the requirement of photographs for *zagranpasporta* for the first time. AVPRI, f. 157, op. 455a, d. 21a, ll. 23–325 (petitions and correspondence regarding individuals entering and departing the country, 1915).

64. "Ob ispolnenii voinskoi povinnosti inostrantsami, vstupivshimi v Russkoe poddanstvo," *Osobyi zhurnal Soveta ministrov,* September 13, 1914, in *Osobye zhurnaly Soveta ministrov Rossiiskoi Imperii: 1914 god* (Moscow: Rosspen, 2006), 369–71.

65. RGVIA, f. 2005, op. 1, d. 24, ll. 414–417 (memorandum of the extraordinary meeting of the Council of Ministers at Stavka, June 14, 1915). The document is published in Eric Lohr, "Novye dokumenty o rossiiskoi armii i evreiakh vo vremena Pervoi mirovoi voiny," *Vestnik evreiskogo universiteta,* no. 8 (26) (Moscow, 2003): 245–268.

66. GARF, f. 102, II deloproizvodstvo, op. 75 (1916), l. 33 (*Osobyi zhurnal Soveta ministrov,* March 15, 1916); GARF, f. 215, op. 1, d. 429, l. 14. AVPRI, f. 157, op. 455a, d. 21a, ll. 1–325 (petitions and correspondence on individuals entering and departing the country, 1915); AVPRI, Posol'stvo v Vashingtone, op. 512/1, d. 338, ll. 8–220 (materials on the call-up of military-obligated Russian subjects). For an example of measures on the eve of the war to expand oversight over foreigners living in border regions, see RGVIA, f. 1343, 8, 107, l. 10–11.

67. *Vestnik vremennogo pravitel'stva,* no. 2 (March 7, 1917), 1.

68. "Ob otmene veroispovednykh i natsional'nykh ogranichenii (March 20, 1917)," *Pravo: ezhenedel'naia iuridicheskaia gazeta,* March 30, 1917, 508–509.

69. Rochelle Goldberg Ruthchild, *Equality and Revolution: Women's Rights in the Russian Empire, 1905–1917* (Pittsburg: University of Pittsburg Press, 2000), 2–4, 83–86, and 226–230. Australia and New Zealand extended the vote to women in the 1890s and the Grand Duchy of Finland in the Russian Empire did the same in July 1906.

70. RGVIA, f. 1932, op. 12, d. 67, ll. 1–267; Lohr, *Nationalizing,* 140–142.

71. *Sbornik tsirkuliarov Ministerstva vnutrennikh del za period mart-iiun' 1917 goda* (Petrograd: Tip. Ministerstvo vnutrennikh del, 1917), 68.

72. Ibid., 67.

73. "O priostanovlenii ispolneniia uzakonenii o zemlevladenii i zemlepol'zovanii avstriiskikh, vengerskikh i germanskikh vykhodtsev," *Pravo: ezhenedel'nata iuridicheskaia gazeta* 10 (April 11, 1917): 582–583.

74. See Lohr, *Nationalizing the Russian Empire*, 82–83; GARF, f. r-546, op. 1, d. 70, l. 52 (memo on possible claims by Germany against Russia compiled by the Bolshevik committee on financial questions linked to the Brest-Litovsk treaty negotiations, n.d.).

75. For examples, see GARF, f. r-393, op. 7, dd. 5–6.

76. GARF, f. r-393, op. 7, d. 11, l. 9. The army never formally approved of this decision, but does not seem to have actively opposed it. See RGVIA, f. 2005, op. 1, d. 24, ll. 461–465; Oleg E. Kutafin, *Rossiiskoe grazhdanstvo* (Moscow: Iurist, 2004), 153.

6. SOVIET CITIZENSHIP

1. Sergei Kishkin, *Sovetskoe grazhdanstvo* (Moscow: Narodnyi komissariat iustitsii RSFSR, 1925), 22.

2. Golfo Alexopoulos, "Soviet Citizenship, More or Less: Rights, Emotions, and States of Civic Belonging," *Kritika: Explorations in Russian and Eurasian History* 7, no. 3 (2006): 489.

3. Mark Abramovich Plotkin, *Legal Status of Foreigners in the USSR* (Moscow: USSR Chamber of Commerce, 1934), 19.

4. Vladimir Vladimirovich Egor'ev, Georgii Nikolaevich Lashkevich, Mark Abramovich Plotkin, and Boris Danilovich Rozenblium, *Zakonodatel'stvo i mezhdunarodnye dogovory Soiuza SSR i soiuznykh respublik o pravovom polozhenii inostrannykh fizicheskikh i iuridicheskikh lits* (Moscow: NKIu RSFSR, 1926), 23.

5. Ibid., 93.

6. On the welcoming attitude toward previously oppressed religious groups, see correspondence between diplomatic officials and groups of Molokane and other sects in California about a potential return migration. GARF, f. r-364, op. 1, d. 2, ll. 52–158.

7. Egor'ev et al., *Zakonodatel'stvo*, 22.

8. Kishkin, *Sovetskoe grazhdanstvo*, 6.

9. Egor'ev et al., *Zakonodatel'stvo*, 7.

10. Vsevolod N. Durdenevskii, *Zakon o grazhdanstve Soiuza sovetskikh sotsialisticheskikh respublik*, 52–53, cited in O. E. Kutafin, *Rossiiskoe grazhdanstvo* (Moscow: Iurist, 2004), 149.

11. GARF, f. 3316, op. 2, d. 147, ll. 10–20 (stenogram of the meetings of the VTsIK Constitutional Committee, October 1924).

12. Ibid., l. 27.

13. Rochelle Goldberg Ruthchild, *Equality and Revolution: Women's Rights in the Russian Empire, 1905–1917* (Pittsburg: University of Pittsburg Press, 2000), 2–4, 83–86, and 226–230. The Bolshevik regime also carried for-

ward measures that had been seriously considered under the old regime but not implemented, such as a project to issue wives their own passports and register them separately from their husbands. GARF, f. 102, op. 269, d. 39 (Zhurnaly mezhduvedomstvennogo soveshchaniia, obrazovannogo dlia razsmotreniia proekta 'polozheniia ob udostoverenii lichnosti, ob uchete naseleniia i o pasportakh', 1914–1915).

14. GARF, f.r. 393, op. 1, d. 66, l. 22. One may find *raison d'etat* in these measures. Because mixed marriages tended to be overwhelmingly of Russian women to foreign men, the rule helped to maximize the number of people maintaining RSFSR citizenship and minimize the number of foreigners on Soviet soil, always a central concern of Soviet citizenship policy.

15. Yuri Felshtinskii, "The Legal Foundations of the Immigration and Emigration Policy of the USSR (1917–27)," *Soviet Studies* 34, no. 3 (1982): 329.

16. GARF, f. r-393, op. 43a, d. 1722, l. 2.

17. Felshtinskii, "The Legal," 331.

18. Plotkin, *The Legal Status*, 31–32.

19. In the Treaty of Brest-Litovsk, the Germans demanded the protection of all properties of German and Austrian subjects. Central Powers negotiators in June 1918 conceded that Bolshevik nationalization was a general policy affecting citizens and foreigners alike, and in a basic error allowed any properties acquired by the state prior to July 1, 1918, to be exempted from the strict requirement that all German and Austrian properties be returned to their previous individual owners. The declaration of the nationalization of all industry and frantic nationalization of all remaining firms and shares belonging to Germans and Austrians was announced on June 28 and implemented in chaotic, rapid fashion to beat the July 1 deadline. See Eric Lohr, *Nationalizing the Russian Empire: The Campaign against Enemy Aliens during World War I* (Cambridge: Harvard University Press, 2003), 202; Silvana Malle, *The Economic Organization of War Communism, 1918–1921* (Cambridge: Cambridge University Press, 1985), 59–61; RGIA, f. 23, op. 28, d. 3194, l. 1; GARF, f. r-393, op. 7, d. 1.

20. *Izvestiia Vserossiiskogo tsentral'nogo ispolnitel'nogo komiteta sovetov krestianskikh, rabochikh, kazach'ikh i krasnoarmeiskikh deputatov i Moskovskogo Soveta rabochikh i krasnoarmeiskikh deputatov,* June 7, 1921, no. 196, p. 80. The Cheka was the first secret police organization created under the Bolshevikg on December 20, 1917.

21. Alon Rachamimov, *POWs and the Great War: Captivity on the Eastern Front* (Oxford, New York: Berg, 2002), 38.

22. Rachamimov, *POWs and the Great War,* 192; Reinhard Nachtigal, "The Repatriation and Reception of Returning Prisoners of War, 1918–22," in

Matthew Stibbe, ed., *Captivity, Forced Labour and Forced Migration in Europe during the First World War* (London and New York: Routledge, 2009), 168.

23. Rachamimov, *POWs and the Great War*, 193–194. Moreover, while Germany had installed a friendly government in Ukraine in 1918, it was in no rush to force the repatriation of German and the much more numerous Austrian POWs from there because of the strategic importance of Ukrainian grain and the significant role Austro-Hungarian POWs had adopted as agrarian laborers in Ukraine, where agricultural labor was in short supply. Nachtigal, "The Repatriation," 161.

24. Ibid., 162.

25. Ibid., 163.

26. Rachamimov, *POWs and the Great War*, 192.

27. For details on the agreements, see *Prava i obiazannosti inostrantsev, optantov i bezhentsev po mezhdunarodnym dogovoram i soglasheniiam i po postanovleniiam sovetskoi vlasti s oktiabria 1917 po 1921 g.* (Petrograd: Tip. Otdela upravleniia petrogubispolkoma, 1921), 29–33; Zoia S. Bocharova, *Russkie bezhentsy: problemy rasseleniia, vozvrashcheniia na rodinu, uregulirovaniia pravovogo polozheniia (1920–1930-e gody): sbornik dokumentov i materialov* (Moscow: ROSSPEN, 2004), 21.

28. Edward F. Willis, *Herbert Hoover and the Russian Prisoners of World War I* (Stanford: Stanford University Press, 1951), 13–14.

29. Hannes Leidinger and Verena Moritz, *Gefangenschaft, Revolution, Heimkehr: Die Bedeutung der Kriegsgefangenenproblematik für die Geschichte des Kommunismus in Mittel- und Osteuropa 1917–1920* (Vienna: Böhlau Verlag, 2003); Inge Pardon and Waleri Shurawljow, eds., *Lager, Front oder Heimat. Deutsche Kriegsgefangene in Sowjetrussland 1917 bis 1920*, 2 vols. (Munich: LKG Saur, 1994).

30. GARF, f. r-393, op. 7, d. 3.

31. Arkady Lavrovich Sidorov et al., *Pervaia mirovaia voina 1914–1918* (Moscow: Nauka, 1968); Mark von Hagen, "The Great War and the Mobilization of Ethnicity," in Barnett R. Rubin and Jack Snyder, eds., *Post-Soviet Political Order: Conflict and State-Building* (London and New York: Routledge, 1998), 34–57.

32. John F. N. Bradley, *The Czechoslovak Legion in Russia, 1914–1920* (Boulder and New York: Columbia University Press, 1991).

33. By Nachtigal's estimates, this included about 13,000 Austrian POWs via Ukraine and 7,000 via Vladivostok in 1921–22. See Nachtigal, "The Repatriation," 166.

34. *Texts of the Russian "Peace"* (Washington DC: GPO, 1918), 8; "*Soglashenie mezhdu RSFSR i Germaniei ob otpravke na rodinu voennoplennykh i in-*

ternirovannykh grazhdanskikh lits obeikh storon," in *Sovetsko-Germanskie otnosheniia ot peregovorov v Brest-Litovske do podpisaniia rapall'skogo dogovora: Sbornik dokumentov* 2 (Moscow: Izd. politicheskoi literatury, 1968): 178–180.

35. GARF, f. 1318 op. 1 d. 1025, ll. 241. A proposal was discussed early in 1918 to grant an amnesty to Ukrainians, Poles, Lithuanians, Latvians, Jews, Muslims, and others native to the region of the theatre of military activity who had been deported to the interior of the country for "so-called treasonous activities."

36. GARF, f. 1318 op. 1 d. 1025, ll. 217–230; GARF, f. 393, op. 1, d. 66, l. 13 (Tsentroplenbezh to NKVD, June 10, 1918).

37. GARF, f. r-393, op. 1, d. 66, l. 3. (NKVD circular, signed by Unshlikht, June 6, 1918). This order specified that such individuals should be sent to the nearest concentration camp.

38. Tomas Balkelis, "In Search of a Native Realm: The Return of World War One Refugees to Lithuania, 1918–24," in Nick Baron and Peter Gatrell, eds., *Homelands: War, Population and Statehood in Eastern Europe and Russia, 1918–1924* (London: Anthem Press, 2004), 77; GARF, f. r-393, op. 27, d. 25, l. 305.

39. Sarah Wambaugh, *Plebiscites since the World War, with a Collection of Official Documents*, 2 vols. (Washington, DC: Carnegie Endowment for International Peace, 1933).

40. George Ginsburgs, "Option of Nationality in Soviet Treaty Practice, 1917–1924," *The American Journal of International Law* 55, no. 4 (1961), 924.

41. *Prava i obiazannosti inostrantsev*, 2–3.

42. GARF, f. r-393, op. 43a, d. 1722, l. 5 (NKVD circular, November 2, 1922); Felshtinskii, "The Legal Foundations," 339.

43. Latvia and Estonia frequently tried to deny permission to Jewish optants wanting to enter their countries. GARF, f. 1318, op. 1, d. 679, l. 4 (Narkomat po delam natsional'nostei RSFSR to NKID, August 22, 1921).

44. The treaty included the term *Rzech Pospolita,* referring to the Polish-Lithuanian state prior to the partitions of 1772–95. *Prava i obiazannosti inostrantsev,* 4–7.

45. *Prava i obiazannosti inostrantsev* 4, 6–7; GARF, f. r-393, op. 21, d. 1, l. 1 (NKVD to Sibrevkom, n.d., "The procedures for optation of Polish citizenship").

46. *Prava i obiazannosti inostrantsev*, 5, 40.

47. See GARF, f. r-393, op. 27, d. 26, l. 274–276 (NKVD to VTsIK RSFSR, May 1, 1921).

48. There was some diversity in this requirement. The Polish-Soviet treaty did not compel optants to depart, but gave the two governments the power to

compel them to depart. If they exercised this right, optants were given six months to leave. Most of the other agreements required all optants to leave the country within one year from the date of the granting of the optation petition. See Ginsburgs, "Option of Nationality," 934.

49. It was possible to appeal for extensions of the deadline. The Soviet-Latvian agreement was the only one that lacked a clause requiring the optant to depart by a certain deadline.

50. GARF, f. r-393, op. 43a, d. 1699, ll. 1–11 (case of one hundred "kochuiush-chikh Serbov" families).

51. Fridtjof Nansen, *Conference of Government Representatives to Consider Proposals for the Settlement of Refugees in Overseas Countries, Armenian and Russian Refugees* (Geneva: Imp. Kundig, 1927); Jane Carey, "Some Aspects of Statelessness since World War I," *The American Political Science Review* 40, no. 1 (1946): 115.

52. GARF r-393, op. 27, d. 26, l. 326 (Rules for Estonians in the Red Army opting for Estonian citizenship, May 2, 1920). In order to prevent this, the Latvian-Soviet agreement explicitly noted that optants were to be freed from all military service requirements.

53. GARF, f. r-393, op. 43a, d. 1466, l. 117 (Inotdel OGPU to NKVD, February 26, 1926).

54. GARF, f. r-393, op. 27, d. 27, l. 13 (Tsentroevak to Moscow Gorsovet, September 1, 1921); GARF, f. r-393, op. 21, d. 1, l. 19.

55. GARF, f. 1318 op. 1, d. 830, ll. 5–7. For comparative perspective, see Peter Sahlins, *Unnaturally French: Foreign Citizens in the Old Regime and After* (Ithaca: Cornell University Press, 2004).

56. GARF, f. r-393, op. 27, d. 27, l. 66 (NKVD report, September 8, 1921). The same file contains angry protests from Estonia about the denials and the slow pace of allowing individuals approved to opt for Estonian citizenship to actually leave the country.

57. GARF, f. r-393, op. 21, d. 1, l. 33–35.

58. On the growing efficacy of the border police and controls over border crossings, see Andrea Chandler, *Institutions of Isolation: Border Controls in the Soviet Union and Its Successor States, 1917–1993* (Montreal: McGill-Queen's University Press, 1998).

59. The number of individuals identified as "Russian" by place of birth in the United States increased by more than seven times from 1910 (57,900) to 1920 (392,000). See Vladimir M. Kabuzan, *Emigratsiia i reemigratsiia v Rossii v XVIII-nachale XX vek* (Moscow: Nauka, 1998), 219.

60. *Russkaia voennaia emigratsiia 20-kh–40-kh godov: dokumenty i materialy*, vol. 3 *Vozvrashchenie* (Moscow: Geia, 1998), vol. 1, 17–54, 348–350.

61. *Russkaia voennaia*, 9–13. See the editorial by editor in chief Iu. Steklov in *Izvestiia*, November 23, 1921.

62. *Russkaia voennaia,* 13.

63. "Postanovlenie VTsIK, November 3, 1921," in *Russkaia voennaia,* 70–71.

64. *Russkaia voennaia,* 75–80, 107–108; GARF, f. r-393, op. 43a, d. 9, l. 37.

65. Bocharova, *Russkie bezhentsy,* 22.

66. Paul Robinson, *The White Russian Army in Exile, 1920–1941* (New York: Oxford University Press, 2002), 75.

67. GARF, f. r-364, op. 3, d. 1. For example, after long negotiations, 1,500 Cossack followers of Nekrasov during the civil war were denied entry into the country due to a mix of official hostility to their return and concerns about the expenses.

68. Bocharova, *Russkie bezhentsy,* 22.

69. Ibid., 23.

70. Postanovlenie SNK "O konfiskatsii vsego dvizhimogo imushchestva grazhdan, bezhavshikh za predely RSFSR," *Dekrety Sovetskoi vlasti,* vol. 11 (Moscow: Gos. izd. politicheskoi literatury, 1977), 245–246.

71. Zoia S. Bocharova, "Dokumenty o pravovom polozhenii russkoi emigratsii 1920–30-x godov," in *Istochniki po istorii adaptatsii rossiiskikh emigrantov v XIX–XX vv., sbornik statei* (Moscow: RAN, Institut rossiiskoi istorii, 1997), 63–64; George Ginsburgs, "The Soviet Union and the Problem of Refugees and Displaced Persons 1917–1956," *American Journal of International Law* 51, no. 2 (1957), 329–330; *Russkaia voennaia,* 81.

72. Vladimir Vladimirovich Egor'ev, *Pravovoe polozhenie fizicheskikh i iuridicheskikh lits SSSR za granitsei (sistematizirovannye materialy s kommentariiami)* (Moscow: Narodnyi komissariat iustitsii RSFSR, 1926), 30–35.

73. Timothy A. Taracouzio, *The Soviet Union and International Law: A Study Based on the Legislation, Treaties, and Foreign Relations of the Union of Socialist Soviet Republics* (New York: Macmillan, 1935), 121; Plotkin, *The Legal Status,* 22.

74. GARF, f. r-393, op. 41, d. 18 (protocols from the sessions of the presidium of VTsIK on naturalization and on the implementation of the VTsIK decree of December 15, 1921 on the deprivation of Russian citizenship).

75. Peter Gatrell, "War, Population Displacement and State Formation in the Russian Borderlands, 1914–1924," in Baron and Gatrell, eds., *Homelands,* 26; Iurii Aleksandrovich Poliakov, ed., *Naselenie Rossii v XX veke,* vol. 1 (Moscow: Rosspen, 2000), 134–142; Bocharova, *Russkie bezhentsy,* 20.

76. GARF, f. r-393, op. 43a, d. 1722, ll. 3–4 (NKVD circular to governors on rules for repatriates returning as a result of amnesty according to the decree of December 15, 1921).

77. Ginsburgs, "The Soviet Union," 329.

78. Bocharova, *Russkie bezhentsy.*

79. Ibid., 18–19.

80. Mass denaturalization became a prominent tool of extremist regimes in interwar Europe. Nazi Germany and Romania both denaturalized their resident Jewish populations in the 1930s. See Joshua Starr, "Jewish Citizenship in Rumania (1878–1940)," *Jewish Social Studies* 3, no. 1 (1941): 57–58; Martin Dean, "The Development and Implementation of Nazi Denaturalization and Confiscation Policy up to the Eleventh Decree to the Reich Citizenship Law," *Holocaust Genocide Studies* 16, no. 2 (2002): 217–242.

81. Galina Iakovlevna Tarle, "Emigratsionnoe zakonodatel'stvo Rossii do i posle 1917 goda (analiz istochnikov)," in *Istochniki po istorii adaptatsii*, 51; Iurii A. Poliakov, *Sovetskaia strana posle okonchaniia grazhdanskoi voiny: territoriia i naselenie* (Moscow: Nauka, 1986), 119.

82. Tarle, "Emigratsionnoe zakonodatel'stvo," 52; Larisa Shatsillo, "'Eto byla strannaia mera': O vysylke iz Sovetskoi Rossii predstavitelei intelligentsii v 1922 g.," *Rossiiskie vesti*. Moscow, no. 49 (March 10, 1994), 6.

83. See the essays by Chirot and Reid in Daniel Chirot and Anthony Reid, eds., *Essential Outsiders: Chinese and Jews in the Modern Transformation of Southeast Asia and Central Europe* (Seattle and London: University of Washington Press, 1997).

84. GARF, f. r-393, op. 43a, d. 9, l. 200 (Zampred GPU Iagoda to NKID Zamnarkoma Litvinov, secret, December 26, 1922).

85. Chandler, *Institutions of Isolation*.

86. See Golfo Alexopoulos, *Stalin's Outcasts: Aliens, Citizens, and the Soviet State, 1926–1936* (Cornell: Cornell University Press, 2003).

87. Alexopoulos, "Soviet Citizenship," 493.

88. Ibid., 488.

89. GARF, f. 102, op. 269, d. 39 (Zhurnaly mezhduvedomstvennogo soveshchaniia, obrazovannogo dlia razsmotreniia proekta 'polozheniia ob udostoverenii lichnosti, ob uchete naseleniia i o pasportakh', 1914–1915). This inter-departmental committee was also seriously considering unifying the internal passport with the *zagranpasport* to creat a single document for all identification and control over movement.

90. Marc Garcelon, "Colonizing the Subject: The Genealogy and Legacy of the Soviet Internal Passport," in Jane Caplan and John Torpey, eds., *Documenting Individual Identity: The Development of State Practices in the Modern World* (Princeton: Princeton University Press, 2001), 91.

91. Al'bert Baburin, "K predistorii sovetskogo pasporta (1917–1932)" *Neprikosnovennyi zapas* 2 (2009): 144–147.

92. GARF, f. r-393, op. 27, d. 18, ll. 14–17, 37.

93. Kronid Liubarskii, "Pasportnaia sistema i sistema propiski v Rossii," *Rossiiskii biulleten' po pravam cheloveka*, no. 2 (1994), 14–26.

94. Chandler, *Institutions of Isolation.*

95. GARF, f. r-393, op. 43a, d. 1700; GARF, f. r-393, op. 43a, d. 1467, ll. 6–19.

96. GARF, f. 3316, op. 2, d. 147, l. 61 (stenogram of the meetings of the VTsIK constitutional committee, October 1924); GARF, f. r-393, op. 33, d. 24.

97. Bocharova, *Russkie bezhentsy,* 23.

98. Chandler, *Institutions of Isolation,* 69.

99. GARF, f. r-393, op. 43a, d. 1466, l. 117 (Inotdel OGPU to NKVD, February 26, 1926).

100. GARF, f. 3316, op. 2, d. 147, ll. 1–3 (stenogram of the meetings of the VTsIK constitutional committee, October 1924).

101. Terry Martin, *The Affirmative Action Empire: Nations and Nationalism in the Soviet Union, 1923-1939* (Ithaca: Cornell University Press, 2001).

102. GARF, f. 3316, op. 2, d. 147, l. 32.

103. Ibid., ll. 32–37.

104. Ibid., l. 48.

105. "Polozhenie o soiuznom grazhdanstve," text in Kishkin, *Sovetskoe grazhdanstvo,* 93.

106. Mikhail O. Reikhel', *SSSR: ocherki konstitutsionnykh vzaimootnoshenii sovetskikh respublik* (Kharkov: Narodnyi komissariat iustitsii, 1925), 128–147; S. A. Kotliarevskii, *SSSR i soiuznye respubliki* (Moscow: Gosudarstvennoe izdatel'stvo, 1924), 12–17.

107. Martin, *The Affirmative Action Empire.*

108. GARF, f. 3316, op. 2, d. 147, l. 60.

109. Ibid., ll. 72–73.

110. There were also large numbers of temporary visitors, as many as 100,000 between 1917 and 1939. Because very few tried to naturalize or immigrate, they mostly fall outside the scope of this analysis. For an excellent study, see Michael David-Fox, *Showcasing the Great Experiment: Cultural Diplomacy and Western Visitors to the Soviet Union, 1921–1941* (Oxford, New York: Oxford University Press, 2011).

111. *Sbornik dekretov, 1917–1918* (Moscow: Gos izd., 1920), no. 56, "O prave ubezhishcha," 28 (15), March 1918.

112. Sergei Zhuravlev, *"Malenkie liudi" i "bol'shaia istoriia": inostrantsy moskovskogo elektrozavoda v sovetskom obshchestve 1920-kh–1930-kh gg.* (Moscow: ROSSPEN, 2000), 26; Kutafin, *Rossiiskoe grazhdanstvo,* 157. In part, this was linked to a Piedmont policy in the Karelian autonomous region and a VTsIK decree of March 16, 1925, that gave the TsIK of the Karelian republic the right to grant personal amnesties to Karelian refugees in Finland, allowing them to return and take Soviet citizenship.

113. For example, see GARF, f. 1318, op. 1, d. 34, l. 1 (report from the head of the military-naval control of the northern fleet, June 19, 1918, complaining about Finns entering Murmansk with documents given by the Narkomnats).

114. Tarle, "Emigratsionnoe zakonodatel'stvo," 42–46.

115. On the concessions policy, see Anthony C. Sutton, *Western Technology and Soviet Economic Development 1917–1930*, 3 vols. (Stanford: Stanford University Press, 1968–1973); N. Liubimov, "The Soviets and Foreign Concessions," *Foreign Affairs* 9, no. 1 (1930); GARF, f. r-393, op. 43a, d. 3 (protocols of the STO on concessions); Jane Degras, ed., *Soviet Documents on Foreign Policy, vol. 1, 1917–24* (New York: Oxford University Press, 1951) 19–20; Vladimir Butkovskii, *Inostrannye kontsessii v narodnom khoziaistve SSSR* (Leningrad: Gos. izd., 1928); N. P. Dergachev, *Kontsessii* (Leningrad: Rabochee izdatel'stvo, 1925). I. M. Bernshtein, *Pravovye usloviia kontsessionnoi deiatel'nosti v SSSR. sistematizirovannye materialy s kommentariiami* (Moscow: Gos. iurid. izd. RSFSR, 1930).

116. RTsKhIDNI, f. 17, op. 2, d. 126, ll. 25, 57–58 (stenograph of the meeting of the Plenum of the Central Committee of the Communist Party, April 2, 1924).

117. GARF, f. r-364, op. 1, d. 4, ll. 147–154; GARF, f. r-364, op. 3, d. 1, l. 33.

118. GARF, f. r-364, op. 3, d. 1, l. 67. On the STO, see Derek Watson, "STO (The Council of Labour and Defence) in the 1930s," *Europe-Asia Studies* 50, no. 7 (1998): 1203–1227.

119. GARF, f. r-364, op. 3, d. 1, ll. 26–31.

120. GARF, f. r-364, op. 7, d. 4, ll. 343–344.

121. GARF, f. 1318, op. 1, d. 42, l. 17.

122. Martin, *The Affirmative Action Empire,* 316.

123. Zhuravlev, "*Malenkie liudi,*" 26; GARF, f. r-364, op. 1, d. 4, l. 162; Ian Matley, "The Dispersal of the Ingrian Finns," *Slavic Review* 38, no. 1 (1979): 1–16.

124. Clarence Clausen, "Dr. Fridtjof Nansen's Work as High Commissioner of the League of Nations" (Ph.D. diss., University of Illinois, 1932).

125. GARF, f., r-364, op. 6, d. 3, ll. 45–46.

126. NARA, RG 59, M316, roll 128 (decimal files 861.55–861.56, 1910–1929), 44–55.

127. GARF, f. r-364, op. 3, d. 1, l. 133 (resolution of the STO committee on immigration and emigration, June 30, 1924).

128. Andrea Graziosi, "Foreign Workers in Soviet Russia, 1920–40: Their Experience and Their Legacy," *International Labor and Working-Class History* 33 (1988): 41. Several of the larger-scale immigrations and return migrations, including the Armenians, Finns, Galicians, and returning Russian White Army veterans were not handled by the STO and thus do not appear in these statistics.

129. NARA, RG 59, M316, roll 128 (decimal files 861.55–861.56, 1910–1929), pp. 45–60.

130. GARF, f. r-364, op. 3, d. 1, l. 122.

131. Ibid., l. 74.

132. Ibid., l. 343.

133. GARF, f. r-364, op. 7, d. 4, l. 103 ("Nekotorye vyvody iz trekhletnei raboty postoiannoi komissii STO po immigratsii," 1925).

134. Kathleen Innes, *The Story of Nansen and the League of Nations* (London: Friends Peace Committee, 1931), 32. Innes estimates 150,000 Armenian refugees in Syria, 120,000 in Greece, and 50,000 in other parts of Europe in 1923.

135. GARF, f. r-364, op. 3, d. 1, l. 26.

136. *League of Nations, Russian, Armenian, Assyrian, Assyro-Chaldean and Turkish Refugees.* Report submitted by the sixth committee of the assembly, Geneva, October 6, 1932. Another 1,783 Armenians were resettled from France by bilateral agreement. See Laurette McKendree, *Nansen Refugees* (M.A. thesis, University of Michigan, Ann Arbor, 1944), 33.

137. On the Piedmont strategy, see Martin, *The Affirmative Action Empire*, 8–9, 36.

138. Dekret SNK RSFSR, August 22, 1921 in Egor'ev et al., *Zakonodatel'stvo*, 23, 562.

139. GARF, f. r-393, op. 1, d. 66, l. 9 (Moscow NKVD memo, May 13, 1918); GARF, f. r-393, op. 7, d. 2, ll. 4–8.

140. Kutafin, *Rossiiskoe grazhdanstvo*, 147; Kishkin, *Sovetskoe*, 23; "Dekret SNK RSFSR, August 22, 1921," in Egor'ev et al., *Zakonodatel'stvo i mezh-dunarodnye dogovory*, 23.

141. GARF, f. r-393, op. 7, d. 4, l. 40.

142. On this point, see Alexopoulos, "Soviet Citizenship," 494.

143. *Sobranie uzakonenii i rasporiazhenii pravitel'stva dal'ne-vostochnoi respubliki.*

144. GARF, f. 1318, op. 1, d. 148, l. 50 (Postanovleniia VTsIK ob uproshenii perekhoda Koreitsev v grazhdanstvo SSSR, 1921–24).

145. Martin, *The Affirmative Action Empire*, 317.

146. Boris D. Pak, *Bor'ba rossiiskikh koreitsev za nezavisimost' Korei, 1905–1919* (Moscow: IV RAN, 2009), 339–349.

147. Ginsburgs, "The Citizenship Status," 18.

148. GARF, f. 1318, op. 1, d. 148, l. 50 (NKVD otdel upr. Dal'revkoma to VTsIK, January 5, 1924).

149. George Ginsburgs, "The Citizenship Status of Koreans in Pre-Revolutionary Russia and the Early Years of the Soviet Regime," *Journal of Korean Affairs* 5, no. 2 (1975), 18. The decline in naturalization was likely also in part a result of the Korean independence movement and the resulting unwillingness

of Koreans in Russia to endanger their ability to return to a future independent homeland.

150. Martin, *The Affirmative Action Empire*, 323–324; Jonathan Bone, "Socialism in a Far Country: Stalinist Population Politics and the Making of the Soviet Far East, 1929–1939" (Ph.D. diss., University of Chicago, 2003).

151. GARF, f. r-393, op. 43a, d. 1651, l. 77 (Dokladnaia zapiska. Sekretno. Nachal'nik administrativnogo otdela NKVD L. P. D'iakonova, September 29, 1928); Henning Bauer, Andreas Kappeler, and Brigitte Roth, eds., *Die Nationalitäten des Russischen Reiches in der Volkszählung von 1897. Quellen und Studien zur Geschichte des östlichen Europa* 32, vol. B. (Stuttgart: F. Steiner, 1991), 211.

152. Jon Jacobson, *When the Soviet Union Entered World Politics* (Berkeley: University of California Press, 1994), 209.

153. *Chetyrnadtsatyi s"ezd Vsesoiuznoi kommunisticheskoi partii: stenograficheskii otchet* (Moscow: Gos. izd., 1926): 20.

154. Richard Day, *Leon Trotsky and the Politics of Economic Isolation* (Cambridge: Cambridge University Press, 1973), 158.

155. Ibid., 119.

156. Alexander Erlich, *The Soviet Industrialization Debate, 1924–1928* (Cambridge: Harvard University Press, 1960).

157. John Sontag, "The Soviet War Scare of 1926–27," *The Russian Review* 34 no. 1 (1975): 6.

158. Sontag, "The Soviet War Scare," 70–75. One of the biggest barriers to the concessions policy was the issue of Bolshevik expropriation of foreign businesses and tsarist-era debt. Trotsky, Sokolnikov, Chicherin, and other opponents of economic isolation thus argued for serious negotiations to ameliorate the issue through at least a partial compensation package. See Kim Oosterlinck and John S. Landon-Lane, "Hope Springs Eternal—French Bondholders and the Soviet Repudiation (1915–1919)," *Review of Finance* 10 (2006): 507–535; Leo Pasvolsky, *Russian Debts and Russian Reconstruction; A Study of the Relation of Russia's Foreign Debts to Her Economic Recovery* (New York: McGraw-Hill, 1924), 236; Louis Fischer, *Oil Imperialism: The International Struggle for Petroleum* (New York: International, 1926), 91.

159. N. S. Simonov, "'Krepit' oboronu strany sovetov' ('voennaia trevoga' 1927 goda i ee posledstviia)," *Otechestvennaia istoriia* 3 (1996): 155–161; L. N. Nikolaev, "Ugroza voiny protiv SSSR (konets 20-kh—nachalo 30-kh gg.): real'nost' ili mif?" in *Sovetskaia vneshniaia politika, 1917–1945* (Moscow: Mezhdunarodnye otnosheniia, 1992), 63–90; L. N. Nezhinskii, "Byla li voennaia ugroza SSSR v kontse 20-kh—nachale 30-kh godov?" *Istoriia SSSR* 6 (1990): 14–30; A. V. Golubev, *'Esli mir obrushitsia na nashu respubliku':*

sovetskoe obshchestvo i vneshniaia ugroza v 1920–1940-e gg. (Moscow: Kuchkovo pole, 2008). For an explanation of why Stalin pushed the war scare, see James Harris, "Encircled by Enemies: Stalin's Perceptions of the Capitalist World, 1918–1941," *Journal of Strategic Studies* 30, no. 3 (2007): 515–521.

160. Jacobson, *When the Soviet Union*, 242; Hiroaki Kuromiya, *Stalin's Industrial Revolution: Politics and Workers, 1928–1932* (Cambridge: Cambridge University Press, 1988), 12–17.

161. Jacobson, *When the Soviet Union*, 245.

162. NARA, U.S. State Department: Records Relating to Relations with the Soviet Union, 861.602/210 "Background Report," 1–23; Simon Liberman, *Building Lenin's Russia* (Chicago: University of Chicago Press, 1945), 178–179; Armand Hammer, *The Quest of the Romanoff Treasure* (New York: W. F. Payson, 1932), 124.

163. NARA, U.S. State Department: Records Relating to Relations with the Soviet Union, 861.602/210 "Lena Goldfields, Ltd." File no. 18.

164. Sutton, *Western Technology*, vol. 2, 28.

165. Vladimir Gsovski, *Soviet Civil Law: Private Rights and Their Background under the Soviet Regime* (Ann Arbor: University of Michigan Law School, 1948), 364; Adam J. Albin, "Joint Venture Law in the Soviet Union: The 1920s and the 1980s," *Northwestern Journal of Law and International Business* 9 (1989): 636.

166. M. Osmova and O. Stulov, "Inostrannyi kapital u nas novoe, khorosho zabytoe staroe?," *Kommunist* 18 (1990), 51–59; V. I. Kasianenko, "Leninskie idei ob aktsionernom predprinimatel'stve," *Voprosy istorii KPSS* 9 (1990), 17–34.

167. For the most comprehensive analysis of the TACs, and an attempt to assess their impact, see: Sutton, *Western Technology*, vol. 2.

168. Sabine Dullin, "Les protecteurs. Le rôle des guards-frontières dans la surveillance des frontiers occidentals de l'URSS (1917–1939)," in Sophie Cœuré and Sabine Dullin, eds., *Frontières du communisme. Mythologies et réalités de la division de l'Europe, de la révolution d'Octobre au mur de Berlin* (Paris: La Découverte, 2007), 379–405.

169. GARF, f. r-393, op. 43a, d. 1081, ll. 101 and entire file.

170. GARF, f. r-393, op. 43a, d. 1653. Ibid., l. 39.

171. Kutafin, *Rossiisskoe grazhdanstvo*, 157.

172. GARF, f. r-393, op. 43a, d. 1653. Ibid., ll. 43–48.

173. GARF, f. r-393, op. 43a, d. 1653, ll. 3–34.

174. GARF, f. r-393, op. 43a, d. 1653. Ibid., l. 34.

175. GARF, f. r-393, op. 43a, d. 1651, ll. 20–25; GARF, f. r-364, op. 3, d. 1, l. 278.

176. GARF, f. r-393, op. 43a, d. 1651, ll. 5–16.
177. Ibid., l. 77. The restrictions imposed to save a small amount of hard currency had real personal costs. For example, Zinaida Nikolaevna took ill with a rare case of brain inflammation. She wanted to go to France, where her two brothers lived and could support her. The brothers were artists lacking enough cash to send her assistance in the Soviet Union, but they could provide her with a place to live while she visited a specialist there. In her application, she included a letter of support from the French embassy. The OGPU denied the application on the grounds that the petitioner would leave with hard currency. GARF, f. r-393, op. 43a, d. 1698, l. 427.
178. Zhuravlev, *"Malenkie liudi,"* 27.
179. Graziosi, "Foreign Workers," 39–40.
180. Ibid., 43.
181. Ibid., 49.
182. See Andrey Shlyakhter's forthcoming University of Chicago dissertation tentatively titled: "Smugglers and Commissars: The Making of the Soviet Border Strip, 1917–1939" and his "La contrebande aux frontières de l'URSS dans les années 1920: méthodes d'évaluation et mesures de lutte," in Cœuré and Dullin, eds., *Frontières du communisme,* 406–427.
183. GARF, f. r-393, op. 43a, d. 1653, l. 20.
184. Ibid., ll. 1–42; GARF, f. r-393, op. 41, dd. 9–17.

CONCLUSION

1. The French Revolution, Peter Sahlins has convincingly shown, came in the midst of fundamental changes that started in the mid-eighteenth century and concluded in 1818. The American Revolution was an important event in the history of American citizenship, but certainly not transformative. See Peter Sahlins, *Unnaturally French: Foreign Citizens in the Old Regime and After* (Ithaca: Cornell University Press, 2004).
2. See the following landmark articles: Gijs Kessler, "The Passport System and State Control over Population Flows in the Soviet Union, 1932–1940," *Cahiers du Monde russe* 42, nos. 2-4 (2001), 478; David Shearer, "Elements Near and Alien: Passportization, Policing, and Identity in the Stalinist State, 1932–1952," *The Journal of Modern History* 76 (2004): 835–881; Nathalie Moine, "Passeportisation, statistique des migrations et contrôle de l'identité sociale," *Cahiers du monde russe* 38, no. 4 (1997): 587–600. Kessler and Shearer argue that the analogy with serfdom is incorrect because the Soviet passports aimed to register and control urban populations and fence off cities and border areas from a rural influx, which was very different from the imperial aim of maintaining peasant ties to the village

commune even if they moved to a city. This is correct for the postemancipation era. I think that the analogy holds better when comparing to the era of serfdom. The Soviet passport system marked much of the country out of bounds for peasants, closing off the main escape route from the coercive labor system of the collective farms, thus *de facto* serving the same function as the pre-1860 passport system, as a means to hold peasants to their localities.

3. Mervyn Matthews, *The Passport Society: Controlling Movement in Russia and the USSR* (Boulder: Westview Press, 1993), 27–33.

4. Ibid., 35.

5. Shearer, "Elements Near and Alien," 839.

6. See article 3 of the April 22, 1931, decree which reiterated that "every person in the territory of the USSR is regarded as a citizen of the USSR in so far as his citizenship of a foreign state is not proved."

7. Tim Tzouliadis, *The Forsaken: From The Great Depression to the Gulags: Hope and Betrayal in Stalin's Russia* (London: Little, Brown, 2008), 48–50, 62–64, 104–105; Sylvia R. Margulies, *The Pilgrimage to Russia: The Soviet Union and the Treatment of Foreigners, 1924–1937* (Madison: The University of Wisconsin Press, 1968), 108–111.

8. O. E. Kutafin, *Rossiiskoe grazhdanstvo* (Moscow: Iurist, 2004), 159.

9. The citizenship law of April 22, 1931, had reasserted that foreign workers and peasants were granted "all the political rights of USSR citizens." M. A. Plotkin, *Legal Status of Foreigners in the USSR* (Moscow: USSR Chamber of Commerce, 1934), 12.

10. Keith Sword, *Deportation and Exile: Poles in the Soviet Union, 1939–48* (New York: St. Martin's Press, 2004), 1–2.

11. Nora Levin, *The Jews in the Soviet Union since 1917* (New York: NYU Press, 1988), 348, 372.

12. Catherine Gousseff, "Des migrations de sortie de guerre qui reconfigurent la frontière: ouverture et refermeture de l'URSS avant la guerre froide," in Sophie Cœuré and Sabine Dullin, eds., *Frontières du communisme. Mythologies et réalités de la division de l'Europe, de la révolution d'Octobre au mur de Berlin* (Paris: La Découverte, 2007), 428–442.

13. Yaacov Ro'i, *The Struggle for Soviet Jewish Emigration, 1948–1967* (Cambridge: Cambridge University Press), 252–261.

14. Bruce F. Adams, "Reemigration from Western China to the USSR, 1954–1962," in Cynthia Buckley and Blair Ruble, eds., *Migration, Homeland, and Belonging in Eurasia* (Washington, DC: Woodrow Wilson Center Press, 2008), 183–202.

15. Gennadii P. Dol'zhenko, *Istoriia turizma v dorevoliutsionnoi Rossii i SSSR* (Rostov: Izd. Rostovskogo universiteta, 1988), 150; Dennis B. Shaw, "The

Soviet Union," in Derek Hall, ed., *Tourism and Economic Development in Eastern Europe and the Soviet Union* (London: Belhaven Press, 1991), 137.

16. Anne E. Gorsuch and Diane P. Koenker, eds., *Turizm: The Russian and East European Tourist under Capitalism and Socialism* (Ithaca: Cornell University Press, 2006); V. E. Bagdasarian, ed., *Sovetskoe zazerkale: inostrannyi turizm v SSSR v 1930–1980-e gody* (Moscow: Forum, 2007).

17. Alan Dowty, *Closed Borders: The Contemporary Assault on Freedom of Movement* (New Haven: Yale University Press, 1987), 74–75.

18. Shawn Salmon, "To the Land of the Future: A History of Intourist and Travel to the Soviet Union, 1929–1991" (Ph.D. diss., University of California, Berkeley, 2008).

19. Judith Matz and Margery Sanford, *Separated Soviet Families* (Miami: South Florida Conference on Soviet Jewry, 1976).

20. G. A. Razina, N. I. Rotova, and Iurii V. Sigachev, "Ne priznaem vashego prava na akt nasiliia nad nami": k istorii lisheniia sovetskogo grazhdanstva g. P. Vishnevskoi i M. L. Rostropovicha," *Istoricheskii Arkhiv* 5 (1993): 161–186.

21. Hall, ed., *Tourism and Economic Development*, 22–26.

22. Victor Zaslavsky and Robert Brym, *Soviet Jewish Emigration and Soviet Nationality Policy* (London: Macmillan, 1983), 1, 12.

23. Oleg V. Budnitskii and Olga V. Belova, eds., *Evreiskaia emigratsiia iz Rossii, 1885-2005* (Moscow: ROSSPEN, 2008).

24. Despite this constitutional right, local authorities have managed to continue to sharply limit the legal ability of citizens to settle where they wish. See Matthew Light, "Regional Migration Policies in Post-Soviet Russia: From Pervasive Control to Insecure Freedom" (Ph.D. diss., Yale University, 2006).

25. Ibid., 74.

26. Rossiiskaia Federatsiia, Federal'naia sluzhba gosudarstvennoi sluzhby. http://www.gks.ru/wps/wcm/connect/rosstat/rosstatsite/main/population /demography/# and http://www.gks.ru/dbscripts/Cbsd/DBInet.cgi. Both accessed March 26, 2012.

27. Migration Policy Institute, Migration Information Source. Accessed March 21, 2012. http://www.migrationinformation.org/feature/display.cfm ?ID=62.

28. Light, "Regional Migration," 9; Lowell Barrington, Erik S. Herron, and Brian D. Silver, "The Motherland Is Calling: View of Homeland among Russians in the Near Abroad," *World Politics* 55, no. 2 (2003): 290–313; Oxana Shevel, "National Identity and International Institutions: Refugee Policies in Post-Communist Europe: A Comparative Study of the Russian Federation, Ukraine, the Czech Republic, Poland, 1990–2001" (Ph.D. diss., Harvard University, 2003).

29. Ineta Ziemele, *State Continuity and Nationality: The Baltic States and Russia* (Leiden: Martinus Nijhoff, 2005); Gwendolyn Sasse, *The Crimea Question: Identity, Transition, and Conflict* (Cambridge: Harvard University Press, 2007), 148–149.

30. Shevel, "National Identity," 15; Light, "Regional Migration," 11; S. A. Gannushkina, ed., *Priobretenie grazhdanstva RF i legalizatsiia inostrannykh grazhdan v Rossii (Materialy vosemnadtsatogo seminara, provedennogo v ramkakh programmy 'Migratsiia i pravo' pravozashchitnogo tsentra 'Memorial' 28–30 Oktiabria 2004 goda)* (Moscow: R. Valent, 2005), 6-33; Anastasiia Nikolaevna Golovistikova, *Kommentarii k Federal'nomu zakonu ot 31 Maia 2002 g. No. 62-FZ 'O grazhdanstve Rossiiskoi Federatsii'* (Moscow: Eksmo education, 2005), 58–102.

31. Oxana Shevel, *Migration, Refugee Policy, and State Building in Postcommunist Europe* (Cambridge: Cambridge University Press, 2011), 92–93. Legally stateless former Soviet citizens were allowed to apply for Russian Federation citizenship under a simplified procedure that waived the standard five-year residence requirement. This clause was particularly directed toward residents of Latvia, Estonia, Abkhazia, and Transdnistria in Moldova who had not acquired citizenship in their states.

32. An important part of this policy turn was the sudden "securitization" of discourse and practices relating to immigration both in Russia and throughout the world in the early 2000s. For an excellent analysis see Mikhail A. Alexseev, *Immigration Phobia and the Security Dilemma: Russia, Europe and the United States* (Cambridge: Cambridge University Press, 2006).

33. Shevel, *Migration, Refugee Policy*, 94–96.

34. *Independent International Fact-Finding Mission on the Conflict in Georgia, Report Commissioned by the European Union Council*, chaired by Heidi Tagliavini (September 2009), vol. 2, 146–184. The Tagliavini report strongly argues that the populations of South Ossetia and Abkhazia were given a reasonable six-month period to opt out of ascribed collective naturalization as Georgian citizens according to a 1993 law. Given that Georgia had a strong ban on dual citizenship, the report argues that international and Georgian law both prohibited recognition of these populations as Russian citizens unless they were formally released from Georgian citizenship (see p. 154). See also Scott Littlefield, "Citizenship, Identity and Foreign Policy: The Contradictions and Consequences of Russia's Passport Distribution in the Separatist Regions of Georgia." *Europe-Asia Studies* 61, no. 8 (October 2009), 461–482.

35. The policy has also faced practical barriers, including the desire of many to use their Russian citizenship as a means to migrate to the Russian Federation. Various administrative measures have attempted to deprive these new

citizens of the ability to acquire a residence permit in the Russian Federation, but such actions undermine the international status of this category of passport, and have proven difficult to enforce. Rebecca Chaimberlain-Creanga and Lyndon Allin, "Acquiring Assets, Debts and Citizens: Russia and the Micro-Foundations of Transnistria's Stalemated Conflict," *Demokratizatsiia* 18, no. 4 (2010): 329–356; Florian Mühlfried, "Citizenship at War: Passports and Nationality in the 2008 Russian-Georgian Conflict," *Anthropology Today* 26, no. 2 (2010): 8–13.

36. Light, "Regional Migration," 92.

37. Moya Flynn's study of Russian migrants from former Soviet republics to the Russian Federation found government support very sparse and integration into normal economic and social life very difficult. See Moya Flynn, *Migrant Resettlement in the Russian Federation: Reconstructing Homes and Homelands* (London: Anthem Press, 2004).

38. Grigory Ioffe and Zhanna Zayonchkovskaya, "Immigration to Russia: Why It Is Inevitable, and How Large It May Have to Be to Provide the Workforce Russia Needs," NCEEER Working Paper, contract number 824–05g, January 21, 2010, pp. 1–3; Nicholas Eberstadt, *Russia's Peacetime Demographic Crisis: Dimensions, Causes, Implications* (Washington, DC: National Bureau of Asian Research, 2010).

39. A yearly quota of around half a million was set in 2003 on the migration of seasonal foreign laborers. Suren A. Avakian, *Rossiia: grazhdanstvo, inostrantsy, vneshniaia migratsiia* (Sankt-peterburg: Iuridicheskii tsentr, 2003), 219.

40. Leonid Leonidovich Rybakovskii and N. I. Kozhevnikova, *Otsenka vozmozhnykh i neobkhodimykh masshtabov privlecheniia immigrantov v Rossiiu* (Moscow: Institut sotsial'no-politicheskikh issledovanii RAN, 2010).

41. Valerian Valerianovich Obolenskii, *Mezhdunarodnye i mezhkontinental'nye migratsii v dovoennoi Rossii i SSSR* (Moscow: Ts.S.U. SSSR, 1928), 108, 110.

42. Shevel, *Migration, Refugee Policy*, 73–133.

43. Alexseev, *Immigration Phobia*, 95–147; Maria Repnikova and Harley Balzer, *Chinese Migration to Russia: Missed Opportunities* (Washington, D.C.: Woodrow Wilson International Center for Scholars, 2009).

Acknowledgments

The research and writing of this book was supported by fellowships from the Davis Center for Russian Studies at Harvard University, the Kennan Institute for the Advancement of Russian Studies, and the National Council for Eurasian and East European Research.

I would like to thank Harvard's Davis Center for funding a conference that I organized on citizenship in Russian history and the editors of *Kritika: Explorations in Russian and Eurasian History* for editing and publishing an excellent set of papers that emerged from the conference in two special issues of the journal. Dean Peter Starr, the College of Arts and Sciences at American University and my much-missed department chair Bob Griffith helped me carve out time to write by providing generous research support and flexibility in research leaves and teaching schedules. Henry Hale and the Center for European, Russian, and Eurasian Studies at George Washington University provided an excellent place to write and interact with other scholars.

Participants in workshops and seminars provided insightful comments and critiques at the Davis Center for Russian Studies, L'École des hautes études en sciences sociales, the Kennan Institute, the Harriman Institute at Columbia University, the Washington DC Russian History Seminar, the American University History Forum, the University of North Carolina, the Humboldt University (Berlin), Albert-Ludwigs-Universität (Freiburg), the German Historical Institute in Moscow, the Ballinstadt Emigration Museum (Hamburg), the Watson Institute for International Studies at Brown University, the Institute for Global Studies at the University of Minnesota, and the Kiev Mohyla Academy. David Brandenberger's comments on the whole manuscript were a great help. Michael David Fox, Robert Geraci, David Goldfrank, Dominic Lieven, Terry Martin, Alexei Miller, Alexander Semyonov, Roman Szporluk, and the sorely missed Richard

Stites provided particularly helpful and extensive comments and critiques. I would also like to thank Mustafa Aksakal, Harley Balzer, Oleg Budnitskii, Juliette Cadiot, Timothy Colton, David Engerman, Alison Frank, Anton Fedyashin, Max Friedman, Peter Holquist, John Klier, Mary D. Lewis, Dominic Lieven, Kelly O'Neill, Marshall Poe, Randall Poole, Blair Ruble, Andrey Shlyachter, Ben Tromly, and Paul Werth for their help and support. Huge thanks are due to one of the anonymous outside reviewers for ten single-spaced pages of extremely helpful comments and critiques. Thanks to Omer Bartov, David Brandenberger, Tobias Brinkmann, Juliet Cadiot, Gia Cagliotti, Ulrike von Hirschhausen, Jörn Leonhard, Terry Martin, Alexei Miller, Nathalie Moine, Kelly O'Neill, Susanne Schattenberg, Gleb Tsipursky, Louise McReynolds, Alexander Semyonov, and Eric Weitz for inviting and hosting me at a range of interesting seminars and conferences where drafts and ideas in this book were discussed.

The professionals at the Library of Congress European, Law, and microform reading rooms provided much help and created an incomparable working environment. The staff at the State Archive of the Russian Federation, the Russian State Military Archive, the Russian National Library, and the Russian State Historical Library were extremely efficient and helpful. The National Archives and Records Administration showed me that archival research can be easy. The interlibrary loan service at American University generously and quickly responded to my many requests.

Andre Hand at the Estonian Institute was a great help with the cover art. It has been an honor to again work with Kathleen McDermott and join the impressive list of books in Russian history that she has brought to publication. Edward Wade skillfully managed the editing process. Simone D'Amico, Yuliya Iskhakova, Abigail Kret, and Christina Ling provided excellent research assistance. Grad students in my course on citizenship showed me that laws and theories don't fascinate everyone as much as they do me; I hope that this book is more interesting to more people as a result. Thanks to everyone for waiting a couple extra years for this book while I played with my boys Alexei and Andrei. This book is dedicated to my wife and best friend, Anya Schmemann.

Index